"*Literature is news that stays news*"

Ezra Pound,
ABC of Reading

*Books that are
always news
at* Waterstone's

GRANTA 53, SPRING 1996

EDITOR Ian Jack
DEPUTY EDITOR Ursula Doyle
MANAGING EDITOR Claire Wrathall
EDITORIAL ASSISTANT Karen Whitfield

CONTRIBUTING EDITORS Neil Belton, Pete de Bolla, Frances Coady,
Will Hobson, Liz Jobey, Blake Morrison, Andrew O'Hagan

Granta, 2–3 Hanover Yard, Noel Road, London N1 8BE
SUBSCRIPTIONS: TELEPHONE (0171) 704 0470 FAX (0171) 354 3469
EDITORIAL: TELEPHONE (0171) 704 9776 FAX (0171) 704 0474

SALES AND BUSINESS MANAGER Kate Griffin, FINANCE Geoffrey Gordon,
ASSOCIATE PUBLISHER Sally Lewis, SUBSCRIPTIONS Rhiannon Thomas,
OFFICE ASSISTANT Angela Rose

Granta US, 250 West 57th Street, Suite 1316, New York, NY 10107, USA
US PUBLISHER Matt Freidson

PUBLISHER Rea S. Hederman

SUBSCRIPTION DETAILS: a one-year subscription (four issues) costs £21.95 (UK),
£29.95 (rest of Europe) and £36.95 (rest of the world).

Granta is printed in the United States of America. The paper used in this publication
meets the minimum requirements of American National Standard for Information
Sciences—Permanence of Paper for Printed Library Materials, ANSI Z39.48-1984. ⊚

Cover design by The Senate.
Photograph: PA News
ISBN 0-14-014132-4

Graham SWIFT

Last Orders

Sometimes you know from the very first words of a book that you are reading an author whose work is going to last.

These are the books and authors we select as Harvill Panthers.

Peter Høeg
Miss Smilla's Feeling for Snow

"It is freezing, an extraordinary -18°C, and it's snowing, and in the language which is no longer mine, the snow is *qanik* - big, almost weightless crystals falling in stacks and covering the ground with a layer of pulverised white frost..."

Borderliners

"What is time?
We ascended towards the light, five floors up, and split up into thirteen rows facing the god who unlocks the gates of morning..."

Giuseppe Tomasi di Lampedusa
The Leopard

"*Nunc et in hora mortis nostrae. Amen.*
The daily recital of the Rosary was over. For half an hour the steady voice of the Prince had recalled the Sorrowful and the Glorious Mysteries..."

Boris Pasternak
Doctor Zhivago

"On they went, singing 'Eternal Memory', and whenever they stopped, the sound of their feet, the horses and the gusts of wind seemed to carry on their singing."

Great books - from first to last

HARVILL | PANTHER

CONTENTS

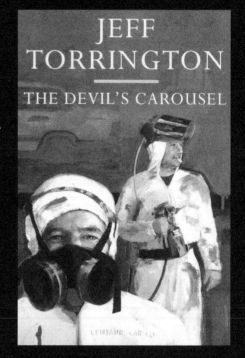

INTERESTING IF TRUE

The Herald, 31 May 1951

PHILLIP KNIGHTLEY

Phillip Knightley

The end of the war in the Pacific came just before I left school. My matriculation grades were not good enough for an arts course at Sydney University, so my mother said that while I thought about whether to re-sit some subjects, I had to go to work. Consolidated Press, owned by Sir Frank Packer, father of Kerry, publisher of the *Sydney Daily* and *Sunday Telegraph* and the *Australian Women's Weekly*, was looking for copy boys, and I started there on the night shift—six p.m. to midnight. The copy boys sat in a row on a wooden bench facing a series of buzzers, watched over by the head copy boy, who was at least sixty-three. If a buzzer went, the boy at the top of the bench ran to answer the call, and the whole line moved up one. But the reporters and sub-editors seldom used the buzzers. They simply roared 'BOY!', and you tracked down the source of the roar. We were called copy boys because we carried copy—the handwritten or typewritten material for publication—from one part of the newspaper office to another and finally down to the composing room where it was set for printing.

But this was only part of our duties. We ran errands for reporters: collected their laundry, bought them hamburgers and sandwiches, put them on the train or tram when they were drunk, lied to their wives and girlfriends about their whereabouts and escorted in and out of the building the many women who called to see Sir Frank Packer. In return for all these extra duties, we hoped that some of the skills of our heroes would rub off on us, and that one day we would be rewarded with a cadetship. Four years as a cadet and you became a fully trained journalist able to shout 'BOY!' yourself.

The king of the reporters' room was a lanky, sallow-faced man called Sam White. White not only had the glamour of having been a war correspondent in the Middle East, but he wore the first pair of suede desert boots ever seen in Sydney. This was a brave thing to do because the toughest cop on the vice squad, Sergeant 'Bumper' Farrell, the man who chewed off a fellow Rugby League footballer's ear during a scrum, had decreed that only poofters wore suede shoes and therefore anyone caught wearing them could be arrested for homosexuality, then a terrible crime in Australia carrying a sentence of life imprisonment.

Unfortunately, Sam White was not there long enough to teach us much. There is a mean streak in many Australians, a desire to punish anyone who seeks to soar above the crowd. Someone who had been overseas had to be brought back down on his return. No one actually said to Sam, 'Just because you've been a war correspondent, mate, don't think you can bludge back here. You're on court rounds.' But the chief of staff did send him to Darlinghurst Court where the biggest case would have been about pimping, prostitution, or consorting with known criminals, a catch-all charge that made it possible for the New South Wales police to arrest just about anyone, any time. Sam stuck it for a week, then came into the office late in the afternoon, flung his copy on to the subs' table, announced, 'This isn't fucking journalism,' and resigned. He left a week later for Europe, settled in Paris and found the fame he justly deserved.

The reporter with the most envied job was Dave Barnes who ran the *Sunday Telegraph* Beach Girl competition. During the summer months Barnes spent several hours every day wandering along Sydney beaches looking for candidates for that week's beach girl. When he found one, the *Sunday Telegraph* photographer would either take her picture on the sand or ask her to come into the newspaper studio later that day. At the end of the summer the paper's readers voted for the beach girl of the year. Barnes took his job seriously and, as far as I know, never took advantage of the power it gave him. I cannot say the same for the photographers. Swimming costumes in those days were usually one piece and very modest. The photographer, alone with the beach girl in the office studio, would take the discreet shot that would be used in that week's newspaper. Then he would say, 'Now let's have one for the boys in the darkroom,' and insist that the girl drop the top part of her costume and expose her breasts. That so many agreed to do this was a revelation to me. 'They can't resist the camera,' the photographers would say cynically as they produced their collection for the copy boys and made us tremble with lust.

One day there was a printers' strike. The journalists' union called the reporters out in sympathy, and the reporters told the copy boys to come out too. In the Irish pub on the corner of

Park and Castlereagh Streets, they lectured us about worker solidarity. 'There are only two classes in this world,' said one of the sports writers, 'bosses and workers, and you lot are workers.' The worst creature on earth, beneath all contempt, he said, was a scab. Anyone who stayed at work when his mates were out on strike was a dirty, rotten bastard, lower than a fucking snake's belly, probably a Pom, and should never, ever be forgiven. There was once such a journalist, they said, who defied the union and stayed at work to help the management produce the paper. When he finished his shift in the early hours of the morning and tried to catch the night tram home, the conductor threw him off. The next day when he tried to get a beer, the barmaid would not serve him. His regular restaurant turned him away at the door. And when the sanitary men, who in those days collected your full lavatory pan and replaced it with a fresh, empty one, heard about the scab they let him stew in his own shit. Here was an example, they said, of Australian worker solidarity and, like a lot of other things in Australia, it was the best in the whole bloody world. These events, it turned out, had happened years before, but the reporters spoke of it as if it were yesterday, and their hatred for the scab, who was still being punished, was undiminished. It all made a powerful impression on the copy boys.

After a year as a copy boy there was still no chance of a cadetship because returning servicemen had priority for any spare jobs. But they all preferred the city, so I began writing to editors of rural newspapers asking if they had a vacancy for a first-year cadet who knew his way around a newspaper office. The *Northern Star*, a daily paper in Lismore, a flourishing dairy-producing centre in northern New South Wales, said yes.

My mother found me accommodation at Miss MacNamara's Boarding House for Professional Young Gentlemen and Ladies, a big, pre-First World War wooden house with a rusting, corrugated-iron roof on which the drumming of rain during the wet season was sometimes so loud it kept those on the top floor awake half the night. Miss MacNamara, a white-haired spinster in her mid-seventies, promised to keep an eye on me. We slept two to a room—men in one part of the house, women in another—and

11

ate in a big communal dining room served by two waitresses who were even older than Miss MacNamara. The other guests were police constables, nurses, office workers and schoolteachers. There was one other journalist, a Scots migrant called James Cleary who had clearly run away from something nasty in the Old Country.

I think it was at Cleary's suggestion that the editor threw me in at the deep end: the annual meeting of the Country Women's Association, the weekly swimming carnival, the opening of a new baby health centre, the monthly meeting of the Returned Servicemen's League, weddings, funerals and twenty-first birthday parties. When the one woman reporter, Gwen Lyle, went on holiday I even wrote her weekly column 'Roundabout, by Suzanne'. It was wonderful training. The idea of interviewing someone on the telephone never occurred to us—we went out and met people face to face. We were part of the community. We knew everybody, and everybody knew us. If I got someone's second initial wrong, he would stop me on the street to complain. If I got the whole story wrong, I would never hear the end of it. The *Northern Star* taught me to be accurate; that people had feelings; and that you could not use your privileged access as a journalist to come into their lives, suck them dry and then leave again. You had personal and civic responsibilities, especially to people such as Alderman W. G. Walker, the mayor. Alderman Walker was a popular figure and good at his job but he was poorly educated, and his grammar made his speeches something of a joke to anyone who listened to what he actually said. One day, when he was particularly incoherent, I handed in a verbatim report of his speech as a joke. The editor was furious. What if the story had made its way into the paper by accident? The mayor's reputation would have suffered, and so would that of the newspaper. Was this what I wanted? In future I would do as everyone else did—without changing the mayor's meaning, I would polish up his speeches in all my reports. Why? Because it was not a journalist's job to make fools out of honest public figures. If they were dishonest, that was another matter, but if I wanted to get on in journalism then the gratuitous humiliation of other people was not the way to do it.

But even at that stage of my career there were indications

that not everything the reader learned from his paper was necessarily true. On one long, hot, humid summer afternoon, Cleary got up from his typewriter and announced that he was going for a milk shake. 'Here,' he said, handing me a file, 'it's time you had a turn doing the stars.' I looked at the folder. It was labelled THE WEEK AHEAD: YOUR FUTURE IN THE STARS, BY TAURUS. Until then I had believed that the *Northern Star* had some regular astrologer who wrote the weekly column. Now it appeared the reporters did it. Cleary noticed my bewilderment. 'Don't worry, it's easy,' he said. 'Go down to the file room and dig out a copy of the paper from ten years ago. Copy out its stars column then mix it around a bit.' He headed for the door, then stopped. 'One other thing. Don't give the same people bad stars two days running.'

At the end of a year in Lismore I was restless. I felt that I had learned all that the *Northern Star* had to teach me. Cleary, in a rare communicative mood, said that it did not matter what you did to earn a living because the best training for journalism was life. 'Piss off from here,' he said. 'Get any old job. You'll always be able to come back to reporting.' The very next day there was an advertisement in the *Sydney Morning Herald*. 'British company requires trainee South Sea Island traders. Young men with initiative and a sense of adventure are invited to apply for long- and short-term contracts.' To a nineteen-year-old steeped in Conrad and Somerset Maugham the challenge was irresistible, and after a long interview in the Sydney offices of Morris Hedstrom—at which they seemed more interested in what sport I had played at school than in my academic achievements—I got the job and left for Fiji the following month.

In those early post-war years, before tourism, the few people who wanted to go to Fiji did so in six or seven leisurely days on old steamships that had been rescued from troop-carrying to reopen the San Francisco–Sydney run. But my new employers splashed out on a seat for me on the Pan-American clipper plane which boasted bunks that folded out of the cabin ceiling. After a few drinks and a freshly cooked meal, the stewardess made up your bed, you snuggled down between crisp sheets to the comforting roar of the engines and woke up in Nadi, Fiji's international airport. A day's taxi ride over dirt roads past miles of sugar-cane fields took you to Suva, the capital. It was exactly as I had expected—straight out of *Lord Jim*.

It was fortunate that Suva was so romantic because being an island trader turned out to be unspeakably boring. Morris Hedstrom bought copra from the Fijians and, in return, sold them British-manufactured goods. My job was to keep track of all those goods. I met the 'home' ship when she came in, helped supervise the unloading, entered the stock and, at regular intervals, did the stocktaking. Indian clerks, descendants of the Tamil labourers Britain had imported in the nineteenth century to work the sugar plantations, did the counting. I did the sums: six dozen and three four-inch brass countersunk screws at one pound seven and six a gross equals what? After an hour or so of this in those pre-calculator days, I would doze off at my desk, at first guiltily and then, when I noticed everyone else nodding, with equanimity. I made a vow then that I would never take a clerical job again.

I fled after six months. Not from the islands, but back to journalism. A group of local businessmen decided to try to break the newspaper monopoly enjoyed by the *Fiji Times and Herald*, whose editor, a former New Zealand schoolteacher called Len Usher, was trying to mould it into a South Pacific version of *The Times* of London. The idea was that the new paper should be more like the *Daily Mirror*. The backers bought a flatbed press which the London Missionary Society had imported a hundred years earlier to print bibles, recruited a new editor from New Zealand and found a sub-editor in the unlikely person of Bryan Hanrahan, a former officer from the Gurkhas who had washed up in Fiji after a good war in India. They called their paper the *Oceania Daily News* and, with a flash of inspiration based on the fact that Fiji is just to the west of the International Date Line, where the world's time starts, gave it the slogan: 'The First Paper Published in the World Today'. Theoretically, every day it would scoop not only the *New York Times*, the *Washington Post*, *Le Monde* and *The Times*, but every other newspaper everywhere. The challenge was irresistible. I gave up island trading and became its only reporter.

The first paper printed in the world that day

The job brought me into contact with a Fiji that I had not known existed. Underneath an apparent calm and orderly exterior, all sorts of strange things were going on. The Indian community, which made up nearly half the population, seethed with internal violence, usually over land disputes, or arranged marriages that had gone wrong, or quarrels over dowries. Judging from the court cases I covered, the favourite method of settling these arguments was not litigation but to break someone's legs with an iron bar.

Life as a reporter in Fiji was wonderful. I covered everything, and even started a gossip column, 'Round the Town with Suzanne', which turned out to be a terrible error of judgement. At first informants fell over themselves to tell me what was really going on in the colony—politically, socially, sexually. In innocence, I wrote it all: 'Who was the lady in the red polka-dot dress seen emerging from bushes near the Cable and Wireless station in the early hours last Thursday accompanied by Mr R—?

15

And did her husband know?' The circulation of the *Oceania Daily News* soared.

My first inkling that not everyone enjoyed reading 'Suzanne' came when I went as a paying passenger on a boat to Levuka, the old capital, on the island of Ovalau. There we were to meet up with the Yacht Club for a weekend cruise. Just before the boat left Suva, I wrote a small item for the *News*. I still have the yellowing clipping: 'Big event of the year for Yacht Club-ites is the cruise this weekend. Known as the closing weekend, it provides an excuse for a party on Saturday night. There's some very tall (or are they?) stories around town of the amount of liquid ballast some of the boats are to carry.' This was a perfectly justifiable reference to the heavy drinking for which Yacht Club members were renowned, but in the middle of the night I was seized from my berth by a bunch of drunken heavies chanting, 'Suzanne is a dirty old man. Oink, oink. Suzanne is a dirty old man.' I put up a token resistance for honour's sake and then surrendered. They carried me to the end of the pier and threw me into the sea. When I clambered out, they gave me some rum and told me to be careful what I wrote lest I confirm the Fijians' worst views of the whites.

Word of this, and of the lady in the polka-dot dress, must have reached Government House because I received a telephone call—could I have afternoon tea with the governor's secretary? He turned out to be a tall, languid young man, not much older than me, a little like the British attaché in Evelyn Waugh's *Scoop*, and we had a chat over Darjeeling and Osborne biscuits in a drawing room that looked as if it had been transposed intact from Mayfair. He handled it brilliantly. He began by asking me how journalism worked. Who thought of a story? How did you go about getting it? Who decided how long it would be? Gradually he steered the talk around to an item I had written about a hurricane which in December 1948 had devastated some of the outer islands in the Fiji group. I had used the Weather Bureau's code name for the hurricane, 'Margaret'. It was a brilliant story, he said, but he felt that the use of a woman's name for the hurricane tended to detract from the seriousness of the disaster. 'In fact, dear boy,' he said, 'one has to be careful about using women's names in general. Things like that could damage our reputation in the eyes of the

Fijians and cause problems. I know His Excellency is very keen that we are seen to be beyond reproach. I'm sure you understand.' And he actually winked.

Not long after that the Fiji Legislative Council enacted the Press Correction Bill which gave the governor the power to order the publication of 'a short factual statement of any report held to be incorrect or distorted'. Any editor who refused to publish the correction would be liable to a fine of five hundred pounds and six months' imprisonment. If the correction was still unpublished after a conviction, the newspaper would be deemed seditious and, presumably, closed down.

The editor of the *News*, a tough professional, would undoubtedly have chosen jail. But it never came to that because he left soon afterwards for a better job in Australia, and the *News* fell apart. The new editor, another New Zealander, drove Hanrahan, the sub-editor, mad with lectures on pedantic points of grammar. Late one night, overcome by the heat and tension, Hanrahan listened to half an hour on the use of the pluperfect, then snatched a painting off the editor's wall and smashed it over his head. Understandably, the editor fired him. The printers, who had more to do with Hanrahan than the editor, went on strike in his support. The clerical staff, who had more to do with the editor, went on strike in his support. Since I comprised the whole of the editorial staff, I had to choose which picket line to join, and since I was a paying guest in Hanrahan's house, I joined him. The proprietors, under pressure from the governor not to allow either strike to succeed because of the example it might set the native workers, sacked everyone and shut down the paper for ever.

2

I sailed to New Zealand and worked for a time as a wharf labourer and as a 'linesman' for the New Zealand Post and Telegraph Department (the job was deceptively titled—it meant digging ditches for cables). When I got back to Australia there were still no jobs on any of the Sydney newspapers, so in desperation I appealed to Sir Keith Murdoch (father of Rupert

Murdoch), the media magnate, who ran the *Herald*, the only afternoon newspaper in Melbourne. I wrote to him personally and told him that I had met two of his reporters in Fiji, where they had been offloaded from a Swedish oil tanker diverted from its original destination, San Francisco, to Indonesia. The reporters had been working as ships' stewards and were hoping to make it to London, Fleet Street, fame and fortune, in much the same way as young Keith himself had done thirty years earlier. Murdoch replied by telegram asking me to meet him on his next trip to Sydney. I did and was hired as a fourth-year cadet. I hitched a ride to Melbourne on an interstate freight truck and started work the following week.

It was my first experience on an afternoon newspaper, and the system was as rigid as in any military establishment. The chief of staff and his deputy started work at five a.m. and ploughed through the morning newspapers—the *Age*, the *Argus* and the *Sun-Pictorial*—looking for stories that could be expanded or developed. A newsroom diary listed all forthcoming events, and those occurring that day were added to the list of possible stories. By the time the first reporters arrived at seven-thirty a.m., the assignments had been compiled and the straightforward ones set out in typewritten notes which were placed in each reporter's mailbox. Reporters allocated complicated assignments were given a personal briefing from the chief of staff or his deputy.

As well as general reporters, of which I was one, there were 'roundsmen', senior journalists who looked after specific 'beats'. The western roundsman looked after the western end of the city, which included the railways and the transport unions; the police roundsman covered crime; the court roundsman the courts; the state roundsman the goings-on at the state parliament; the shipping roundsman met incoming ships; and the industrial roundsman covered all industrial disputes. Sometimes a story straddled two areas, and then there were fierce battles between roundsmen defending their territories.

One day I had been assigned to shipping because it was the regular roundsman's day off. It was late afternoon, nothing was happening and the final edition—the *Herald* produced five a day—was due to press in about an hour. A passenger ship from

Malta had docked that morning carrying wives and relatives of Maltese men who had emigrated to Australia ahead of their families to set up home. These men, many of whom had not seen their families for a year or more, had arrived at the wharves before dawn to meet the ship.

Despite the post-war immigration scheme that had brought hundreds of thousands of southern Europeans to Australia, local officialdom remained very suspicious of them. Immigration officials acted as if every document the immigrants carried had been forged; customs automatically assumed that they were all smuggling drugs, arms and alcohol; and the quarantine officers knew for certain that they would be carrying sausages full of foot-and-mouth disease or other typically foreign organisms.

So while wives, children and parents lined the ship's decks and waved to their menfolk waiting patiently on the wharf in the sun, these officials slowly and painstakingly worked their way through the immigrants' documents and baggage. I left the wharf at noon to do other shipping stories and then decided to go back and see if it had all concluded smoothly. I walked through the dock gates into a riot—the Maltese were storming the ship. A customs officer who had tried to stop them entering the customs' examination hall had had his ear bitten off and was staggering around with a bloodstained handkerchief clasped to his head. The Maltese were winning, but over the noise of battle could be heard the distant whine of police sirens.

Was this a police rounds story or a shipping one? Once the police arrived the police roundsman would not be far behind, and his office car was equipped with two-way radio so he could dictate his story direct to the *Herald*. But until he arrived it was a shipping story, my story—if I could find a telephone and send it. At the far end of the customs hall, well away from the fighting, was an empty office. The door was locked, but a hard push sprang the catch. I got on the telephone and told the chief of staff what was happening. Then I dictated five paragraphs to the copy-takers—fast touch-typists, all women, who worked with earphones, typing one paragraph to each short sheet of paper, then ripping it from the machine to pass to the sub-editors for processing.

I had just started the sixth paragraph when two customs

officers burst in. 'Get the fuck off the phone,' the first one said, reaching for it. 'I'm from the *Herald*,' I said. 'I'm sending my story.' He wrenched the telephone from me. 'Dave,' he said, 'chuck this bastard out.' Dave escorted me to a loading ramp and made me jump down to the street. As I walked through the wharf gates, I saw the *Herald* police rounds car arrive, and the roundsman leap out and run towards the riot which appeared to be petering out. He was too late. I had my first scoop.

Whether word of this reached Murdoch or not I never knew. But a week or so later his secretary called me to her office and said, 'Sir Keith likes to meet new members of the editorial staff. He's going to Canberra for a couple of days tomorrow. He wants you to go along as his secretary. It's a good chance to see how he runs his papers. Here's your ticket. You'll be staying at the Rex. He'll be at the farm but he'll be in touch with you when he needs you.' In Canberra I checked in at the hotel and waited. Sir Keith rang early next morning and said he would pick me up in an hour. I watched a procession of government limousines and the occasional Bentley. Would Murdoch have a Bentley or a Rolls? Finally a battered, dirty, utility truck pulled up with Murdoch in the passenger seat and a young man about my age driving. Murdoch got out, I got in and squeezed my knees around the gear shift. 'This is my son, Rupert,' Murdoch said. We shook hands, and the truck lurched off for the Indian High Commission.

I had, of course, heard of Rupert because there had been rumours in the reporters' room that he was going to fill in some of his time between finishing at Geelong Grammar School and going up to Oxford by working as a cadet on the *Herald*. My first impression was that he was an image of his father. He had the same sturdy build, the same features, the same wavy hair. He had also inherited his father's relaxed, easy manner—what someone was later to describe as 'deadly charm'. 'Have you been to Canberra before?' he asked. I confessed I had not. 'If Dad doesn't need you this afternoon, I'll show you around. The War Memorial's well worth a visit.'

At the High Commission, Murdoch, the High Commissioner and his wife chatted over tea while Rupert and I waited patiently. The High Commissioner was pressing the Murdochs to come to a reception that evening to mark India's national day. Murdoch was protesting that the reception was black tie and he did not want to drive back to the farm to change. Finally he yielded. 'OK,' he said. 'We'll come. We'll buy something in town.' Ah, I thought, how wonderful to be rich. Your dinner jacket is back at the farm when you need it, so you simply buy another. When we got back into the truck and drove to the Rex, Murdoch got out, fished in his pocket for his wallet, drew out a single pound note and handed it to Rupert. 'Buy a couple of black ties for tonight,' he said.

Murdoch had lunch with the prime minister, Sir Robert Menzies, and I went along to hand out the cigars and field telephone calls. Then he dictated a letter to his fellow newspaper proprietor Sir Lloyd Dumas of Adelaide. It gave a summary of what had been discussed over luncheon, including four or five paragraphs on what the prime minister had said about the likelihood of an alteration in the currency exchange rate between Britain and Australia, and advice on what Dumas should do to take advantage of this inside information. I could have sworn that Murdoch said that, according to Menzies, a 'revaluation' (which would strengthen the Australian pound) was likely in the next three months, and that was what I typed, signed on behalf of Murdoch and posted. But when I mentioned it to a business reporter on my return to Melbourne, he alarmed me by saying, 'That can't be right. A devaluation is on the cards, but certainly not a revaluation.' I spent an anxious three months worrying that when the devaluation occurred, Sir Lloyd Dumas would lose a fortune, and the blame would be traced back to me. In the event nothing at all happened: Sir Lloyd Dumas never complained, but I felt the first splinter of doubt about the effect of political and economic information.

The most glamorous round at the *Herald* was of course the police one. The chief police roundsman was Alan Dower, a tall, distinguished man with a military moustache and bearing, whose act at parties was to borrow a broomstick, pretend he was on the parade ground and carry out drill as ordered by an imaginary sergeant major. His deputy was Lionel Hogg, who could well have been a detective himself had he not opted for journalism. It was Hogg's job to give an occasional lecture to the cadets on the mysteries of reporting. One sticks in my mind. 'A little twist to the most mundane of stories can turn it into a front page lead,' Hogg began. 'Now take what happened to me last week. The police got a call to a restaurant where the chef had just beaten off an armed robber. I interviewed him and asked him how he had done it. He said he chucked a plate of food in the man's face and the guy ran away. That's a pretty boring story. But I noticed that the restaurant was a Hungarian one. So I asked the chef what the plate of food had been. He said that in the excitement he hadn't noticed. So I wrote a lead that said the chef of a Hungarian restaurant had foiled an armed robber by chucking a plate of Hungarian goulash in his face. It made page one.' We thought about it for a second or two; then one of the cadets said, 'But, Lionel, that wasn't true.' Hogg laughed. 'No,' he said, 'but it should have been.'

Hogg arranged for each cadet to accompany a night police patrol car crewed by three detectives so we would get a feel for police work. On my night we crawled around the darkened inner suburbs of Melbourne hoping that the radio would crackle to life with some exciting crime in our area, but the only message we got was an order to check out a man sleeping on a bench in a park near the state parliament building. He did not speak English, and the detectives were losing their patience with him, so I felt justified in intervening and with some schoolboy French discovered he was a crew member of a ship in harbour and had missed the last bus back to the docks. Instead of being grateful, the police became wary of me. Squashed between two of them in the back seat of the squad car, we maintained an uneasy silence until they spotted an old drunk urinating against a tree in St Kilda Road.

'Dirty bastard,' the driver said. 'Teach him a lesson.' The two detectives in the back of the car jumped out. One grabbed the old man's hat and flung it far into park. The other began methodically kicking him in the backside as the old man staggered away mumbling protests and then fell over. The detective gave him one final kick and came back to the car. The exercise must have made them hungry because we headed off to the city centre and stopped at a late-night restaurant. The proprietor, a Greek, came hurrying up. 'Oyster soup and steaks, Tony,' one of the detectives said, 'and put some bloody oysters in the soup.' When we were leaving, I made an effort to pay for my share. 'Put it away,' one of the detectives ordered. 'It's on the house. We look after Tony, he looks after us.'

Did I write any of this? Did I tell the *Herald* readers that their police were less than perfect? I did not. Hogg had made it clear that we were guests in the squad car and that anything that happened had to remain confidential, otherwise the cosy relationship between the police and the *Herald* police roundsmen would be endangered.

The most eccentric reporter on the *Herald* was John Pitcairn. He appeared in the reporters' room one day, a slight, red-haired figure with a drawling British accent. He had been on a tour of the Pacific, he said, and had just arrived in town from Tahiti. He peppered his chat with French words, spoke confidently about the international situation and told tall stories about all the Tahitian chiefs he knew and how obliging their daughters had been. Yes, he was related to the Pitcairns of Pitcairn Island, and his family knew the Murdochs. In fact, he said, he was staying in Rupert Murdoch's room while Rupert was up at Oxford.

Pitcairn was often late for work because Sir Keith Murdoch gave him a lift in his car, and Murdoch started work later than the newsroom. The *Herald* executives did not quite know what to do with Pitcairn. They did not want to be seen to be easy on the boss's guest but neither did they want him to complain to Murdoch, and the feeling was that, being English, Pitcairn could not be trusted. Pitcairn went about his duties oblivious to it all. Some days we both drew suburban court reporting, and the courts were often close enough for us to meet for lunch. He began to tell me stories of life in the Murdoch household. Most of them were mundane family gossip, but one I remember well.

According to Pitcairn, the British Council had asked Murdoch if he would entertain the distinguished British author Eric Linklater, who was visiting Australia under the auspices of the Council. Murdoch readily agreed and asked Pitcairn to prepare him a little brief on Linklater's achievements. Pitcairn boiled it down: he had served as a private in the Black Watch, had a wartime career in the Directorate of Public Relations in the War Office, been rector of Aberdeen University, a lieutenant-colonel in Korea. He provided a list of all Linklater's books, plays and films and then added what would turn out to be an unfortunate line—that Linklater was a connoisseur of fine French wines.

Pitcairn said that, for reasons he never understood, Murdoch had taken an instant dislike to Linklater, and the dinner had proceeded in an atmosphere of deep chill. After one particularly long silence, Murdoch suddenly said, 'I understand, Mr Linklater, that you are something of a wine buff.' Linklater replied that he liked good wines and, yes, he did know a little about them. 'Ha,' said Murdoch, pouncing, 'then perhaps you could tell us what we have been drinking this evening?' And he gestured to the middle of the table where the Murdoch family butler/chauffeur Ted Pentecost had placed a wine bottle wrapped in a snowy-white napkin. Linklater picked up his glass, drank in the aroma, took a sip and rolled it around his mouth before swallowing it. 'Well,' he said tentatively, 'a claret, of course. Not a distinguished vineyard. Certainly not from a chateau. Recent vintage. A perfectly drinkable table wine. In fact, delicious.'

A delighted smile spread over Murdoch's face. 'Really,' he said. 'Then no doubt you'll be surprised to know, Mr Linklater, that you've been tasting one of the best wines in my cellar, one I myself drink regularly. We're talking about a Château Pape Clément, a *grand cru classé*. Bottled by the chateau itself, of course. Pentecost, show Mr Linklater the label.' Everyone turned to look at Pentecost who was standing frozen, white-faced, eyes glazing over. Everyone, that is, except Murdoch, who was watching Linklater. 'Come on, Pentecost,' Murdoch said impatiently. 'Show him.' Pentecost moved slowly to the table, lifted the bottle, peeled off the napkin, and robot-like turned the label towards Linklater. Linklater peered at it. 'Yes, well,' he murmured, 'as I said.' Murdoch suddenly caught on. Pentecost had deceived him, probably not every night, but certainly this time. He clenched his jaw, changed the subject, pretended nothing untoward had happened and quickly brought the evening to a close. Pitcairn claimed not to know what Murdoch later said to Pentecost but insisted that the man did not lose his job.

3

After I had been at the *Herald* for nearly two years I thought I would try Sydney again. In the 1950s it was the journalistic capital of Australia and, so everyone said, a great place to be a reporter. But there were no jobs in journalism in Sydney, and my savings quickly ran out. I tried selling vacuum cleaners door-to-door. I worked part-time for an advertising agency writing copy for a new brand of refrigerator: 'Colda refrigerators keep your food colder longer. Its powerful compressor unit and high-technology insulation fight off summer heat. Don't run the risk of sickness from spoilt food. Make sure your children grow older with Colda.' I lasted long enough to decide that advertising was not for me either—there was something of the door-to-door vacuum-cleaner business about it, something shifty.

The *Sydney Daily Mirror* came to my rescue. I had bombarded its news editor, Charlie Buttrose, with job applications, and his secretary rang one day and asked if I could come in for a week's trial as a D-grade general reporter. The *Mirror* and its Sunday stablemate, *Truth*, were owned by Ezra Norton, a newspaper tsar in the Citizen Kane mould. Norton had made his money from *Truth*, which specialized in divorce cases and attacks on the Roman Catholic Church. Norton's father, a fiercely anti-British immigrant from Ireland, realized that, unlike in Britain, New South Wales law allowed anyone to publish all the evidence in divorce hearings. There were very limited grounds for divorce in the state at that time. You could either wait three years after the spouse had left home and then sue for desertion, or go for a quick divorce on the grounds of adultery. Adultery won easily. But the courts, again unlike those in Britain, would not accept as evidence an overnight stay at some Brighton love hotel. In Australia, the couple, either by arrangement or ambush, had to be caught in the actual act of illicit sex.

This provided regular employment for an army of private detectives who specialized in springing out from hotel wardrobes, or from under beds, or in crashing through windows, camera with flash gun in hand and a ready quip such as 'Hello, hello, what's going on here?' The private detective would then describe the event in great detail to the divorce court judge, and it all would be reported in the next issue of *Truth*, usually under a joky headline. Thus, when the international golf star Norman von Nida was caught with his lover on the back seat of a car near the golf club's seventeenth fairway, the *Truth* headline read CHAMP GOLFER CAUGHT IN WRONG HOLE.

Truth reporters prowled the courts looking for other juicy sex stories, especially ones involving Roman Catholic priests. In an effort to show some good taste these were not given funny headlines but alliterative ones. So a case of homosexual relations between a member of the Marist Brothers order and a teenage pupil carried the headline BEASTLY BROTHER IN BED WITH BOY.

Anyone in conflict with the Catholic Church could be assured of support from *Truth*. Some orders of nuns ran laundry businesses in Sydney suburbs, and novices were expected to work long hours at tubs and ironing machines. Every now and then a novice would realize that she did not have a vocation and would leave surreptitiously at night, scaling the high fences surrounding the order's headquarters. In *Truth* jargon, it was a case of ANOTHER NUN OVER THE WALL AT ARNCLIFFE.

Norton hated Freemasons almost as much as he hated Roman Catholics. Not long after joining the *Mirror*, the editor, Len Richards, sent for me and said, 'Mr Norton has a job for you. Come on. We'll go and see him at the city office.' Norton's office was spacious and elegantly furnished, but I did think it odd that he had two busts of Napoleon on his desk. Norton was short, dark complexioned, immaculately groomed and had expensive taste in suits. He got up as we came in, walked around to the front of his desk and shook hands. Then he gestured to two chairs and returned to his own. We waited. Suddenly Norton turned to me and said, 'That was a fucking Masonic handshake you gave me, wasn't it?'

I was stunned. Honesty seemed the only defence. 'Yes,' I said.

'Well, listen to me, sonny,' Norton said. 'If you want to get on in my fucking papers, then you don't go around giving fucking Masonic handshakes. I don't want any fucking Masons on my papers and I don't want any fucking Catholics. All I want

Phillip Knightley as a reporter on Truth

is fucking reporters. Is that fucking-well clear?' I was stunned but managed to say it was.

'All right,' Norton said. 'Now what do you know about Professor Macmahon Fucking Ball?'

I said I knew that Ball was professor of political science at Melbourne University, one of the few such departments in Australia.

'Well, I reckon he's a fucking commo,' said Norton, 'and

27

we're going to get him. I want you to do me a dossier on him. Everything you can find out. And then we'll fucking well crucify him in *Truth*.'

On the way back to the *Mirror*, I asked Len Richards what I should do. 'Exactly as Mr Norton says,' he replied. 'It'll never be published. Too libellous. But if you don't do it, Mr Norton'll sack you.' I asked around. Richards was right. Norton had a reputation for terrorizing and sacking people. His chief accountant, a mild, confident and beautifully mannered Englishman called Harold Parrot, had been reduced to a quivering wreck by Norton who would ring him at least once a day and shout down the telephone, 'Is that you Parrot? Then get down off your fucking perch and come and see me.' The news editor of *Truth* was an amiable Irish old-timer called Jack Finch whose face had been turned a deep rosy red by years of drinking. He too went in fear of Norton, who would ring him late on Saturday as he was busy getting the paper to bed, and roar, 'What's the lead, beetroot puss?'

Norton also had a reputation for feuds that sometimes became violent if he had had enough to drink. He hated Frank Packer with great passion, probably because the two were so alike—both newspaper owners, both horse-racing enthusiasts, both big drinkers. Norton resented the fact that during the war Packer had been given a commission in the Australian army and he worked out a bizarre revenge. He ordered a *Truth* photographer to go to the races every Saturday and photograph Packer enjoying himself there. Sunday after Sunday for several months *Truth* published this photograph with a caption that never changed: 'Captain Frank Packer at Randwick races yesterday. Captain Packer will be leaving for the front shortly.' Norton ceased tormenting Packer only after the two met in the members' bar at the races and began wrestling, one trying to strangle the other by tightening his necktie, although who was being strangled by whom depended on who was telling the story.

Not wishing to cross Norton so early in my career, I set about compiling a file on Professor Macmahon Ball and what Norton alleged were his communist connections, pretending to myself that if I stuck to the truth it could be called journalism. I gathered all the academic reference books and then began telephoning his friends and enemies and finally contacted Macmahon Ball himself. The tactics were not very different from those used today by journalists on quality newspapers who want to write an anonymous 'profile' of someone in the news. But in my case, I had to disguise the real purpose by pretending to be working on a survey of academics and their lifestyle. It took me a week or so to finish, and then I sent it off to Norton and never heard another word about it. I learned later that he had dozens of files on all sorts of prominent Australians whom he disliked and had never published any of them.

Although my main work was for the *Daily Mirror*, I used to do an occasional Saturday shift for *Truth* and stood in as its news editor from time to time. It was easy to fill the main part of the paper with the usual divorce cases and Saturday's sport, but the front page was always a problem. Unlike British Sunday newspapers, no one on *Truth* began working on a major news story until Friday or Saturday, and if nothing sensational had emerged by Saturday afternoon, panic followed.

One week I had two reporters working on an exposé of Sydney's milk suppliers, an idea I had sold to a reluctant Jack Finch who was worried Norton might have some farming friends. Government regulations specified that the butterfat content of the milk had to be a certain minimum level. Dairy farmers had told *Truth* that they produced rich milk well above that level, therefore the milk suppliers must be watering the milk down to the minimum legal requirement. *Truth* reporters had bought sample bottles of milk from all over Sydney, and *Truth* had paid to have the butterfat content analysed. If one or two bottles had been watered down to a level below the legal minimum, we had a story. The trouble was that we had not started on the story until Thursday, and the laboratory did not come up with the results until late Friday afternoon. Every single bottle was above the minimum butterfat level.

The race now began to find a replacement front page lead. At four p.m., we had nothing. Jack Finch's face had become so red that I feared he would explode. 'For Christ's sake find something,' he said. 'You're an imaginative fellow. Use your fucking imagination.' Then he went and hid in his office. I went through the week's newspapers for a fourth time. There was a small item from Wednesday's *Sydney Morning Herald* about a youth convicted in a suburban court for indecent assault. He had used the evening rush-hour crush on a suburban train as an excuse to press his groin against the girl squeezed against him in the corridor. To my everlasting professional shame—I can plead only that I was just twenty-four and very ambitious—I obeyed Finch and used my imagination. I invented a story about a pervert known to his victims and the police only as the Hook. The Hook, who was unemployed, spent his days travelling the Sydney train network armed with a length of wire cunningly contrived from an old coat-hanger. The wire ran over his right shoulder and down his coat sleeve where it stopped in a hook just short of the cuff. While pretending to read a newspaper, he would sidle alongside an attractive and unsuspecting girl as she stood in a crowded train, drop his shoulder to extend the hook which he would then slip under the girl's skirt, surreptitiously raising it to reveal her thighs. The Hook would then draw his device back up his sleeve and continue reading his paper, a picture of innocence. I quoted an anonymous police officer as saying that suburban police had been inundated with complaints but that they did not know where to begin their inquiries. An equally anonymous girl spoke of her horror at discovering her skirt rising mysteriously above her stocking top, vowing never to travel by train again until this pervert was caught. Finally I got a staff artist to draw his impression of the Hook at work. The more I worked on my fairy story, the more I enjoyed it. There were no inconvenient facts to get in the way of a perfect narrative. Like Lionel Hogg said—it was how it should have happened. Finch was delighted and made only one change to my copy—he had the Hook active that very Saturday evening among crowds heading into Sydney for a night out. Then he wrote a headline: HOOK SEX PERVERT STRIKES AGAIN.

It made a good front page and had the opposition struggling desperately to catch up. Some rival journalists may have guessed that it was an invented story but knew better than to try to tell that to their news editors. I learned later that they spent hours telephoning duty officers at Sydney suburban police stations trying to find one who either knew of the Hook or would brand the story a fake, but, of course, all any of them could say was that, no, no one at his station had heard of the Hook, but he could not answer for the others.

I came into the *Mirror* on Monday confident that I had got away with it. *Truth* did not believe in bylines ('No fucking journalist is going to get fucking famous at my fucking expense,' said Ezra Norton) so there was unlikely to be any comeback from the police unless someone at *Truth* told them who had written the story. My telephone rang, and a voice laden with authority said, 'Sergeant Williamson here. Did you write that stuff about the Hook?' He obviously knew, so there was no sense in lying. 'Yes,' I said. 'Right. Well, I just want to thank you and let you know that we got the bastard this morning.' Had I heard right? 'Got him?' 'Yeah. Arrested him at Punchbowl station. Caught him in the act. You might want to write about it.' I checked with the police roundsman. They really had got him.

Over the next few weeks, I waited for the Hook to appear before a magistrate, but he never did, and I did not want to press my luck by asking the police about him. Thinking about it, as I still do from time to time, I came up with several explanations. It could have been a copycat crime: some idiot read the *Truth* story, decided that he would emulate the Hook and got caught on his first time out. Or there really had been a Hook out there, and my imagination paralleled the truth. Or the Sydney police, who had a reputation for massaging crime statistics to polish their public relations, got rid of a case which promised to be a PR disaster by arresting some pathetic minor sex offender and nominating him as the Hook. I decided that the last explanation was the most likely and, filled with guilt, I swore that would be the first and last time I would ever make up a story. This was not an easy vow to keep, because I soon fell in with the Fleet Street Royal Press Corps, which made up stories all the time.

The Royal Press Corps had come for the Queen's tour of Fiji, New Zealand and Australia in December 1953 and January 1954. The *Mirror* was ambivalent about it. It was the first time a reigning monarch had visited Australia, and loyalist newspapers such as the *Sydney Morning Herald*, which tended to import Englishmen as its editors, had become very excited and were planning extensive coverage. But Norton was a republican and anti-English and was certainly not going to follow the *Herald*'s lead. So in the end the *Mirror* decided on a compromise. It would assign a junior reporter to the job, and under no circumstances would any story refer to Her Majesty as 'Queen of Australia'. I was junior enough and I had lived in Fiji, where the *Mirror*'s coverage was going to start, so I got the job and left for Suva the following week.

The British press had been travelling with the royal party from London. To an impressionable colonial who had grown up on British B-movies, all these Fleet Street reporters appeared to have come straight from West End casting. A lot of the men were either half drunk all the time or fully drunk half the time. At one stage of the tour I shared a room with Patrick O'Donovan of the *Observer* who was usually sober in the early part of the week, when he did not have to write anything, and then drunk on Friday and Saturday, when he did. In Wellington, New Zealand, he typed his story lying full length on the hotel floor because he was incapable of sitting on a chair without falling off it. When I had to take his copy to the Cable Office because he had passed out, I naturally had a peep at it. It turned out to be legible, coherent, irreverent and funny. I decided that O'Donovan drunk was a better reporter than some of the others sober.

Also staying in my hotel was a reporter named Gwen Robwyns from the London *Daily Mirror*, and since our papers had the same name, the staff sometimes confused our incoming messages. This introduced me to the confusing world of 'cablese', a language invented by desk-bound foreign editors ostensibly to save money (cables were charged by the word), but actually to lend them and their empire of foreign correspondents an aura of secret romance.

PROROBWYNS EXFORNEWSED CANST FILE EARLIEST FRIMORN GMT UPWARDS EIGHTHUNDRED HOW HM COPING HEATWISE STOP BBC SAYS DUKE EXPRESSED CONCERN PROHER HEALTH ETDEMANDING SCHEDULE

CUTS STOP WHAT SAYST OTHERS QUERY ADVISE WHEN
AUCKLANDWARDING ENDS

PROROBWYNS EXFORNEWSED YOUR HM HEALTH PAGEONE
.LEAD STOP OTHERS HAD UPCHASE LATER EDITIONS STOP
CONGRATS PROGOOD WORK STOP ONFORWARDING EXES
SYDNEY ENDS

It was catching. Within days I had a cable from the *Mirror* in Sydney.

SUN SAYS QUEEN WILL SIT CROSSLEGGED ON GROUND AT
TONGAN FEAST AND EAT ROAST PIG WITH FINGERS STOP
WHY YOU NO FILE THIS STORY QUERY SMITH

Suddenly I understood the art of being a foreign correspondent: it was not reporting what had happened today— the agencies did that; it was telling the reader what was going to happen tomorrow, or the day after. It did not matter if what you confidently predicted did not then happen because by that time you and the reader had moved on to the next prediction. For example, the Queen did not sit cross-legged on the ground at the Tongan feast—she sat in a chair—and she ate her roast pig with a knife and fork, as did her host, Queen Salote of Tonga, but I did not get a cable from Smith saying:

YOU RIGHT ABOUT QUEEN AND FEAST STOP SUN WRONG
AND HAS APOLOGIZED TO READERS STOP WELL DONE ENDS

So after that I left the reporting of the record to Reuters, the Associated Press, the Press Association, the Australian Associated Press and all the other agencies and instead concentrated on the strange little happenings, the accidents, the faux pas, the social oddities and the mechanics of a royal tour.

As the tour progressed, I developed a theory, later confirmed on other royal tours, that there was an unwritten agreement between Buckingham Palace and the press. It was as if the Palace had said to Fleet Street, 'You need us to bring in your readers, most of whom love royal stories. We need you to tell the Queen's subjects what she is up to and what a wonderful person she is. So you can write anything you like about the royals—as long as you don't question the actual institution of the monarchy.' So Fleet Street cheerfully made up all sorts of stories about the royal family—arguments, rifts, romances, pregnancies—and Buckingham Palace seldom denied them, never banned or even remonstrated with the reporters concerned, and even laid on a cocktail party or two during tours so that the press could actually meet the people they had been writing about.

Being on tour was a corrupting experience. You were your own boss and, providing you did not miss a major story, your office left you alone. You stayed in the best hotels, ate the finest food—all on expenses. How could I go back to reporting suburban courts after all this?

The *Mirror* had a London office, so I began lobbying for a posting there. The editor-in-chief quickly disillusioned me: Mr Norton did not approve of sending journalists abroad, especially to Britain. If, however, I was to get to London at my own expense and turn up at the *Mirror*'s bureau there, then no doubt a job could be found for me. I arrived in London just before Christmas 1954. The *Mirror*'s office turned out to be in Red Lion Court, rather than Fleet Street, but it was a start.

4

The *Mirror* office in London reflected Ezra Norton's Irish ambivalence about Britain. On the one hand, he recognized that London was still the major centre of overseas interest for most Australians and that his newspapers would have to cover what happened there. On the other, he refused to buy a service from any of the big news agencies because he felt that they would reflect too British an attitude. So he created his own service, staffed it with Australians and expected them to cover Britain from an Australian point of view. But having done this, he began to wonder if he could trust them. On the eve of war he had sent a flamboyant New Zealand-born journalist, Eric Baume, to report from Britain. Baume had run 'The *Daily Mirror* World Cables and *Truth* Special Service' out of a suite at the Savoy and had written the front-page lead of the first issue of the *Mirror* on 12 May 1941. Baume had employed Lady Margaret Stewart, daughter of Lord Londonderry, as a war correspondent and feature writer, and Norton suspected, correctly, that Baume was having an affair with her. When Baume wrote that he had been introduced to George VI by the Secretary of State for War, Oliver Stanley, Norton decided that Baume had been well and truly 'duchessed'—Norton's description of how the British establishment seduced Australians away from their anti-English stance by sucking them into aristocratic circles. This view was confirmed when, after the war, Norton told the London office to stress in their stories the theme 'Britain is done for', and Baume proved less than enthusiastic.

Baume was recalled, and the enlarged London office was staffed with Australian reporters assigned to cover the British scene—but ordered to have as little contact with the British as possible. It worked like this: the London editor was George Hawkes, a former Australian army officer. Under him was Keith Hooper, a former Australian war correspondent, who had the title of chief sub-editor. There was one feature writer, Eric Jessup, a former clerk in the British navy who had taken his discharge in Australia and had worked there as a jackaroo. Then there were seven journalists, of whom I was one. Because of the time difference between London and Sydney, five of us worked from six p.m. to midnight, and two from midnight to six a.m. We sat around a big U-shaped table and 'stole' stories from all the British newspapers. Of course, we did not 'steal' them intact—that would have been illegal; we took the facts, and—this is the creative part—we rewrote everything. We shuffled paragraphs around, putting the first paragraph second, paraphrasing the third, turning a direct quotation into an indirect one or vice versa, adding a sentence or two from the same item in another newspaper. Then Hooper went through the rewritten story, added a touch or two of his own and handed it to the teleprinter operator, a Cypriot-born Armenian called Victor Krikorian who had served in the British army in Cyprus, who sent it off to Sydney. Even Jessup's feature stories were scarcely original, since he gathered all the facts from the *News of the World* clippings library to which Norton had reluctantly subscribed. This recycling of news occasionally produced strange results. Sometimes we so thoroughly rewrote a story that by the time it appeared in the *Sydney Daily Mirror*, where it had been given the tabloid treatment by a Sydney sub-editor, it looked fresh and original. Then the Australian correspondents of the British newspapers would pick it up and send it to London just in case Fleet Street had missed it. And every now and then, in its new form, it got back into the very paper whence it had originated.

The work was mind-numbingly boring, relieved only when Sydney—which thought everything in Britain ran like it did in Australia, only on a bigger scale—made some impossible request, usually at eleven a.m. Sydney time, which was two a.m. in London:

EXSMITH RING BUCKPALACE ASK REAL REPEAT REAL REASON WHY MARGARET NO MARRY TOWNSEND. Or

EXBLUNDEN UPWAKE HOMESECRETARY ASK WHETHER INTENDS HANG RUTH ELLIS ENDS

We spent a lot of time devising replies that disguised the fact that Buckingham Palace did not have a twenty-four-hour answering service, and that no one knew the home secretary's private number and would not dare ring it if he did.

Very occasionally something out of the ordinary raised new questions for me on the nature of journalism, particularly the one that journalists argue over all the time: what is news? I was wandering through Harrods one afternoon, filling in an hour or two before work, and found the pet department. It seemed to have everything—puppies, kittens, hamsters, birds, rats, even snakes. And there in a remote corner, huddling in his cage, was a small kangaroo, looking as homesick as I was. I had to write about him. I painted a real tabloid picture: Australia's national emblem, brutally removed from the sunny plains of New South Wales, shivering in the English winter, waiting for some rich Englishman's spoilt child to demand brief possession of him as a Christmas plaything before committing him to his fate with the Royal Society for the Prevention of Cruelty to Animals. 'Nice piece,' said Hawkes, and then we all forgot about it. Four days later, Hawkes handed me a teleprinter message from Sydney:

PROHAWKES TRUTH READERS GREATLY DISTRESSED
KANGAROO PLIGHT HAVE CONTRIBUTED FORTY POUNDS
STERLING PROHIS RESCUE STOP BUY HIM FIND GOOD
HOME FILE EIGHT HUNDRED WORDS AND PIX HAPPY ROO
WITH NEW OWNER STOP FINCH

'Here,' said Hawkes. 'It's your story. Draw forty quid from
Miss Dwyer and go and buy the bloody kangaroo.'

'But what'll I do with him when I've bought him?' I asked.

'That's your bloody problem,' said Hawkes.

One of the other journalists, Rex Lopez, came to the rescue.
The Duke of Bedford had recently opened his stately home to
visitors, and one of the attractions was a small zoo. 'The Duke'll
take him,' Lopez said. 'Ring his gamekeeper.' I did, and it was all
arranged very quickly. I would buy the kangaroo and have him
crated and sent by rail. The gamekeeper would meet the train, the
kangaroo, a photographer from the Keystone Press Agency and
me. We would have a cup of coffee with the Duke, Duchess and
one of their sons, and then they would pose with the kangaroo in
the stables. It was amazing what a Duke would do in those days
for a bit of publicity.

I went down to Harrods and found a poncy sales assistant in
the pet department. I broadened my Australian accent. 'Listen,
mate,' I said, 'I've got some friends from Sydney coming over for
dinner on Saturday and I want to give them a bit of a treat—
kangaroo-tail soup, freshly made. Have you got any kangaroos?'
His expression did not flicker. 'We do have one, sir,' he said.

'I'll take him,' I said.

'Will that be cash or account?'

'Cash,' I said.

'And will sir be taking him with him, or does sir want him
delivered?'

The gamekeeper was at the station, and back at the stately
home the Duke and Duchess were charming over coffee. Then we
adjourned to the stables. A wooden box with a large Harrods label
stood near the door. The Duke and Duchess arranged themselves
alongside it, the gamekeeper began levering it open with a crowbar
and the photographer levelled his Speed Graphic. 'Maybe Your

Grace could give him a bit of a pat,' I suggested. At that moment the lid of the box came off. There was a thump, a brown blur, another thump and a glimpse of a kangaroo's tail disappearing over a six-foot wall in the stable yard. 'Shit,' said the photographer, 'he's bolted.' He had indeed. I wrote a lame story for Finch about the kangaroo taking happily to the wild acres of the Duke's estate, and the Duke's insistence that the animal could not be photographed in case it disturbed the settling-in period. I learned later that the kangaroo had come from a breeding farm on the Isle of Man, was accustomed to the British climate and must have found some other kangaroos on the Duke's estate because there were soon so many that they had become a nuisance. Should I have told those *Truth* readers the real story?

It did not take me long to find out that everyone else in the *Daily Mirror* and *Truth*'s London office was as bored with the job as I was, but since they had been at it longer, they had all found other interests to keep them occupied. The only reporter trying to get on in journalism was Lopez who wanted to make the leap from Red Lion Court into Fleet Street. He kept quoting the example of Murray Sayle, an Australian reporter who worked on the *People*, as proof that it could be done. One Saturday night he took me round to Sayle's flat in Notting Hill Gate. Sayle, a tall, raw-boned man with a large broken nose, ran a salon where expatriates gathered to rail against the English and discuss ways of beating the system.

Sayle was our beacon. Three years earlier he had knocked on just about every door in Fleet Street before getting a week's trial on the *People* as assistant to the legendary crime reporter Duncan Webb. Webb was then in the middle of exposing the Messina brothers, five Maltese who ran most of London's brothels. Webb would establish that some West End address was being used by prostitutes. Then he would trace the ownership of the premises back to the Messinas. The first step was often the most difficult, and Webb himself could no longer do it—the Messinas had rumbled him, and his picture was on display in every brothel in London. This is where Sayle came in. As Webb explained it to him: 'I need someone who couldn't be me, and couldn't be a copper. As a big wool man straight off the boat, looking for a bit of the old you-know-what, you'd be perfectly convincing, digger.' And how did one actually establish that premises were being used for prostitution?

'You have to get a definite offer of sex,' Webb had told Sayle. 'Get them to disrobe and name a price. Like, how much for a short time and how much for an all-nighter. Don't actually hand over any cash, though. Sam [the *People*'s managing editor] would never stand for throwing the firm's money around like that. Then you make some sort of excuse and leave.'

Sayle had gone on to prosper for the *People*—leaving only to write what is arguably the best novel on journalism, *A Crooked Sixpence*—and remembered Webb with admiration: 'Webb set a standard of honest reporting later to flower in various Insights, Daylights and other group-grope investigative journalism which has chewed up so many Finnish forests. But no one ever did it better, or produced a worse set of bad guys than the Messinas.'

But in 1955 the Australians in the *Sydney Daily Mirror* office could be encouraged only by the thought that since Sayle had broken into Fleet Street, then maybe, one day, we would too.

The Australian Rugby League football team, the Kangaroos, were touring Britain, which brought an unexpected break from the routine of Red Lion Court. Everyone in the London office had been too long out of Sydney to appreciate what big news this was back home when, in the early hours one morning, the teleprinter chattered out a message for Hawkes:

EXRICHARDS SUN BEATING US HOLLOW ON KANGAROOS
STOP UPSTEP COVERAGE IMMEDIATELY ENDS

A few hours later I was on my way to Ilkley in Yorkshire where the Australian team was staying. I was to cover their last test match in Britain and then tour France with them. Within days I faced the dilemma of all sports reporters: do you write what really goes on and then get so frozen out by the players and officials that you never get another story, or do you keep your mouth shut, write anodyne nonsense and enjoy being accepted as a non-playing member of the team?

On the first night, before I had presented myself to the Kangaroos' manager, I was dining anonymously in the hotel's small restaurant. Four Australian players were at the bar when a local businessman and his attractive wife walked in and were shown to their table. 'Hey, darling,' said one of the Australians to the woman, 'would a quick fuck be out of the question?' The woman blushed, and her husband immediately pushed his chair back and stood up. So did the four Australians at the bar. The man registered their size, realized who they were and thought better of whatever he had been planning. He took his wife by the arm and left. I mentioned the incident to the hotel manager, who said that his takings had dropped dramatically because none of his regular customers would come to the restaurant or the bar for fear of Australians. I did not write the story.

It got worse in France. After a match at the Parc des Princes the team decided to visit a brothel in Montmartre. The man from the *Sydney Sun*, Ian Arnold, and I decided to go along. A few modest Kangaroos went off to private bedrooms, but most of the action took place in one large room with two seasoned women and one famous forward taking part, and ten players and two journalists as the audience. The forward was drunk and could not perform. The two French women did their professional best, without success. '*Il n'arrive pas jusqu'au demain matin,*' one of them complained when what seemed like half an hour's oral sex failed to produce any result. The forward now became aggressive and demanded his money back, threatening to drop-kick both women between the banister posts. The manager, a small man wearing a green leather apron, appeared in the doorway, assessed the scene, went away and returned remarkably quickly with an equally small French policeman. He was not in the least troubled by the size of the opposing team. He began to speak quietly in French, saying that it would be best for everyone if the Australians now left. If, however, they did not wish to do so, then he explained, his voice rising, they could stay. He would then beat their heads to a bloody pulp, an action he graphically described and even illustrated, pounding to pieces with his baton a small bedside table. This was language the Australians understood, and Arnold and I watched in amazement as they filed quietly out of the room and on to the street. We did not write the story.

The French players were equally unpolished. One of them, a Catalan called Poux, had a French wife who was the image of Brigitte Bardot, then every male's erotic fantasy. In a bar in Perpignan, with the pastis flowing freely, Poux watched quietly as one Australian after another made a crude pass at her. Then he punched out the bottoms of two wooden chairs and, as an encore, challenged the Australians to a test of manhood. He took a heavy ceramic ashtray from the bar, held it flat against the wall, and then head-butted it until it broke in two. The Australians abandoned the Bardot lookalike to prove that they too had foreheads of steel. The game stopped only when the bar ran out of ashtrays. Everyone appeared at breakfast the next morning with large red weals in the middle of their foreheads. I did not write the story.

A few nights later I asked a friendly and apparently civilized French sports writer whether it was always like this with visiting players and whether he ever wrote about it. He looked surprised. 'Is always like this,' he said. And he did not write about it because his editor and his readers would wonder what the news value was. That night I saw him trying to punch a fellow journalist who had disagreed with his match report and, two days later, wielding a folding steel chair, he led a pitch invasion of spectators anxious to get their hands on a Kangaroo who had stiff-armed a Frenchman. I did not write this story, either. That is the way it goes, then and now. While sports writers give the impression of being only too willing to criticize sportsmen, it's all froth and bubble—they never write the most interesting stories because they have to live and travel with the people they write about.

After the Kangaroos tour I began to wonder if I was cut out to be a journalist. Compared with any nine-to-five job, journalism was all a big adventure: excitement, freedom of movement, a chance to use your wits and initiative, a sense of being, if not a part of mainstream events, a close-up observer. But it could also be seedy. To do it well you had to betray the trust of too many people. You winkled your way into their presence, won their confidence, got them to tell you things they should not and then exposed them to the world at large. I was amazed that people could be so innocent as not to realize the journalist's intention. A colleague went to interview an elderly, retired couple and the next day exposed them as one-time Soviet spies. When the story appeared, he sent them a big bunch of flowers and a note in appreciation of their help. He showed me their reply. Part of it read: 'Your flowers cheered us up enormously on what was otherwise a most miserable day.' It did not occur to them that the flowers had come from the very man who had made their day so miserable.

Pondering this, an advertisement in the local newspaper caught my eye. 'Be your own boss. American vending machines can pave your way to a fortune.' In an attic in Soho, a slick salesman convinced me that five machines dispensing peanuts, strategically placed in pubs around London, could bring me fifty pounds a week, nearly three times what I was earning at the *Mirror*. All I had to do was to buy the machines at two hundred pounds each and contract to buy the peanuts only from him. I took Lopez on as a partner, and we persuaded five publicans in the East End—'Big drinkers down there,' Lopez said—to allow us to install the machines. A week later we returned to top-up the peanuts, empty the cash, pay the publican his ten per cent and bank our money. We ran into a barrage of abuse: the peanuts were stale, the machines gave out only twenty-five nuts for a shilling and the customers were incapable of putting one hand under the dispensing spout while turning the operating handle with the other, so peanuts showered all over the pub carpet and then were trodden deep into the pile. 'Get it outta here,' said the licensee of the Iron Bridge in the Old Kent Road, 'before I chuck it out and you after it.' Lopez and I tried to get our money back from the Soho entrepreneur. 'No money back, lads,' he said. 'Not company policy.' But what about the stale peanuts? 'Stale they may be,' he said. 'But they're a bigger nut.' In the end he agreed to swap our peanut machines for ones dispensing bubblegum. But we had already lost heart and instead of doing deals with newsagents to place the bubblegum machines outside their shops, we installed them in our flat and adjusted the money slot so that drunken guests could help themselves.

Sayle advised us to stick with what we knew, so three of us, Lopez, Philip Harris and I, started Global News and Features—a worldwide agency that offered to provide discriminating subscribers a range of news stories, feature articles, columns and photographs. The problem of where to obtain all this editorial material was easily solved—we had it all to hand in the *Mirror* office where officially we still worked. We would take all the material that came in from newspapers, wire services and picture agencies, then tailor it for our subscribers. We rented an office in Chancery Lane with one desk and a telephone manned during office hours by Harris. We designed a lavish brochure listing Global News and Features offices in all the major capitals of the world, actually addresses of friends and relatives. We sent the brochure out to every newspaper in Britain along with a sample sports column written by Jimmy Jones, the former tennis champion. Nobody answered, nobody rang. Then in the second week, the features editor of the *Birmingham Post* telephoned. Would we get our office in Paris to cover the French motor show for him? Certainly—two thousand words and a selection of photographs for a hundred pounds. The trouble was that our man in Paris was a friend's mother who made dolls for a living, and we had neither the time nor the money to go to Paris to cover the motor show ourselves. So our editorial staff swung into action. Lopez got all the press releases from the Paris organizers of the motor show and began to rewrite them as if he were there. I persuaded a darkroom assistant at Keystone to superimpose a photograph of me alongside the new car Renault had unveiled in Paris. Then we sent the whole package express to Birmingham: a personal report on the Paris motor show by Phillip Knightley. The telephone rang the next evening. It was the *Birmingham Post* features editor, and he was very angry. 'What do you take me for, lad, a bloody idiot? I've read all the Paris handouts and I can spot a rewrite a mile off. Is this all you've got to offer?' I said I would get on to our man in Paris and see what he could do. That was Global News and Features' only assignment, but it was not the end of our venture.

Six weeks later Hawkes announced that the entire editorial staff was suspended while a special investigator—sent from Sydney by Norton—examined the office's work practices and established the truth or otherwise of some serious criminal allegations. Norton had somehow learned about Global News and Features and thought that the whole office was involved. The investigator invited me to submit a statement confessing everything. There was no sense in denying it, so I did, but added a sentence that saved me from the sack and perhaps prosecution. It said, 'All I was trying to do was to take the first step to becoming a newspaper baron. Since Mr Norton is one himself I am sure he will understand the attractions.' We all escaped unscathed—except poor Victor Krikorian, the Armenian teleprinter operator. Unknown to most of us, he had been moonlighting at the Soviet news agency Tass, and in the atmosphere of confession engendered by Norton's investigator someone had betrayed him. Hawkes got a secretary to ring Tass and ask for Victor, and since the Tass staff were used to women ringing him at all hours, the call was put through. When Victor came on the line, he heard not the voice of one of his girlfriends, but that of Hawkes. 'Victor,' he said, 'you're sacked.' Hawkes did not know it at the time but he did Krikorian a favour. He rose through the ranks at Tass to be an economic journalist and, eventually, adviser to the Soviet government on international commodity prices and then, when the USSR collapsed, a successful antique dealer in Surrey.

I decided to leave town. I went to Victoria Station and asked the ticket clerk for the longest railway journey he could sell me. 'Vladivostock—but it'll take you six months to get a Soviet visa,' he said. Otherwise? 'Basra on the Persian Gulf. Orient Express to Istanbul, the Taurus Express to Baghdad and then the metre gauge to Basra. End of the line.' I bought a second-class single for forty pounds, put journalism behind me for the moment and set off for the end of the line.

BRAND LEADER

Financial Times, 27 January 1994

FINTAN O'TOOLE

Tony O'Reilly, chairman, president and chief executive of Heinz   IRISH TIMES

On the morning last December that Tony O'Reilly spoke at a conference in Belfast, his own newspaper the *Irish Independent* ran two full pages about the event. One of them was dominated by a stark black-and-white advertisement. At its centre was a map of Ireland. Around the map was the distinctive triple-bordered shape of a label familiar to devotees of tomato ketchup and baked beans. Within the borders were five large letters spelling HEINZ. There was nothing else—no slogan, no exhortation: just this strange map of a small island in the Atlantic. Inside the jagged contours of its coastline, this country had no political boundaries, no features, no landmarks of history, none of the resonant names or contested zones of a place emerging from a dark and tangled past. It was a clear, uncomplicated space, a brand image, a label that could be stuck on a billion sauce bottles.

As he rose to speak that morning in the Europa Hotel, against a backdrop of cobalt blue emblazoned with the logo of Independent Newspapers and an abstract painting of the globe, Tony O'Reilly seemed the perfect citizen of an Ireland that had escaped from itself. He had been introduced as the Irish head of a multinational company, H. J. Heinz, with expected sales this year of nine billion dollars, as a man who 'encapsulates perfectly' the theme of the conference—global economics. And that image had been driven home by his own newspapers over many years. His *Sunday Independent* once devoted an eight-page colour supplement to him, headlined A MAN FOR ALL CONTINENTS, with no fewer than seventeen photographs of the proprietor: Tony O'Reilly with Henry Kissinger, Tony O'Reilly with Margaret Thatcher, Tony O'Reilly with Valéry Giscard D'Estaing, Tony O'Reilly with Robert Mugabe, Tony O'Reilly stepping off his corporate jet, Tony O'Reilly with his beautiful first wife and six beautiful children.

In Belfast that morning he laid out the colour supplement of his own personality for the admiring gaze of his audience, every inch the smiling public man, at ease in the way that only someone who has been a star since he was barely out of school can be. A rugby international at the age of eighteen, he still has the height and bearing of a sportsman, even if the smooth beauty of his youth has now become rugged, its effect more imposing than dazzling. Because he seems to take his own air of authority for granted, he can afford to be charming, even gossipy, knowing that nobody will take advantage of the sense of intimacy he creates.

He is a man for whom there is no clear distinction between the private and the public self, a man whose acquaintances all remark on the fact that almost every meal in one of his houses in Pittsburgh or in Ireland seems to be a public event, shared with friends, contacts, associates: people who are, for one reason or another, being wooed. One former colleague remembers the brilliant mixture of private charm and public purpose: 'I found him big, expansive, talkative. He tells funny stories; he's charming; he makes you feel that his wealth, his big house and his ambience are yours to enjoy, that you're being given privileged and undivided access to it all. You need that kind of charm and loquaciousness and those gifts in business and in public life, and he's got them in abundance. You find yourself with a sense of intimacy with him in your conversation, because he's indiscreet, and he speaks in a mischievous way about people he knows, so you feel quite close to him. And then you hear that if any of his staff fail to call him "Doctor O'Reilly", he hangs them up by their heels and pours boiling pitch down the front of their trousers.'

The contradiction is present even in his name. He is universally known as Tony, except in his own newspapers, where he is always referred to as 'Dr A. J. F. O'Reilly', the doctorate being a Ph.D in food marketing awarded by the University of Bradford in 1980 for a thesis he submitted on the launch of Kerrygold butter, his first great business coup. Yet in reality Tony and Dr A. J. F. are indistinguishable in the persona of a man with whom the whole world is on intimate terms.

Even in front of his formal audience in Belfast, he presented that same package of public and private, knowing that the details of his own career had already acquired the aura of legend. Many of his listeners could have rattled off its milestones. The birth of Anthony John Francis O'Reilly in Dublin on 7 May 1936 as the first and only child of an apparently respectable middle-class couple, his mother a housewife, his father a customs official. His education at a fee-paying Jesuit school, followed by a law degree at University College Dublin. His glorious rugby career in which he

Tony O'Reilly the rugby international   IRISH TIMES

played twenty-nine times for Ireland. His membership from the age of nineteen of the British Lions, the all-star touring team made up of the best rugby players from Ireland, England, Scotland and Wales, and the swashbuckling tours of South Africa, New Zealand and Australia through which he made a name for himself on three continents. The sure-footedness with which he bartered that

49

sporting fame into an equally dazzling corporate career, first as a managing director of the Irish state dairy and sugar companies, then on to his present pinnacle as chairman, president and chief operating officer of H. J. Heinz, and chairman and controlling shareholder of Independent Newspapers in Dublin and a range of other Irish-based companies. His first marriage to Susan Cameron, an Australian with whom he had six children, including triplets. His second marriage to Chryss Goulandris, a member of a hugely wealthy Greek shipping dynasty which has become an important ally in his business ventures. His Georgian mansion, stud farm and estate at Castlemartin in County Kildare, Ireland, and his other homes in Dublin, West Cork, Pittsburgh (where Heinz has its headquarters) and the Bahamas. His foundation of the Ireland Fund, a multinational charitable trust that funds projects in both parts of Ireland.

He littered his speech in Belfast with anecdotes drawn from most of these chapters of his own legend, reminding his audience that he was himself his own message. And all the time his own story was made to seem a parable of globalization, of a man rising from a specific time and place into a great network of worldwide power. Even his jokes were global—flow charts parodying management styles in China, Britain, Italy, Saudi Arabia, Latin America, Ireland and the United States appearing on the screen beside him as he performed his accomplished warm-up act.

In the face of this tour of far horizons, the petty details of Irish history, so recently strewn in the shape of twisted metal and torn flesh on the streets outside the hotel, dissolved into insignificance. Facing an audience of besuited businessmen drawn from both sides of the Irish border and both sides of the Protestant–Catholic divide, he felt confident enough to tease them with a small political joke. His lecture, he announced, would be called 'The island of Ireland—united'. He paused just long enough to hear the strain in the room, the jerk of raw nerves being touched by the cruel point of politics. And then, his craggy face broken by a small smile, he picked up his sentence: ' . . . to a global economic system.'

After the jokes, he started to talk about history. He explained to the members of his audience, with the help of slides, and as if they didn't know this, that we are at the end of the twentieth century. The century, he said, is a triptych. In the first panel are two brutal world wars. In the second is a forty-five-year period of geopolitical equilibrium and dramatic economic growth. And in the third, 'here we are', in a new age of 'capital ruthlessly seeking the best rate of return', of 'the emergence of the global consumer'. The twentieth century, he said, was dominated by ideological competition, but the twenty-first will belong to commercial competition.

The slide showing now was made up of a large picture of O'Reilly's friend Nelson Mandela and a smaller one of Yitzhak Rabin and Yasser Arafat shaking hands, with the caption 'The Collapse of Communism and the Promise of Peace'. It looked like the end of history, and he mentioned that Francis Fukuyama wrote a book of that name after the demolition of the Berlin Wall.

For Tony O'Reilly, the great symbolic event of the last decade was not so much the fall of the Wall as the opening of the first McDonald's in Moscow. It was, he has said, not just a new product launch; it was 'a social and cultural event of international proportions.' While others were thinking about the peace dividend at the end of the cold war or about the triumph of democracy, he was thinking about the beginning of global marketing and the arrival of the new, placeless consumer, belonging to a world where allegiances to brand names have replaced the more dangerous and visceral loyalties of history and geography.

He looks and sounds like a man who has made a nonsense of history and indeed of geography. His deep voice carries an Irish accent that has been levelled out by a quarter of a century in America so that it seems to echo with only the faintest undertone of time and place. His easy mimicry, the way he slips, in his jokes, into perfectly tuned Belfast or Dublin, or English or American accents, serves merely to emphasize the neutrality of his own voice, to draw attention to the fact that local inflections are something he can put on or take off at will. And everything he said that morning in Belfast seemed to suggest that he really believes that history is over, that the business of the world, now and for evermore, is business.

But something—perhaps the fact that he was speaking in a

hotel that was known until recently, in spite of the antiseptic internationalism of its decor, as the most bombed building in Europe—seemed suddenly to make him doubtful. History did not really end, he mused. It 'emerged from the permafrost of communism. Theological nationalism is re-emerging.' It was an anomalous moment of doubt and it passed quickly. He moved on to talk with his usual certainty about the scarce and demanding nature of capital, about the need to get governments off the back of business, about the beneficial effects of the North American Free Trade Agreement in allowing Heinz to keep wages down. But somehow, the moment lingered as an undercurrent of fear. Even Tony O'Reilly can't mention theological nationalism in Belfast without reminding his audience that there are other forces in the world besides global competition. And even he knows, from his own life, something about those forces.

Had any of the businessmen at that conference in Belfast been present in November 1982 at a function in the Abbey Theatre in Dublin to honour the novelist Peadar O'Donnell, they would have been amazed to find Tony O'Reilly not merely present but more or less running the show. O'Donnell embodied in many ways a past that few of them would have wanted to recognize. As well as being a distinguished writer, he was also the last surviving member of the executive of the old Irish Republican Army. He was a Marxist radical, a fiery trade union organizer and professional agitator. And he was, for five years in the 1940s, Tony O'Reilly's mentor. When O'Reilly started his tribute to O'Donnell by declaring that the old man had 'almost reared me', many of those present thought at first that it was another of O'Reilly's jokes, that the punchline would be coming soon.

There was no punchline. O'Donnell's nephew and namesake was O'Reilly's best friend at school, and the two boys spent all their summers in O'Donnell's big house in the countryside near Dungloe in County Donegal. 'Peadar was Uncle Peadar to me,' O'Reilly told his audience, 'and his wife was Auntie Lil . . . I remember Peadar's glittering conversation, and the notion that we were both interested in Marx: he in Karl, I in Groucho.' The predictable joke, intended to dismiss the strangeness of this icon of multinational capitalism adopting a communist uncle, could not hide the vestiges of rapture in the memory of golden times: 'I learned how to fish there, how to row and how to drink altar wine.' Those, he recalled, were 'sunlit days, and both glittering and glamorous as well'. For once he had nothing clever to say, no pronouncements to make. For once he allowed the distance between the president of Heinz and a certain kind of Irish past to stretch over a terrain not of triumph but of loss.

O'Donnell was just one of three veterans of Ireland's bloody wars who helped to shape O'Reilly's early life, and the memory of the other two was less golden. When he was born in 1936, in a state still struggling to emerge from the bloody circumstances of its birth, Tony O'Reilly was named after his mother's brother, Tony O'Connor, who was always to be his favourite uncle. Uncle Tony was a man who had seen history at first-hand. In the savage civil war that followed the Anglo–Irish treaty of 1921, fought between those who accepted the establishment of an Irish Free State within the British Empire and those who wanted to hold out for a republic, the O'Connors took the Free State side. Tony O'Connor himself joined the Free State army when it was established, and he later wrote that before he was twenty he had killed at least a dozen fellow Irishmen in the wild country-road skirmishes that constituted the civil war, rising in the process to the rank of sergeant.

He survived the war but he was always haunted by the memory of a day in January 1923 in Athlone, where he had grown up and played as a child with a 'tall, slender and dark-haired' boy. For more than fifty years, he carried with him the secret of what had happened to that boy. In 1975, when O'Reilly had ascended beyond the internecine hatreds of a small nation and was already president and chief executive of H. J. Heinz, he let the secret out.

O'Reilly had by then reached a point from which he could look back on Irish history, with all its entanglements, as a joke. In 1970, for instance, when he was managing director of Heinz UK, he had made an extraordinary comeback, after an absence of fifteen years, to play rugby for Ireland against England at Twickenham. In the programme for the match, he wrote a burlesque of Anglo-Irish history in which even the massacres of Cromwell could be laughed about: 'To the English it is a game of rugger—to the Irish a historical pageant, the continuation of centuries of loose rucks, crooked into the scrum, and bad refereeing, including a particularly nasty period when England were strong up front and had Oliver Cromwell at fly-half, "a very mean fella with the boot and elbow and distinctly anti-clerical when he got you on the ground", as a decaying Irish wing-forward was heard to remark.'

For O'Connor, though, history was not a game, but a personal burden, a story he would like to forget but was compelled to remember. Even then, it was too painful to be told bluntly and was wrapped in a thin layer of fiction, as a novel called *He's Somewhere In There*. Its status was deliberately confused in a foreword confessing that the story, in spite of its fictional form, was 'a factual account of the Western Sector during the Irish Civil War'.

If the line between fact and fiction is unclear, so too is that between history and news. The memories of bloody death that came spilling out between the covers of the book had an awful familiarity in 1975, in the middle of the worst period of sectarian murder in the Northern Ireland conflict. The sense of violence as a cycle, an inescapable undertow, even 'a way of life', is continually present in Tony O'Connor's memory.

What he used the novel to recount was his own betrayal of his friend Johnny, the boy he used to play with in Athlone. He and Johnny were neighbours and best friends. Johnny joined the IRA and, when the truce with the British was declared, emerged from the underground as a glamorous hero. Wanting to be like him, O'Connor joined the new national army. As soon as he was in, the army split, and Johnny disappeared into the diehard faction, leaving O'Connor behind, caught in a nightmare of carnage.

After seven months of war, his comrades brought in six captured republicans, Johnny among them, and decided to shoot them. O'Connor was forced to watch as his friend was killed, afraid to speak or to plead: 'Through a mist of tears I tried hard to restrain, I looked over at Johnny with the life gone out of him. Those gay eyes would smile no more, and he would be buried in a lost grave thirty yards from the handball alley where we had played so often.'

He was haunted ever afterwards, not just by the deed, but by its secrecy: 'Only those involved would know they were gone. There would be no listings in daily orders, no newspaper reports. It could be months or years before relations heard what had happened to their rebel husbands or sons. Talk was dangerous, and the men who were unlucky enough to form part of any firing party were always given separate, speedy postings to various camps around the country. Even then, one careless slip would result in them being trailed and a bullet-ridden body found in a ditch.'

When Johnny's mother came to ask about her son, O'Connor said nothing, but fifty years on, he reflected that Johnny would remain: 'Forever and forgotten, like those with him will be forgotten. They fought for a cause that failed, and how it failed! And they will be forgotten because Ireland, in its own shame, cannot afford to remember them.'

By the time the book appeared, O'Reilly already controlled Independent Newspapers, the largest newspaper group in Ireland. The book's oblique commentary on news—on the force of facts that do not appear in the newspapers, on the way today's news headlines are yesterday's dark secrets, on the things that societies cannot afford to remember and speak about—must have struck O'Reilly with peculiar force. All the more so because he had his own intimate secrets of subterfuge and betrayal to protect.

In March 1987 Tony O'Reilly handed over a piece of England to Margaret Thatcher. Having bought Cape Cornwall, a mile of English coastline, he presented it to Mrs Thatcher at a public ceremony, remarking that it was especially piquant that an Irishman should be presenting the title deeds to a piece of 'English land' to a British prime minister, and that he did so with a special sense of privilege. It was an odd but telling moment, a half-comic, half-serious reversal of those poignant end-of-empire scenes such as the surrender of Dublin Castle to Michael Collins in 1922 or the handing over of Irish ports to Eamon de Valera in 1939, when O'Reilly was a small child. It was an act of historic cheek, but also an act of great confidence, a public sign that here was an Irishman who didn't have to watch out for himself in England.

This confidence was new among Irishmen. A story that exemplifies older attitudes happened one night in the Second World War. Brendan Bracken, the British minister for information, was introduced at the Ritz to Major-General Emmet Dalton, like Tony O'Connor a veteran of the Irish civil war. It was ostensibly an encounter between a successful Englishman and an Irishman who had taken arms against England. When he had stood, successfully, as Tory candidate for North Paddington in 1929, Bracken had himself described in the local papers as being 'of Anglo-Irish stock . . . born in Bedfordshire nearly thirty years ago. He has residences in North Street, Westminster, and in Bedfordshire, Scotland and Ireland. He graduated from Oxford University.' He was, in other words, exactly the sort of person who might own, as he did, a controlling interest in the *Economist* and the *Financial Times*.

But Dalton recognized Bracken and said to Lord Milton, who was introducing them, 'Brendan and I know one another of old. We were schoolmates in Dublin.' Bracken tried to look puzzled. How could a wealthy Bedfordshire man of Anglo-Irish stock have been to school with a lower-middle-class Irish rebel? Dalton became angry. 'If you don't remember me, Brendan,' he said, 'I bloody well remember you and those corduroy trousers which you wore day in day out until you stank to high heaven. The smell is not out of my nostrils yet.'

Bracken was the most spectacular example of what an Irishman once had to do if he wanted to be an English press baron. Brought up Catholic and Irish in Dublin, the son of a Fenian revolutionary, he reinvented himself as an English toff. When he first arrived in England, he pretended to be Australian. He stayed in Oxford for a while, so that he could subsequently pass himself off as a graduate of Balliol. And he acquired for himself a set of impeccably Tory and imperialist views, impressing Winston Churchill as a soulmate and indispensable ally.

The problem with such a feat of camouflage was that it entailed a constant risk of exposure. The power involved in being the owner of newspapers was limited by the possibility of being a victim of

Tony O'Reilly presents Mrs Thatcher with the deeds to Cape Cornwall TOPHAM/PA NEWS

newspapers. In 1944 Lord Beaverbrook sent a reporter to Ireland to uncover Bracken's true background. Bracken used his powers as minister for information to excise from the *Evening Standard* references to his father's record as an Irish rebel. Even so, there were always people like Dalton who knew him when his trousers stank.

When, in a dawn raid in early 1994, O'Reilly bought twenty-five per cent of Newspaper Publishing, publishers of the London *Independent* and *Independent on Sunday*, he became the first Irishman since Bracken to own a large chunk of an English media group. As a keen reader of English history, he knew enough about his predecessor to recognize the similarities between himself and Bracken. Like Bracken, O'Reilly came from a family with a history of Irish nationalist connections. Like him, he grew up in the

Catholic middle-class suburbs of north Dublin. Like him, he was educated by Irish Jesuits. And like Bracken, he idolized Churchill.

Bracken's connection with Churchill was so strong that there were false but widespread rumours that he was the prime minister's natural son. O'Reilly's connection was second-hand. Churchill was his 'great hero', and he quoted him regularly in his speeches. 'His life to me,' O'Reilly once told the BBC, 'was and continues to be an inspiration.' Asked what he had taken from Churchill, he replied, 'I think he was a very selfish man. He believed he was the epicentre of all that was happening. He was . . . a truly conceited man. He felt he was very important, and I suppose that is one of the principle criteria of success—to believe in yourself so strongly that you are the epicentre of all that is happening.'

O'Reilly could have turned into a milder version of Bracken. The rugby writer Terry Maclean, covering the Lions rugby tour of New Zealand in 1959, noted O'Reilly's attitude to those English members of the side who came from upper-class backgrounds. It was, he wrote, 'a strange regard, almost amounting to envy, for those fortunate folk who move through the world with a lordly calm based upon a secure place in the scheme of things.' His idolization of Churchill, his avid reading of biographies of other British prime ministers such as Disraeli and Gladstone, his lord-of-the-manor posturing at his Castlemartin estate, all bear witness to that strange regard. When the band played 'Land of Hope and Glory' as he entered the village hall in Kilcullen, near Castlemartin, for his fiftieth birthday party, it was not an entirely inappropriate anthem.

But O'Reilly never had the opportunity that Bracken had to reinvent himself. His rugby career made him a star before he was twenty, a visible international symbol of Ireland. Disguise, even had he wanted it, was impossible for a red-haired boy in a green shirt, ducking and weaving before cheering crowds. And besides, O'Reilly had darker, more intimate secrets to conceal than Brendan Bracken ever had. Disguise invites revelation, and early in his career, O'Reilly was vulnerable to revelations.

When he was seventeen, O'Reilly discovered that he was not, as he had always believed, an only child. In his last year at school, one of the priests who taught him took him aside and told him that his parents were not married, that his father had another wife and other children—three half-sisters and a half-brother whom he had never seen. The priest may have told him all of this because he wanted to spare him the shock of later revelations, or he may have been concerned that Tony was considering, as most bright Irish boys did at some stage, entering the priesthood. An illegitimate child could not be a priest.

That rule reflected a wider prejudice in an overwhelmingly Catholic society obsessed with sexual purity. The Irish state made it explicit in law that illegitimate children were second class. The Legitimacy Act of 1931, passed just five years before O'Reilly was born, allowed that a child born out of wedlock might inherit its mother's property if she died without making a will, but it refused to grant any such rights of succession to the estate of a child's natural father who would be, after all, much more likely to have money.

Only in 1964 did Irish law give statutory expression to the notion that an unmarried woman had the right to be regarded as the guardian of her child. Even then, the stigma of illegitimacy retained the sanction of law. Not until 1987 was the legal concept of illegitimacy abolished in Ireland. Well past the age of fifty, O'Reilly, as well as being the richest man in Ireland was also, secretly, a second-class Irishman.

O'Reilly's position was in one sense less shameful than that of the child of an ordinary unmarried mother: he was cherished and recognized by both his natural parents. But in another sense it was more darkly secretive. For most illegitimate children, the sin was acknowledged and open, the shame explicit. There was, at least, little else to be revealed. But for him, his public identity was a subterfuge. His parents pretended to be married and concealed the existence of a whole other family. His cupboard contained not a skeleton, but several living reminders of what was being hidden: his half-siblings. Not only was the existence of his father's other family a secret, but so was the fact that he himself knew about it. He told neither his father nor his mother that he shared their private knowledge until the early 1970s. For twenty more years after that, until he allowed his official biographer Ivan Fallon to reveal the truth, he watched as every profile of him in a magazine or newspaper around the world repeated the official lie that he was an only child.

One can never know how much one's inner life is shaped by social circumstances, and no one else can ever guess. But it is hard to avoid the belief that something of his anomalous origins must be present in what Tony O'Reilly has become. It may be there in his obsessive, driven hunger for success: this is a man who, already one of the highest paid managers in America, used his spare time to build a private industrial empire and to pursue the dream of becoming a global media mogul. It may be there in his attitude to Ireland, the peculiar mixture of distance from a society and intimate knowledge of its workings that belongs to a secret outsider who looks like the ultimate insider. And it must be there in the overwhelming desire to control news, to have power over image and information.

If the Ireland that Tony O'Reilly grew up in had had any of the tabloid newspapers that he now controls—newspapers such as the *Sunday World* or the Irish edition of the British *Daily Star* (a tabloid which he controls jointly with Express Newspapers in London and which is further downmarket than Murdoch's *Sun*) —they would certainly have revealed his secrets. Rugby had made him a glamorous public figure, fair game for prurient curiosity. If, at any time in his youth, his family background had been revealed, it would have caused not just personal hurt but probably fatal damage to his public career. His success depended on media reticence, on the maintenance of a clear distinction between the private realm and the public.

In 1962, for example, when O'Reilly was head of the Irish Milk Marketing Board, and his car hit a cyclist as he was driving back from a rugby match, he was able to arrange through his father's contacts with the local hospital and the local newspaper to have the incident kept quiet, and no newspaper reported it, even though he was one of the best-known men in Ireland. In the most intimate way imaginable, he learned the meaning of news. He learned that the ability to control what can and cannot be said about you is an indispensable form of power. For such a man, the ownership of newspapers would always be more than a business.

None of this has had any discernible effect on his attitude to news values, and his tabloid papers have been no better, if no worse, than those belonging to Rupert Murdoch, whom he affects to regard as a barbarian at the gates. He publicly defended the *Sunday World*, for instance, when some Independent Newspapers shareholders attacked it at the company's annual general meeting. One of them complained particularly about an article about female bus conductors in Dublin, then a new phenomenon and an important test case for women in traditionally male roles, which appeared under the headline RANDY CLIPPIES. It was, the shareholder said, 'a cheap and scurrilous attack on the sexual morality of an easily identified small group of women in this city.' O'Reilly told him, though, that 'just because of the somewhat prurient nature of some of its publications', there was no reason why the *Sunday World* should not be part of Independent Newspapers. 'In many cases,' he remarked, 'we try to lead public taste, but in most we follow it.'

In April 1993, the *Sunday Independent* ran what purported to be an interview with Bishop Eamon Casey, who had fled Ireland after admitting that he was the father of a child. Had it ever taken place, the interview would have been a worldwide scoop. But in fact, as the paper subsequently admitted, it had not taken place. O'Reilly, when asked about this, merely said that he was 'out of the country' when the story ran and that he had not read it or been briefed by his executives about it before it appeared. He wasn't, he said, involved in making editorial decisions 'in that way'.

But he is certainly involved in other ways. In 1973, he bought control of Independent Newspapers in Dublin for just one million pounds. The company now has assets of five hundred million pounds and effectively controls businesses worth a billion. Slowly at first and then quite suddenly, Independent Newspapers has expanded beyond Ireland and into Britain, France, Portugal, Mexico, South Africa, Australia and New Zealand. Since the beginning of 1994, Independent has acquired sixty per cent of the Argus group, South Africa's largest newspaper chain; forty-three per cent of Newspaper Publishing in Britain; fifty-five per cent of Australian Provincial Newspapers; twenty-five per cent of Irish Press Newspapers in Ireland; and forty-four per cent of Wilson and Horton, the largest newspaper group in New Zealand. It also has extensive interests in cable television in Ireland; radio and television in Australia; and outdoor advertising in Portugal, France and Mexico. And it is clear that O'Reilly intends to expand his empire: he tried to buy the Fairfax group in Australia in 1991 but lost out to Conrad Black, and has made little secret of his interest in both the Mirror and Express groups in Britain.

'I have never sought to exercise any personal political power in the newspapers,' he has always claimed. Guarantees of editorial independence were an important part of his failed bid for the Fairfax group, and of his attempt to gain control of Newspaper Publishing in Britain. But he does hold a three-day strategy meeting every year which his editors as well as his managers are expected to attend. And he talks on the phone every day to Independent's deputy chairman, John Meagher.

When Independent Newspapers tried to gain a majority shareholding in the Irish *Sunday Tribune*, O'Reilly had to convince the Competition Authority there that the company would not limit the newspaper's editorial independence. The authority was shown a quotation from O'Reilly, inspired by the style book of the *Washington Post*, of which he was then a director, in which he stated that 'In a world where the ownership of newspapers is increasingly concentrated amongst a smaller group of names . . . the newspaper's duty is to its readers and to the public at large and not to the private interests of the owner.' The Authority was also told that Independent Newspapers had agreed an editorial charter for the *Tribune* guaranteeing editorial independence. But it was unconvinced by either of these submissions. Nobody seriously doubts that O'Reilly's influence, however passive, is pervasive.

In refusing him permission to take a majority stake in the *Sunday Tribune*, the Competition Authority pointed out that his proposal for an editorial charter would have little real effect: 'There would not seem to be a possibility . . . that an editor could be completely independent of the proprietor of the paper, and it seems unlikely that this could ever be properly established. At the end of the day, the editor is constrained by commercial and financial considerations, which can be conclusive. The editor may exercise self-censorship, deliberately or unconsciously. There may be direct interference by the proprietor, or influence may be imposed in more subtle ways, and an editor may take heed of the proprietor for fear of losing his job.' In fact, in early 1994, Independent's two directors on the *Tribune* board supported a successful motion to sack the paper's editor Vincent Browne, who had attacked the *Sunday Independent* in print over the Bishop Casey affair.

In spite of such concerns, Tony O'Reilly has now reached a position in Ireland where, as the Competition Authority expressed it in 1995 in another report on his dealings—this time his investments in the rival Irish Press group—'the possibility cannot be ruled out that in a relatively short period of time, the only remaining Irish newspapers will be those owned in whole or in part by Independent Newspapers plc.' The authority found, in this instance, that O'Reilly's investment in another Dublin daily, the *Irish Press*, which closed in 1995, was made to prevent it being taken over by another newspaper group 'which might be expected to compete more vigorously in the market for newspapers and newspaper advertising.' The rhetoric of free-market competition that trips so easily off O'Reilly's lips is somewhat undermined by the authority's finding that his Irish Press investment 'amounts to an abuse of a dominant position' in the market place.

The complex relationship between politics, money and the control of newspapers that O'Reilly embodies is best illustrated in the hysteria over oil exploration off the coast of Ireland in the 1980s. While the national debt rose beyond twenty billion pounds, and the rate of unemployment went beyond twenty per cent, while all the country's dreams of prosperous modernity turned sour, ordinary people in rural Ireland started to see statues of the Virgin moving, waving, weeping, floating. But while the doctors and dentists, the solicitors and small businessmen of the cities sneered at them, they too looked to their own icon to perform a miracle. Instead of prayers and candles, they turned for salvation to O'Reilly.

Such was the charisma, the allure, the sheer magic of O'Reilly's name, that at his call Irish investors poured fifty million pounds into five deep holes in the Atlantic seabed off the coast of County Waterford, into which O'Reilly himself put five million pounds of his own money. The oil crisis of 1979 had sent the Irish economy into a downward spiral, and people believed that O'Reilly would find oil under the sea and save the nation. When Atlantic Resources, O'Reilly's oil company, made its shares available on the Dublin stock market in April 1981 there were, as all the newspapers agreed, unprecedented scenes of mayhem. Throughout the mid-1980s there were bouts of hysterical exultation and suicidal depression as the price of shares in Atlantic Resources fluctuated wildly. The prices of the shares depended on speculation in the newspapers, and O'Reilly owned many of them.

There was more than money at stake. Oil would save Ireland from debt and allow it to take its place in the Reagan–Thatcher revolution. Thatcher, O'Reilly said, had used the revenues from North Sea oil to 'purchase the silence of the non-working classes'—meaning the unemployed. If he too struck oil, it would 'enable us to pay the bill, as it has enabled Mrs Thatcher to pay the bill while she put into effect the structural changes that are going on in Britain.'

The oil rush could not be disentangled from O'Reilly's position as the largest owner of newspapers in Ireland. In a rare moment of genuine indiscretion, he told *Forbes* magazine in September 1983 that his geologist had chosen six blocks of seabed for exploration. 'Since I own thirty-five per cent of the newspapers in Ireland I have close contact with the politicians. I got the blocks he [his geologist] wanted.'

Even after he got those blocks, however, O'Reilly became increasingly impatient with what he saw as the restrictive terms imposed by the Irish government in its exploration licences. Garret FitzGerald, who headed that government for most of the period, had been a friend of O'Reilly's since the early 1960s, but he felt the effects of O'Reilly's anger.

O'Reilly had supported FitzGerald's liberal, mildly social-democrat politics, and, according to FitzGerald, 'once he acquired Independent Newspapers, he remained very supportive.' In 1982 when Charles Haughey was in power and there were allegations that his government was interfering with the independence of the police, FitzGerald 'was in touch with' O'Reilly 'over the political situation'. 'In talking to him over that period it was kind of on the assumption that he had some degree of influence over the newspapers, I suppose,' Fitzgerald recalls. 'I certainly would have been seeking his assistance in terms of the papers at that time. If I was ringing him, it wasn't just for a general chat.

'When we were in government, he remained supportive to a degree, but towards the end there's no doubt that the *Independent* swung somewhat, and I think the oil thing was a major factor. He felt that the terms we were imposing for oil were too tough and he wanted them changed. The pressure was expressed rationally enough in terms of the need to modify the terms. I didn't feel there was improper pressure. But I felt as time went on he was getting more and more frustrated and he was allowing this to influence his overall judgement. He became irritable and angry. And I didn't think he was very helpful to us afterwards as a result.'

There is a sense in which Tony O'Reilly has always been in the media, even when he was not yet in the newspaper business. He is a self-made man, a folk hero of capitalism who has built a personal fortune of five hundred million pounds from a standing start. But he is a hero of capitalism's unheroic age. His genius is not for making or inventing things, but for buying cheap and selling hard.

Though he heads a great industrial enterprise, his interest is not really in manufacturing at all. In 1986, for instance, he threatened, somewhat rhetorically, to take Heinz out of manufacturing altogether, to buy its food products from factories that could produce them cheaply, and to concentrate instead on selling brands and tastes. He is part of an age of capitalism in which the idea of the entrepreneur as inventor is long past. As a multinational manager, he does two things—he cuts costs and he buys companies. One of his most famous ideas at Heinz was to remove the back label from ketchup bottles, saving four million dollars a year. He has never pretended to be interested in developing new things to sell. He told New York journalists in 1978 that 'The best way to get into new product development is to steal the other guy's ideas. You buy the company.' This is essentially what he does.

Having bought or made the products, he turns them into images. In the last financial year Heinz sold eight billion dollars' worth of food. To do so, it spent $1.7 billion, nearly a quarter of what it earned from sales, on advertising and marketing.

His gift is not so much for thinking up ideas as for selling them. As early as 1966 he was saying things like 'the greatest supermarket in the world is in the United Kingdom housewife's mind.' He sells into the supermarket of the mind, stocking its shelves with images and desires. He has come to believe deeply in the magic of brands, in brand names as a replacement for politics and religion. 'Truly great brands,' he told the British Council of Shopping Centres in 1990, 'are far more than just labels for products; they are symbols that encapsulate the desires of consumers; they are standards held aloft under which the masses congregate.'

His first and most enduring feat of marketing was to turn Ireland itself into a desirable brand. In 1962, when he was twenty-six, he was appointed general manager of Bord Bainne, the Irish milk marketing board. The appointment of a dashing, young sportsman to such a post was itself heavily symbolic. The nationalist dream of economic and cultural self-sufficiency had finally collapsed under the weight of mass emigration. Fianna Fáil, the ruling nationalist party, had abandoned protectionism and invited American multinational companies to invest in Ireland and engineer a belated industrial revolution in a country that was still overwhelmingly rural and traditional.

The atmosphere was not unlike that of Eastern Europe after the fall of communism. O'Reilly's appointment coincided with a number of other signals of change: the IRA's temporary abandonment of a violent campaign for a United Ireland, the inauguration of an Irish television service, Ireland's application to join the EEC. The *taoiseach* (prime minister) Sean Lemass gave a speech urging older company directors to 'consider whether they have not outlived their usefulness and decide to pass their responsibilities over to younger men.' O'Reilly, the most spectacular example of what Lemass desired, was thus himself a kind of symbol, the image of a new Ireland. And this, throughout the rest of his career, is what he has tried to be.

It is this desire that lies behind his refusal to be happy even with his spectacular success at Heinz. Being the bean baron is all very well, but he actually sees himself as very much more than an exemplar of the American corporate dream. He wants to be, at the same time, the embodiment of an Ireland different to that of his adoptive uncle Peadar O'Donnell and his real uncle Tony O'Connor. He wants to be a new Irish brand name, a standard held aloft under which the masses of Irish around the world can congregate; to be, in his own words, 'a representative of the hopes and dreams and aspirations of the Irish around the globe', the man who 'planted the flag of the New Ireland abroad in various forms—Independent Newspapers, capitalism, entrepreneurial spirit, managerial competence . . . The New Ireland which sees we have a right not just to be colonized, but to go to other countries and to harvest and prosper there.'

His position in Bord Bainne was a job of considerable political and economic importance: nearly a third of the Irish workforce was employed in agriculture, and O'Reilly's actions directly affected about half a million people from a population of less than three million. What he did was to invent a symbol of a new Ireland, a symbol of Irish agriculture that could be marketed firstly in Britain and then around the world. The product was simple—Irish butter—and he did nothing to change it. It was the name he put on the wrapping that turned it into money: Kerrygold, a name that had, as the marketing reports put it, 'a definite Irish sound, with overtones of richness and purity'.

In Ireland, the name was nonsensical since Kerry was associated with stony mountains, not green pastures. But soon Irish people too were buying Kerrygold. The golden wrapping, the sonorous name, turned slabs of butter into desirable objects. The allure of the image, the magic of brands, had been released into an emerging Ireland, and O'Reilly was the conjurer.

The old history, the old Ireland, could not be transformed so easily, though. Moving on from Bord Bainne after his triumph with Kerrygold, he was appointed by the Irish government to head an even bigger state enterprise, the Irish Sugar Company.

He replaced the third veteran of the nationalist struggle, and of the civil war, to play a part in O'Reilly's career: General Michael Costello.

In the official summary of his career prepared by O'Reilly's press agent, all the many companies in which he has played a leading role are listed—except one. H. J. Heinz is there of course, as are Independent Newspapers, his investment conglomerate Fitzwilton, Waterford Wedgwood, the minerals and oil company Arcon, Bord Bainne and the Irish Sugar Company. The one exception is Erin Foods. It is easy to understand the omission: Erin is a sensitive subject. But it is hard to understand O'Reilly's career unless you know what happened there.

Costello was a veteran of the old IRA, a protégé of Michael Collins, who promoted him from private to colonel commandant at the age of eighteen after a particularly daring operation during the civil war, in which he took the Free State side. Afterwards he became a general, then the head of the Irish Sugar Company, a large nationalized industry that processed sugar beet. He brought with him the charisma of history and a military attention to detail. More importantly, he applied to the job the idealism of the first generation of nationalist revolutionaries: a deep belief in cooperative effort, in self-reliance and in public service. He came to hate O'Reilly, and, with time, the feeling became mutual.

Costello was fiercely anti-communist, but he was also, almost as passionately, anti-capitalist. He saw 'cooperation' as the 'only alternative to the communist collective or the amalgamation of small farms to form large capitalistic enterprises'. And he tried to create an aggressively commercial but socially progressive food processing industry in rural Ireland by setting up a company called Erin Foods (Erin means simply Ireland, and the symbolism was intentional—Costello saw the company as a national metaphor) as a subsidiary of Irish Sugar. A team of young scientists in Irish Sugar had developed a new freeze-drying technology, which meant that prepared vegetables could be packed, stored outside a fridge (still a rare enough appliance in Ireland then) and reconstituted simply by pouring boiling water over them. Costello intended to use it to sell the produce of Irish agricultural cooperatives and state-owned factories, first to Irish cities and then to the huge British market. To do this he would have to take on the dominant companies in the British processed food market—among them Heinz.

One of Costello's most important allies was an extraordinary Catholic priest, James McDyer. A radical socialist in clerical clothing, McDyer had founded a rural commune in a poor and remote part of County Donegal called Glencolumbkille, and with the encouragement and support of O'Reilly's adoptive 'uncle' Peadar O'Donnell, he persuaded Costello to site one of his vegetable processing factories there. Costello, as Brendan Halligan, a young economist with Erin in the 1960s, recalls, 'dreamed of creating a network of factories, to bring about the stabilization of population in rural areas. He was motivated by old-fashioned nationalism—wanting to develop the economy, seeing resources lying unused and being extremely angry about that, and seeing the depopulation of large parts of the country. He embarked on the Erin dream without the civil service in the Department of Finance or the political establishment really understanding what he was at. When he got to a certain point and he was investing a lot of money which they regarded as losses, they began to understand.' And when they understood what he was doing, they moved to stop him.

In December 1966, Costello left Irish Sugar and Erin Foods and recommended, in his letter of resignation, that 'someone be found who believes that food processing can be run as the Department of Finance wants it run.' That someone was Tony O'Reilly. He was given the job by the leading Fianna Fáil politicians Jack Lynch and Charles Haughey, and by the Department of Finance, which had long distrusted Costello's tendency to put social objectives on the same plane as commercial ones. Officially, O'Reilly was said to be continuing Costello's work, with a brief 'to build the marketing structure that would enable a big expansion to take place in the export drive'. The government assured parliament that 'Erin Foods is now engaged in a vigorous development of the UK market and an expansion of their existing range of products.' In fact, his job was to cut back the operation, stop Erin from competing with private enterprise and tidy up its chaotic books.

Within a month O'Reilly was in touch with Heinz, one of Erin's competitors, to offer a deal. The two companies would merge. Erin would supply Heinz with raw vegetables for processing, and would itself sell Heinz products in Ireland. The Erin offices in Britain would close, and its sales force would be sacked. Two Heinz executives would sit on the Erin board. As for Peadar O'Donnell and James McDyer, they would have to realize that, as O'Reilly later told his official biographer, 'You just can't grow vegetables competitively on the hillsides of Donegal.' O'Reilly and Haughey, now Minister for Finance, discussed the deal on a winter holiday together in the Canaries, and a new company, Heinz-Erin, was formed. Soon after, O'Reilly addressed the workers and small farmers of Glencolumbkille and warned them that they must 'appreciate that the international market place is the supreme discipline in their activities. Heinz-Erin provides such a challenge.'

To Costello, the deal was 'a give-away'. He maintained until his death in 1986 that Erin 'had Heinz beaten as competitors', and that 'Heinz certainly got more out of the deal than Erin Foods, even to the extent of buying Irish vegetables in bulk and shipping them out to factories in Britain where they provide employment which could be better provided here.' He revealed that Heinz had already offered a merger while he was in charge, and that he had rejected it—'Heinz was simply like other foreign firms, looking for something for nothing, or something for very little, anyway. In fact they got something for nothing. Nobody had anything to gain in this country, but naturally enough the people who delivered to Heinz had a lot to gain.'

For Tony O'Reilly, the deal was the beginning of his global career. Less than two years after he joined Irish Sugar and Erin, O'Reilly was negotiating a job with Heinz and in May 1969 became managing director of Heinz UK. Two years after that he was in Pittsburgh as senior vice-president and by 1973 he was president and chief operating officer of Heinz worldwide.

Erin meanwhile went into permanent decline. The merger with Heinz was a commercial failure, and O'Reilly left the company in poor shape. It stumbled on for years as an agency for Heinz in Ireland. In 1990, Heinz, of which O'Reilly was now chairman, president and chief executive, announced abruptly that it was planning to remove the sale and marketing of its products in Ireland from Erin Foods. Erin's chief executive told the press 'I'm extremely disappointed in Tony O'Reilly. I thought Tony had more loyalty to the business.' O'Reilly was unavailable for comment, even to his own newspapers.

When Tony O'Reilly moved to Heinz he made a profound statement about the nature of power in the late twentieth century. He could at that stage have launched a political career that would almost certainly have taken him all the way to the office of *taoiseach*. In the late 1960s, O'Reilly himself was offered political power by both of Ireland's major political parties. The Fianna Fáil *taoiseach* Jack Lynch, who had sponsored him from the start, told him that if he refused the Heinz job, he would make him minister for agriculture in his cabinet. But the rival Fine Gael party also asked him to stand in the 1969 general election. The offer was made by Garret FitzGerald, who says that 'I had the authority of the party to talk to him. I wasn't authorized, so far as I can recall, to say to him that he would be a minister, but he obviously would have had a good prospect of ministerial office given his abilities. But then he got the offer of the Heinz job in England. And he said to me, "Garret, if I get the Heinz job I can make a hundred thousand pounds clear in five years and come back and enter full-time into politics."'

Given a choice between running a multinational company and running a small European country, however, he chose the former. He had seen that once Ireland opened itself up to American multinationals, the idea of national sovereignty, of state control, had become untenable. Years later, when idealistic nationalists came to power in Africa, first Robert Mugabe in Zimbabwe, then Nelson Mandela in South Africa, he would point out to them that they could not run their own economies, that economic nationalism was dead, that they would have to come to terms with the power of scarce and demanding capital.

Shortly after Mugabe was installed in power in Harare, on a Marxist and nationalist platform, O'Reilly went to see him to try to persuade him to allow Heinz to open a plant there. 'We had both been educated by Irish Jesuits,' he later recalled, 'and through this common kinship, we discussed the notion, the model of economic nationalism . . . I was trying to teach him about the limits of economic nationalism.' His arguments about the nature and limits of political power were persuasive—Heinz and the Zimbabwean state established a profitable joint venture, Olivine, making cooking oil and marketing Heinz products.

Equally, in defiance of the fact that he had boasted as late as 1988 that, were he still playing rugby, he would play in South Africa regardless of UN sanctions, and that he would have 'immediate access' to old rugby comrades such as General Magnus Malan, now indicted for murder for his involvement in the establishment of death squads, he quickly established a friendship with Nelson Mandela after the latter's release from prison. Mandela spent Christmas 1993 in O'Reilly's holiday home on the island of Nassau. He too came to accept the limits of political power, among them the necessity to allow a foreign businessman such as O'Reilly to take over his country's largest newspaper group.

Fine Gael and Fianna Fáil were the political heirs of the two sides in the Irish civil war. The fact that both wanted O'Reilly was a sign of how far he had succeeded in creating a persona that transcended history, that seemed finally to lay all the ghosts of the past. In his bright, charming, efficient persona lay the promise of an end to history, of a politics that would be about management, not ideology. But the paradox of that image is that on the one hand it seemed to offer a new Ireland but on the other it embodied an embrace of the global economy in which no Ireland, new or old, could really matter.

From time to time, the idea of a political career for O'Reilly has resurfaced. In 1980 Garret FitzGerald authorized a fresh approach to O'Reilly, testing whether he would agree to stand in the next election. He 'quite possibly' would have appointed him to the cabinet. 'At that stage, he would have had a reasonable expectation of office, if he was going to divert his whole career from where he was. And he would have been very dynamic I'm sure.' But Ireland was now too small a stage. And FitzGerald was subsequently relieved that O'Reilly did not take up his offer: 'He has perhaps come to feel that Tony O'Reilly's interest is Ireland's interest, is the world's interest, the way people do when they get to his stage.'

In 1979 O'Reilly speculated that he might seek to be appointed as a Commissioner of the European Community though 'not in the near term'. In 1988 he fuelled speculation that he would be appointed US Secretary of Commerce by George Bush, for whom he had served as a fund-raiser. But at the same time as he was musing in public on what he might do with the job, he was also making it clear that politicians, even members of the Washington cabinet, have too little power to satisfy him. Unlike Silvio Berlusconi who used his control of large sections of the Italian media to gain political power, O'Reilly has a sharp sense that the global business tycoon and the global media mogul have more power than politicians do. He is also the first person fully to understand that the corporate manager and the media magnate can now be one and the same.

This, more than anything else, is what makes him a representative figure of life at the end of the twentieth century. He belongs to the era of post-industrial capitalism in which a product and its image, commodities and the media through which they are sold, have become virtually indistinguishable. It is an era in which, in O'Reilly's own words, 'the communications revolution and the convergence of cultures have set the stage for truly global marketing.' And in this era the relationship between business and news is that of a closed circle. The mass media obliterate the distinctions of aspiration and taste inherent in national cultures. This in turn allows the same company to sell the same product in the same packaging everywhere in the world: 'Television will further homogenize the cultures of the developed world. It will in turn generate the cosmopolitan aspirations best satisfied by global brands. The capacity for transnational production is available . . . The final step in the process will be mass communication. And the technology of satellite and cable television will make that possible.' When that happens, the news in the broadest sense will be not just a report of what happens, but an agent for making it happen.

Recently, when Tony O'Reilly took over Waterford Wedgwood, he commissioned market research in the United States, the main market for Waterford Crystal. Its object was to answer one question—did the consumers of crystal know that Waterford is in Ireland? If they did, the workers in the factory had some power. They could remain, as they had been for many years, a radical elite in the Irish workforce, knowing that since Waterford crystal had to come from Waterford, their product was proof against global forces, against the ruthless mobility of capital. If on the other hand they did not, Waterford crystal could just as well come from Poland or the Czech Republic, where it could be made much more cheaply. Waterford would, in economic terms, have ceased to be a place and become a brand. It would be possible to do with crystal what the company intends to do with linen this year, selling on the US market cloth produced in China, Belgium and the Philippines under the Waterford brand name. The answer that the research provided was that very few American consumers associated Waterford with Ireland. It was the news that O'Reilly wanted to hear: that the process of branding Ireland that he had begun more than thirty years before had now reached the point where a part of the country had become, finally, no more than a brand, a name without a face, a placeless image, freed at last from history.

FULL DISCLOSURE

Evening Standard, 3 October 1994

ZOË HELLER

Andrew Neil

In June 1994, when the news magazine show *Full Disclosure* was in its second month of development at Fox Television, Andrew Neil, the show's co-executive editor and star correspondent, called a meeting of his staff. Neil had arrived in New York six weeks earlier. His job at Fox was being described as an experimental secondment from his editorship of the British newspaper the *Sunday Times*, and his American staff were still uncertain of what to expect from him. Many of them were imports from the Los Angeles-based *Front Page*, Fox's first attempt at a news magazine show which had been cancelled, after a year's run, in May. Some had never heard of Neil until they read about his appointment in the trade papers, and quite a few were under the impression that he was Australian. There had been some fretful rumour about his political agenda for the show—in particular, his determination to run a story about how heterosexuals are unlikely to get Aids— but no one knew how much authority to attribute to this hearsay. Neil's opinion of his staff was more definite: he wasn't impressed. The story ideas they had presented to him thus far were, he told me, 'very dismal and pedestrian . . . slightly cerebral . . . lacking in storytelling qualities . . . desperate . . . unusable.'

The meeting he had called took place in the conference room of the show's offices at the News Corporation building in mid-town Manhattan. Neil's co-executive producer, David Corvo, a tiny, bearded Californian, got up to speak first. Corvo has a genial, low-key style of management that tends to inspire great loyalty in his employees. Most of the people in the room had worked with him previously, either at *Front Page*, where he was also executive producer, or during his earlier days at CBS News. The speech he gave now was a short and friendly morale-raiser.

Next, Neil stood up. It is an unfortunate fact about Neil's physiognomy that, even in genial mood, he has the menacing, choleric aspect of a man in a pub about to order someone 'outside' for fisticuffs. His complexion is the colour of raw beef. His bristling, squared-up posture suggests imminent combat. Even his hair—odd, wiry stuff that springs up in rebellious tufts from wherever he conscientiously slicks it down—gives an impression of rage. The speech he gave was bellicose. It was time, he told the people in the conference room, for them to pull their socks up.

What they had heard about the 'politically incorrect' perspective of his plans for the show was true, and if any of them felt in the least bit uncomfortable about it they would be better off leaving now. The show, Neil went on, would demand fearless iconoclasm from its staff. If they did their jobs well, the News Corporation building would find itself regularly besieged by pickets protesting the show's political improprieties. 'I want your friends to hate you because of the stories you work on,' he said. At this, there was a sharp intake of breath among his audience. 'Most people were, um, surprised,' David Small, the show's broadcast co-producer, recalled. 'We'd never been given a speech like that before.' When Neil finished speaking, only one staff member felt brave enough to raise his hand. His poignantly literal-minded response suggested just how unfamiliar the staff were with editorial bombast like Neil's. If the show's offices were going to be surrounded by shouting pickets, the young producer asked earnestly, wouldn't the disturbance make it difficult for staff to concentrate on their work?

When Neil made his speech, his show was still called *On Assignment*. It had been conceived as the first step towards building a proper news division at Fox—a long-held dream of the network's proprietor, Rupert Murdoch. While news tends to get lower ratings than light entertainment, it is news, more than any other sort of programming, that gives a network its credibility as a public service, and news anchors that give a network its public face. Murdoch wanted his Connie Chung and Tom Brokaw, his Diane Sawyer and Dan Rather. 'A lot of money is going into this show,' Neil said when I first went to see him. 'It's always been my experience that if Rupert is committed to something and knows it's essential to the overall corporate plan, then money's not a problem, and he's in it for the long haul.' At this point in late June, the show's offices were still under renovation. Wires were hanging from ceilings, walls were wet with paint, and the noise of workmen's drills rose and fell. On Neil's desk, there was a judge's gavel. He had his radio on at a low volume, and Beethoven was providing dim, ambient tootle. He was, he admitted, feeling some trepidation about his new job: 'I've been given a toy train to build as I see fit—and I run it. That's great. But it is also a bit daunting, because it's so huge . . . I mean, I've gone from being a big fish in a small pond to a small fish in a big pond. To get someone from Britain to do a prime-time show and to be on camera as well as be executive producer, that's a huge risk. No one has an idea whether it will work or not.' He ran his fingers over his gavel thoughtfully. 'It might not work,' he said.

The positive aspect of this uncertainty was a spirit of pioneer liberty at large in the *On Assignment* offices. Free from the inhibiting precedents of a long-established news service, staff felt free to challenge assumptions about the function and style of broadcast news. Issues of content and perspective were understood to be up for grabs. Many of the staff were speaking of the show as a crucible for competing ideas of what contemporary television news values were and ought to be. 'We're the new guy,' David Corvo said. 'We're not an institution where news has been practised for thirty years. We should take advantage of that. There's no hierarchy here for us to discuss things with . . . so we can invent it as we go along. That gives us a kind of freedom.'

One of Neil's primary aims for *On Assignment*, he said, was that it should be 'a grown-up show for grown-up people'. The purchase of the rights to the National Football League the previous December had brought an influx of older viewers to the predominantly youthful Fox audience, and Murdoch wanted to increase that trend. Unlike *Front Page*, the new show was to have no tipsy camera angles or kooky graphics. Ron Reagan Jr, the laid-back, ponytailed presenter of *Front Page*, had pointedly not been invited to join the *On Assignment* team. 'The only ponytails we want to have on this show,' Neil quipped weightily, 'will be worn by the drug dealers we're exposing.' Neil wanted *On Assignment* to eschew the meretriciousness and sensationalism of other American news magazines. 'A lot of these other shows are all soft. It's yet another crime story, or a murder in some little town, and these stories have no meaning or purpose—they're just stories. I want to do a series of items that will have a purpose to them, a lesson in them and a policy point.' These hard-hitting, issue-driven items would need to be leavened with judicious injections of 'glamour, show business and populism', but generally *Full Disclosure* would distinguish itself by being tougher, more

79

thoughtful and more bravely controversial than its competition. 'What I'm aiming to do,' he said, 'is produce a show that is not part of the one-party state that American network television is. You think there's a huge diversity, but there isn't really. Network TV—network news—is run by people who share the same assumptions, the same outlook on life, the same reverence for certain institutions and the same disgust for other institutions. I aim to have a go at some of their sacred cows. This country has an establishment. It's not class-based like in Britain, but the media establishment in particular is very much a group of people who write about the same things and hand out prizes to the same people. I think we might just throw a little hand grenade into that.'

In the months that followed, members of the show's senior management tried hard to enlist staff enthusiasm for this aggressive approach. They emphasized Neil's avowed commitment to 'policy point' journalism and repeatedly invoked notions of high-mindedness and 'classy' reporting. 'We're not going to chase after every serial killer, hopefully,' Len Tepper, head of the show's investigative unit, told me. 'Part of my job is to make sure there is a high degree of journalism. We're not going to take short cuts.' At the same time, there was an effort to play down the ideological undertone of Neil's pronouncements. Neil's angle, staff were told, was not so much right-wing as 'sceptical'. 'Within the office, there's a sense that if you're anti-PC, then you're somehow conservative. I don't buy that notion at all,' Emily Rooney, the senior producer of *On Assignment*, said. Soon after this, the words 'politically incorrect' were dropped from office meetings and replaced with the more neutral term, 'contrarian'.

'I think the contrarian approach is a very clever idea,' the show's story editor, Dan Cooper, said. 'I don't view it as an ideological approach. I view it as a fresh way to approach material—I think it could impact us very favourably as a show.' Even on the Aids 'myth' story, which Neil had promoted during his editorship of the London *Sunday Times* and which he was now planning to report himself, the staff were counselled to keep an open mind. Kyle Good, the show's director, admitted she had been 'really offended' by the Aids idea at first and had argued 'vehemently' against pursuing it, but by August, she was calmer.

'I don't have to agree with every story we do here,' she said. 'I'm willing to look at the Aids story when they get it all together and see if they really produce a valid argument.'

In late August I went to see Judith Regan, the woman who had been chosen as Neil's co-anchor on the show. Regan had turned her *On Assignment* office into a flowery dell of femininity, scattered with pieces of French provincial furniture, decorative remnants of antique garden gates and vases of roses. Tiny and fiercely chic, in pale green, size six Calvin Klein, Regan sat at her desk, periodically breaking off our conversation to bark into the telephone headset attached to her coiffure like an Alice band. Regan, one of the star captains of Murdoch's empire, is head of Regan Books, an imprint of the Murdoch-owned HarperCollins, and shortly before joining the *On Assignment* team she signed a multi-media contract with Murdoch, giving her responsibility for bringing in book-related and other sorts of television and movie projects to News Corp. At *On Assignment*, according to David Corvo, she was expected to concentrate on developing contacts and story ideas for the show's 'lighter' side. 'We would like her to become our sort of, you know, Barbara Walters,' he said. Regan herself was hoping, she said, to bring a personal, 'intensely moral' perspective to the show. She explained that she had a 'unique message' to share with her audience. Her origins were working class—her father was a cab driver, her mother a part-time bookkeeper—and she had twice been the victim of domestic violence (she had been battered by two of her former partners, including the father of the two children she was now raising alone). 'There aren't a lot of women in television who've had my life, been through the things I've been through,' she said. 'Most of the women in television don't have children because they couldn't have achieved what they've achieved very easily with children. I would like to become a voice of moral outrage, representing the voice of most women in this country.'

The story she was working on at the time was a piece about young Americans suffering from depression. In it, she planned to argue that responsibility for the damaged psyches of today's young people was borne by the fractured state of the American

81

family At this point, the focus of her piece was the young writer Elizabeth Wurtzel, author of the polemical memoir *Prozac Nation*. Regan's view was that Wurtzel's chronic depression could be traced to her parents'—particularly her father's—neglectfulness. 'You know, if I were to go and interview this guy who basically abandoned her,' she said, 'I would—if I didn't spit in his face, you know—I'd ask him in a very dramatic way, you know, "Tell me, why is it that you didn't see your daughter for ten years? I mean, who do you think you are to bring this person into the world and then abandon her?"'

'I have,' she added, 'a very profound belief in shaming people. Especially men. I think it's the only way you can keep a culture civilized.'

When I asked her how she thought *On Assignment* would distinguish itself from the plethora of other television news magazines, Regan paused. 'Well,' she said, after a moment or two, 'I'm not blonde.' There was another, longer pause while the two of us pondered this fact. 'Tell me,' she continued, warming to her *aperçu*, 'who are the big female news magazine personalities? Come on! Think about it!' She smiled. 'They're all blonde. Walters? She's blonde. Sawyer? Blonde. Pauley? Blonde. Katie Couric? . . . ' She hesitated, remembering that Couric, a presenter on NBC's *Today* show is, inconveniently enough, a brunette. 'Couric,' she said firmly, 'is blondish red. And Connie Chung? . . . OK, she's not blonde, but,'—here she slapped her desk triumphantly—'Connie's Oriental.'

Regan's candid engrossment in the question of coiffure might have seemed a little eccentric, but in fact such matters are far from irrelevant in American broadcast news where the business of 'anchor aesthetics' is taken very seriously. *On Assignment* executives had expressed many misgivings about Neil's Scottish vowels (he was being made to undergo a course of private coaching sessions in order to develop more viewer-friendly elocution), but their much graver concern focused on whether Neil—once described by the British socialite Bridget Heathcoat Amory as 'so ugly it makes you gasp'—could ever find favour with an audience reared on caramel complexions and lantern jaws. Regan was hopeful about her co-anchor. 'I think the American

audience either likes you, or they don't like you,' she told me.
'Look at Robin Leach [the English presenter of *Lifestyles of the
Rich and Famous*]—there's an example of someone who was
certainly not terribly attractive and had an abrasive voice. But for
some reason people responded to him.' Emily Rooney was also
inclined to optimism on this issue. 'We have to figure out a way to
use Andrew's quirky appeal,' she told me, 'because that's what it
is. I mean he's not, you know, Harry the Handsome Anchor Man
from Tulsa. He is what he is. He has this pixie smile and those
great little blue eyes that beam out at you. I mean, he's got an
appeal. The more I look at him and listen to him, the more I
think, you know, there's no reason why that can't work.'

In late August, Neil held a story meeting. He, David Corvo,
Emily Rooney and Dan Cooper went through the show's
current list of ideas and discussed them with the relevant
associate producers. Neil was beginning to get irritated with what
he saw as his staff's 'unwillingness to challenge the consensus',
and part of the aim of the meeting was to help weed out those
without the will or the wit to toe the 'contrarian' line. Some staff
members had already departed voluntarily, having found Neil's
journalistic style unpalatable.

According to David Corvo, however, most of the staff were
not so much recalcitrant about the politics as bewildered. 'I
disagree with Andrew on this,' he said. 'He thinks they're unwilling.
I think they're willing—they just don't get it yet.' Throughout an
entire day, Neil proceeded through the story list, throwing out
ideas with grunts of displeasure and the occasional burst of
sarcastic laughter. 'It's just not a story,' he said over and over again
as he dismissed the painstakingly composed memos presented by
the associate producers. When Regan's 'Young and Depressed' idea
came up for discussion, Neil winced. 'What are you going to say
about this depression?' he asked. 'I would say it's a load of old
bollocks. Let's expose these people.' His colleagues sitting around
the table looked slightly taken aback. 'I just don't see what story
there is here,' Neil said. 'Well,' said the assistant producer who
had been working with Regan on the piece, 'it's a society kind of
story—about people in their twenties who're depressed.'

'Clinically depressed?' Emily Rooney asked sharply.

'Erm . . . yes,' the assistant producer said.

'Is this Elizabeth Wurtzel clinically depressed?' Rooney wanted to know.

'Yes.'

'Definitely?'

'Yes.'

Neil seemed to be growing bored. 'Well, I don't think it's worth doing unless you take the piss out of it. I mean, it says in this memo, "We're going to relate youth depression to the current economic climate." What about the thirties? Why wasn't everyone depressed then?'

'Uh, the difference is,' the assistant producer said, 'it's an in-thing now and, um, more acceptable . . . '

Her face lit up hopefully as she remembered something else. 'We have a man who can talk about the relationship between depression and poor diet.'

'Diet!' Rooney snapped. 'Well, if poor diet causes depression, then why isn't Rwanda depressed?'

'Exactly!' Neil said, clapping his hands.

Rooney blushed with pleasure. 'Why can't we redo this story as one about all the drugs these depressed people are taking?' Neil continued. 'Something about pill-popping . . . '

'I don't think Judith has a sceptical line on this story,' Rooney pointed out.

Neil grunted. 'Then we'll just put a new reporter on it,' he said, turning to the next memo.

Not all the story proposals displeased Neil. 'Ah! Here,' he said, towards the end of the morning session. 'This is a story about Bob Woodson, a black activist who's had a road-to-Damascus experience and turned his back on the black leadership establishment.' He turned to the assistant producer on the story. 'Now, are we sure he will be condemnatory of the existing black leadership?'

'Oh yes,' the assistant producer said eagerly. 'He's a real—forgive the expression—turd in the punch bowl.'

Neil guffawed. 'I like to be politically incorrect, but not *that* incorrect.'

Other suggestions that met with Neil's approval included a story called 'Bosses from Hell' ('Mmm, I could be in this,' he said jovially); a profile of the model Gabrielle Rees ('with some great slo-mo footage of her playing volleyball'); and a story tentatively entitled 'Andrew Lloyd Webber and his Women'. Also being considered at this time, or already shot, were a profile of a seventy-three-year-old American Airlines stewardess; a story about people who perform parachute jumps from the top of tall buildings (highlight: a video recording of a man falling to his death from the top of the London Hilton); a profile of the country singer Tanya Tucker; and a profile of the cat expert who wrote the bestseller *Tribe of the Tiger*. Neil was also rooting for an interview with Heather Locklear, star of the Fox soap *Melrose Place*.

There seemed to be more than a trace here of Randolph Hearst's famous 'tits, tots, pets and vets' formula. Where had all the policy points gone? 'Well, there has to be quite a lot of soft,' Neil said when I put this to him. 'But we've got plenty of hard stuff too—the thing about Bob Woodson, a piece about Mayor Marion Barry in Washington. Then there's the "My dad was a sperm donor" piece, which is both hard and soft. By that, I mean that it's an intriguing story which also raises issues.' Despite these protestations the show seemed to be struggling to make up its mind about where, in the great grey area between low and highbrow, it was going to pitch itself. Although the talk of high seriousness had not altogether subsided, executives were to be heard more and more frequently speaking of 'the need to draw people into the tent'. At the beginning of August, the show's original title, *On Assignment,* had been dropped. 'I never thought we'd go to air with it,' Neil said, 'it was too PBS-ish.' The new title, *Full Disclosure*, sounded good on promos, he said, and it could 'play tabloid or serious'.

Perhaps it was not so surprising that the show should find itself hovering between its original aspirations to 'classiness' and the lure of easy-watching 'fun'. Few who are involved in decisions about content in any form of modern journalism— including the editors of the 'quality' British broadsheets—have not experienced a similar sort of anxious oscillation. Still, the ambitions of *Full Disclosure* seemed to be particularly and alarmingly confused. One gauge of the confusion was the senior staff's differing ideas about how to cover the recently emerged O. J. Simpson murder story. In a conversation that took place two weeks after the murder of Nicole Simpson, Neil told me that if the show had been on air, he would like to have done a piece on wife-beating. (It had recently come to light that Simpson had been previously convicted of physically abusing his wife.) 'The politically correct phrase over here is apparently "spousal abuse", but in fact, it's wife-beating,' Neil said. 'That, to me, was the untold story in the beginning, and I'd have zoomed right in on that. Also, I would have asked, has the trial by media made it impossible to have a fair trial?'

Len Tepper, the head of the show's investigative unit, said he would like to run a piece that tried to evaluate the evidence against O.J. 'We'd ask, What was the key bit of information that came out of the preliminary hearing? Was it the testimony of the chauffeur?' When I spoke to Dan Cooper, the story editor, he spoke admiringly of a report by Barbara Walters the previous week exploring the 'issue' of Nicole Simpson's alleged lesbianism. 'Would there be room for a piece like that on this show?' I asked him.

'Sure!' he said. 'I can't imagine why there wouldn't be—if it's relevant to the case, if our motives are not salacious.'

'Isn't that story salacious, by definition?'

Cooper thought for a long time, before answering. 'Yes,' he finally replied. 'The Simpson case is not out there being enjoyed by everybody because of their interest in spousal abuse—they're interested in it because it's a celebrity murder. But I'm not a snob. Let's get real and understand what we're talking about here. We're talking about putting together information that people are interested in hearing. I don't regard myself as an elitist. I believe firmly that what we're presenting to the audience ought to be presented with respect to what their attitudes and interests are. I don't view what we're doing as being up here in an office building in New York where we know better, telling everyone out there in the United States what they want to know. Nor should we have an attitude that all we're doing is exploiting them in order to deliver them to advertisers. We have a responsibility, but part of the responsibility is to recognize what the big stories are.'

Finally, I spoke to Judith Regan, who proposed doing a

profile of Nicole Simpson. 'I want to talk about how we take this gorgeous, beautiful, innocent little girl and raise her to have her throat slit,' she said. 'You know—what are the forces that really conspired to bring her to that point in her life? What did we teach that little girl, about what to value and what to care about? How did she end up with her throat slit on a driveway in California with those two precious little kids? Nobody is telling that story . . . I think that my approach is probably going to reflect what I've been through personally . . . I'd like to sit down and talk to her parents. They haven't talked to anybody yet. You know, I'd say, "Look, I'm a mother, I have a daughter. I know how I'd feel, you know. I mean, you sat here and watched this girl getting beaten. What did you say to her, you know? I mean, I as a mother, just would never be able to . . . to go into that courtroom without spitting on him. You know. I just couldn't."'

According to David Corvo, such discrepancies in tone and approach were inevitable as long as the show remained off-air. Indeed, by the end of the summer, everyone at *Full Disclosure* felt they had achieved as much as they could by talking and planning. What they needed now was an audience. 'Working in limbo is difficult for people,' Corvo said. 'First of all it's hard to get subjects to play ball when they haven't seen the product, and of course there are lots of current news stories that we can't do because they'll be stale by next week. You can't prepare too long for this kind of thing, or it'll get fusty. You have to go for it, knowing that your first couple of shows won't be your best.' This was in early September, and Corvo had been given no clear indication of when or in which slot the show would be appearing. In the very beginning there had been an idea of running it Sunday nights after the National Football League, in direct competition with CBS's *Sixty Minutes*. This suggestion had been greeted with snarling derision by CBS executives and then rapidly scotched by Neil. 'I thought that idea was crazy from the start,' he said. 'Maybe we could think about it next year, if all goes well, but it would be suicidal to start off like that.'

In late June Corvo had told me he expected to be given a definite air date by the beginning of August. August came and there was no word from Murdoch, but a sign up in the office boardroom proposed an air-date schedule beginning on 26 September. There was talk of the show going on after *Melrose Place* on Monday nights. But by the end of the month Neil was talking about a premiere in mid-October, or possibly January. 'We could go in October, but the fear is that we won't have enough really distinctive stories by then,' he said.

At the start of September, the show began putting its pilot together. Four stories were to be featured: a report on drug-money laundering by Neil; a report on the 'liberalism gone-mad' of the American Civil Liberties Union; a story about two men from Illinois convicted of armed robbery thirty years after their crime; and a profile of Robin Quivers, sidekick of the radio 'shock-jock' Howard Stern. (Judith Regan, who presented the Quivers profile, was about to publish the Quivers autobiography—a fact which she saw as presenting not a conflict, but a felicitous coincidence of interests.) The show's studio segments were filmed at the Lifetime Studios in Astoria, Queens. On the day I went to observe the proceedings, Neil was sporting a new, short haircut with a dark aubergine tint, and an alarming shade of orange panstick. He was rather dismissive of the sessions he had undergone with a television coach: 'She wanted to get me to raise my eyebrows and all that stuff—but I couldn't be doing with it. I'm not an actor.'

The sessions appeared, however, to have had an effect. He was still saying 'grup' and 'cosses' for 'group' and 'causes', but his accent was rather paler than usual, and he had begun to acquire some of the mandatory anchor mannerisms. Introducing serious stories he assumed the corrugated brow of pseudo-*tristesse*, and for lighter items he had begun delivering some very accomplished suppressed chuckles and bemused head shakes.

Kyle Good, the director, was terrifically pleased. 'Are we all getting used to his accent, or does he sound more like an American than ever?' she said. Later, when Neil had finished doing his introductions and links, he came into the control room. Kyle Good, David Corvo, Dan Cooper and Emily Rooney were now studying the pre-recorded 'bumpers'—the plugs for forthcoming items that appear before commercials. Right now, on the monitor before them, was the bumper for the story about the American Civil Liberties Union. 'Panhandlers and sex offenders,' a preternaturally deep American voice intoned. 'Lock 'em up? Not if the ACLU has anything to do with it!' Corvo shifted uncomfortably in his seat. 'Uh, maybe that's a bit strong. I think we've got some work to do on that.'

Neil laughed. 'Oh, I don't think it's strong enough!'

Next Judith Regan came on to the set. There was some delay while cameras and lighting were arranged. In the control room, Dan Cooper stared at Regan on the monitor. 'I think her hair looks fabulous,' he said after a while. 'Am I the only person who feels like that?'

'Kyle?' Regan's voice crackled into the control room. 'How do I look?'

'Great,' Kyle said, looking up at the monitor.

'Better than yesterday?' Regan asked.

'Just as good.'

'What about the hair, Kyle?' Regan asked. 'You like it? Is it better than yesterday?'

'It looks pretty much the same,' Good said, a little wearily. When the cameramen were ready, the business of shooting Regan's autocue introductions began. Nobody in the control room was very keen on the way Regan read. It was felt that she sounded too stiff, that she was emphasizing the wrong words, that she wasn't 'allowing her charisma to translate'. Underlinings were added to the autocue script so that Regan would know where to stress. She read again, but still the people in the control room shook their heads. 'Judith,' Kyle Good said tactfully, 'has got some work to do on presentation.'

The editing of the pilot took up most of September. For the show's signature music, Kyle Good had originally intended to throw out the traditional timpani-and-trumpets herald in favour of a 'sound design'—a musical collage incorporating the noise of computers and telephones—that would communicate the show's iconoclastic but 'classy' concept. This hadn't worked out and at the last minute she was forced to throw in some stock TV current affairs music instead. 'It's a pity,' she said, 'but I guess we're going to end up taking a more traditional route.'

As soon as the pilot was complete, a copy was sent to

Murdoch in Los Angeles, and shortly afterwards Neil and Corvo flew out to receive his comment. In the manner of all dress rehearsals, the *Full Disclosure* pilot was an awkward, nervy affair. Both Neil and Regan had proved rather wooden. 'The general feeling,' one member of the show's senior staff told me, 'is that the anchors are not ready for TV, and we're grateful for the opportunity to try and work with that. It's a general stiffness in manner and speech.' The staff reaction was largely one of disappointment. 'The consensus here,' said one of the show's executives, 'is that the pilot was not particularly strong. To be candid, I would say there was a feeling it was mediocre.' Perhaps the most striking thing about the pilot was how little Neil's contrarian idea had made an impact on the finished product. No one watching this show would have guessed that the guiding principle of its executive producer had been provocation and iconoclasm. The ACLU story was the only item that proposed a distinct point of view but even this seemed less 'controversial' than obscurely het up in tone. The vivid assaults on received opinion that had been promised were nowhere to be seen.

Instead of wanting to clarify and strengthen the 'contrarian' theme, however, the executive response focused on injecting more 'soft' into the mix. The show's problem, David Corvo told me, was a lack of 'fun' items. 'People thought the show wasn't warm enough—that it was a little too aggressive, a little too serious and sombre,' he said. 'Look,' he added a little later, 'we're all a bunch of whores in the end. There is pressure. When I started out at NBC years ago, the news division lost a hundred million dollars a year, but RCA owned us and they saw a news service as their civic responsibility. They took the loss as the cost of their Federal Communications Commission [the body in charge of broadcasting standards] licence. It was the same attitude over at CBS and ABC. But news has to make money now, and inevitably journalism has suffered.'

When I spoke to Dan Cooper, he felt that, in the final analysis, all the brave talk of eschewing tabloid values had been unhelpful. 'If you want to know the truth, I like tabloid,' he said. 'I think tabloid is lively—and I would like to have seen us do something more lively, more spirited and playful.' He stared gloomily out of his window at the midtown skyscrapers. 'It's imperative for us to find a way for this show to be buoyant,' he said. '"Buoyant" is a word I would really stress.'

Everyone was somewhat surprised when Corvo and Neil returned from Los Angeles, bearing the happy news that Murdoch loved the show and wanted it broadcast as soon as possible. According to Corvo, it was one of the most unequivocally positive responses to a pilot he had ever witnessed. 'Rupert said that the stories that were told through the characters were the ones he found the most compelling. But he liked all four stories—he made that very clear. It was a very enthusiastic response. It was like, "How fast can you get it on air?"' The staff were told to get into shape for a premiere at the end of October. 'Rupert wouldn't discuss day and time with us,' Corvo said. 'It's sensitive, because for us to get on, someone else has to fall off, so we understand that. But what he said was, "Be ready to go in a month."' The office, which had become rather sluggish and depressed in recent weeks, was now suddenly revived. 'We've got a new adrenalin pumping,' Emily Rooney said. 'There's a sense of music in the air—we're going into high gear now.' Neil was in a positively bumptious mood. The pilot had not suggested the need for any major changes in the show's strategy, he said. But he was now placing renewed emphasis on 'storytelling skills'. The show needed, 'to develop ways of telling things that'll draw people in.'

At the end of the first week in October Murdoch had still not given Corvo a definite date. Shortly after Neil and Corvo returned from Los Angeles, Murdoch had replaced Fox's chief programmer, Sandy Grushow, with John Matoian, a former CBS executive. No one knew what alteration in the network's programming strategy this shake-up augured, or what Matoian's attitude towards *Full Disclosure* would be. At any rate, the chances of a first air date in late October seemed to be rapidly receding.

The music that introduced the show had still to be finalized. 'The important thing,' Kyle Good said, 'is to get a little bit of melody that after it's heard enough times gets to be known. I mean I can sing Bum-bum-bum-bum—and I know that's ABC. Or NBC has that ding-ding-ding.' (She demonstrated with a little NBC xylophone on her desk.) 'Fox doesn't have that yet, so we're trying to get a few notes of identification.' Corvo and Bruce Perlmutter, the show's broadcast producer, came into Good's office to hear the music, which had been commissioned from Bob Israel, the composer of the ABC news theme. Good synchronized the tape with a video of the show's opening sequence so they could all get a better idea of how the images and music went together. As the music began she sat down at her desk and stared intently at the wall. Perlmutter and Corvo remained standing, clicking their fingers and swaying gently. 'Is the middle piano too wimpy?' Perlmutter asked after the music had been playing for a bit. 'I think it should be more Ba-ba-ba.'

'Yeah,' Corvo said. 'It's too bell-like. We need real positive, American-sounding chords.' Perlmutter and Kyle nodded. Bob Israel had provided variations on the theme to fit the moods of different segments.

'He does sad really well,' Good promised.

'Mmm,' Corvo said, when the sad music played. 'I like it, but again the piano is too tinkly. It's a little too . . . hostile.'

Perlmutter shut his eyes. 'There's not enough da-da-das at the end,' he said, after a bit. 'We need three or four da-da-das before the end.'

Another week went by. Murdoch went on a business trip to Australia and told Neil and Corvo before he left that he wanted Matoian to see the show before he decided on an air date. Morale slumped once again. Neil instructed his assistant to tell me that he wasn't going to discuss the show with me any more. 'Is that because he's too busy or because he doesn't want to?' I asked. 'Both,' she said. The atmosphere of uncertainty and gloom fostered a thousand rumours among the office's staff, including stories of major disagreements between Neil and Corvo. 'It seems there is a conflict in terms of ideology and in terms of taste,' one senior member of staff informed me.

Corvo was trying very hard to keep his sunny side up. 'The length of our development time has not been unusual at all,' he said. 'I've been through this process about five times before this. Some of the kids here are used to going to shows that are up and running, so it's probably a little more frustrating for them. Some of the older producers aren't concerned at all. Hey,'—he leaned back in his chair, raising his hands, palm forwards, in a gesture of resignation—'this is TV.'

On 13 October Dan Cooper, sitting glumly in his office, told me that the show had now 'gone into somewhat powered-down status'. And when Murdoch returned from Australia, the tidings were not good. Matoian had seen the programme and was adamant: Regan and Neil didn't cut it as anchors. The show could not run. His argument was bolstered by the recent ratings figures for the established news magazine shows, almost all of which were down on last year's. 'The feeling is,' Corvo told me, 'it's difficult enough to start a news magazine, but with two unknowns, it's really difficult, and when one of the unknowns is British, it's really, *really* difficult. It's like, who are the people who watch *Melrose Place* going to relate to?'

In the last week of October Murdoch took Neil out to dinner in New York and broke the news: *Full Disclosure* was going to be cancelled. Soon after, a rumour from England wafted about Manhattan suggesting that Murdoch had hired Neil for the *Full Disclosure* project only as a way to lever him out of the *Sunday Times*. Neil did not take up his old job when he returned to Britain. Early in 1996 he launched *The Andrew Neil Show*, which the BBC hopes is the British answer to *Larry King Live*. The programme is broadcast by the BBC's world satellite as well as by domestic transmitters, and in it Neil talks to 'international celebrities' and receives viewers' questions by phone, fax and e-mail.

Back at Fox, some *Full Disclosure* staff left to go to jobs at other networks. Murdoch now decided that what he needed for a credible news service was a strong Washington-based bureau. In the meantime the remainder of the *Full Disclosure* team were put to work researching 'specials'—hour-long 'theme' programmes. 'They have a light-hearted orientation,' explained one assistant producer who was working on a Valentine's Day special entitled 'Dating in the Nineties'. 'It's kind of like the stuff we were doing before, for the news show,' she said, 'except now the reports are longer and more in-depth.'

Two Dead in Car Blast

Detroit News, 22 June 1983

Lynda Schuster

Dial Torgerson, foreign correspondent

I can write about this now only because enough time has passed. I have moved on—covered other stories, lived in other countries, found another man to love. But for a long time it was impossible even to talk about what happened, let alone write about it. For a long time I—who prided myself on my dispassionate journalism, my ability to report shocking details with equanimity—was rendered dumb.

These are the facts. Some time on the afternoon of 21 June 1983 a rented white Toyota Corolla was travelling along the desolate road in south-eastern Honduras that hugs the border with Nicaragua. The car eased past a slow-moving truck and, not long after that, perhaps twenty or thirty metres further on, it strayed too close to the centre of the road. In doing so, the left front tyre made contact with an anti-tank mine that had been planted there.

What happened next is unclear. The tyre might have tripped the mine or, as reporters who later visited the site suggested, someone sitting by the side of the road pushed the detonation button as the Corolla passed. The explosion was tremendous. The force of it shot the car into the air, then split the body in half; the motor, blown out of the chassis, was found a football-field away. The blast left a smouldering crater two metres in diameter in the road.

The two occupants of the car were killed instantly; of this, the coroner assured me. At most, he said, they saw a flash of light; light travels faster than sound, and by the time the detonation reached their ears, the passengers would have been dead. One of them was Richard Cross, a handsome young freelance photographer; the other was Dial Torgerson, a veteran correspondent for the *Los Angeles Times*. Although both Cross and Torgerson were severely mutilated, Torgerson, who was driving, bore the brunt of the explosion. The upward momentum of the charge tore off his legs, lower torso, hands.

Those are the facts. But there is one element of this story that sets it apart from all the numbing war reports I filed from Central America: Dial Torgerson was my husband. We had been married for ten months when he died.

I had met Dial a couple of years earlier, in San Jose, Costa Rica. Ours was not an auspicious beginning. Sitting in the coffee shop of a faded downtown hotel, I was busily concentrating on not becoming hysterical. I had been working for the *Wall Street Journal* for barely a year, and this was the third day of my first foreign assignment.

Unlike my colleagues, who all seemed to have written for their school newspapers since kindergarten, I had majored in Middle Eastern languages and literature as an undergraduate. In my final year, I decided I was too young to die in academia, so instead of pursuing a Ph.D., I entered a graduate programme in journalism. I spent a summer as an intern on a newspaper in Israel, talked my way over the border into southern Lebanon (it was just after the first Israeli invasion) and emerged with a handful of stories. I sent my clips, along with job-application letters, to forty-three US newspapers, and received forty-two rejections. Only the *Wall Street Journal*, then a paper that prided itself on moulding promising young reporters, agreed to take me on.

During my interview with the *Journal*'s editors, I earnestly explained that I wasn't interested in working domestically; I wanted to be a foreign correspondent. They nodded under-standingly and dispatched me to their Dallas bureau. It was a severe shock, going to a place where I was addressed, with true Texan courtesy, as 'little lady'. My beat was agriculture: for months I covered sheep auctions in Oklahoma, wheezed in wheat fields in Kansas, hitched rides on harvesters in Arkansas.

Then—as usually happens in this type of tale—I got a break. The *Journal*'s Dallas bureau was responsible for reporting on Central America. The then-correspondent was suddenly transferred to Los Angeles, and the other reporters in the bureau were engrossed in business beats they didn't want to relinquish, so it fell to me to cover one of the hottest foreign stories of the decade. (These were the early days of Ronald Reagan's administration, when the United States was becoming deeply involved in the region.)

That was why I found myself in a hotel coffee shop in Costa Rica: the country was teetering on the brink of bankruptcy, and the *Journal*'s two million readers back home were waiting to read about it. I knew how to write about winter wheat, but an entire nation? To calm myself I was taking deep breaths through my mouth when my stringer, a brash kid from the States who did odd jobs for several newspapers and boasted an extravagant body odour, suddenly appeared among the potted plants. He explained that today he was working for Dial Torgerson of the *Los Angeles Times*. Did I want to meet him?

Of course I did. I had read about Dial's exploits and remembered in particular how he had foiled the Israeli military censors' attempt to quash a report of war atrocities by flying to London and filing his story from there. It caused a huge furore, and his subterfuge seemed to me a noble thing. I expected to be introduced to a quintessential foreign correspondent—tall, handsome, trench-coated; instead, I was shaking the hand of a small, wiry, middle-aged man in a blue seersucker suit and ugly, squared-off black shoes. What hair he had left was silver, and he walked with a peculiar, slightly rolling gait.

His voice was deep and resonant and lingered over each syllable like a radio announcer's. 'So,' he said, 'what's a nice Jewish girl like you doing in a place like this?'

'Woman,' I replied, rather irked. He looked confused. 'We're called women nowadays.'

Not exactly a transcendent moment.

After I had finished my interviews for the day, and Dial had been taken around town by the stringer, we all met for supper in a pseudo-French restaurant near the hotel. We ordered food—steaks for them, snapper for me—and wine and settled into the cushiony chairs. Then Dial and I began to talk—and I was utterly transfixed. He bewitched me with tales from the Middle East, Africa, the Maghreb. He was a hypnotic storyteller with an actor's phrasing and a Southerner's ear for language (his mother's people came from North Carolina). Platters of food came and went, untouched. Never had I encountered such a union of wit, intelligence, charm.

The poor stringer stolidly made his way through every course while we ignored him. I didn't want the meal to end. Hours later, when we finally had to leave the restaurant, the whole world seemed transformed. The mundane had become magical: the moon-faced vendor trying to sell one last lottery ticket; the dog trotting purposefully down the echoing avenue; even the policeman, leaning against his squad car under a street light, squinting at a comic book.

The next night we met for supper again, this time in a Chinese restaurant. I spent the entire day waiting for those few hours, barely able to concentrate on my work. I was dimly aware of the half-dozen or so other people at our table, journalist friends of the stringer. I was dimly aware of the food that kept passing by on a large revolving tray. But all this was a backdrop to Dial. He and I talked until nearly dawn, moving from the restaurant to a bar to the hotel lobby. Later that morning, Dial departed for El Salvador, leaving a note in my message box: 'Dial Torgerson fell in love at 11.37 p.m., Thursday Oct. 1, in San Jose, Costa Rica.'

So our love affair began: a frenetic, breathless sort of relationship, squeezed in among the wars and coups we had to cover for our respective newspapers. That we would rendezvous in such dangerous places—El Salvador, Nicaragua, Guatemala, Honduras—only heightened our intoxication. A few of Dial's colleagues on the *Los Angeles Times* started muttering to his editors about a conflict of interest, something that Dial dismissed as nonsense: our papers played to very different audiences; we wrote very different stories. My bosses certainly didn't seem worried, for despite my self-doubts I blossomed in Central America. I have never written so much nor, I believe, so well; often I would return from the day's interviews to find a 'herogram'—a laudatory telex from the *Journal*'s managing editor—in my message box.

I was too young then to appreciate the miraculousness of what was happening. I knew only that I had never been in love before; everything about it that had once seemed so trite and silly and that I had derided in others now appeared fresh, meaningful, ineffably sweet. Of course, acquaintances alluded, with exaggerated winks and nudges, to the difference in our ages; even Dial's teenage daughter exclaimed, 'But Lynda, how can you kiss him? He has wrinkles!' They didn't understand that I could never have fallen in love with a younger man. If a man were ever going to grow up—never a certainty—I figured it would take him until at least middle age to discover his humanity. For his part, Dial attracted much ribbing of the ha-ha-you-old-billy-goat sort. A reporter in my bureau, when he learned of our affair, maintained that a man of Dial's age—the same as his own—could be in such a relationship only for reasons of sex and ego. But to me, Dial spoke only of love.

Several months after we met, he wrote from San Salvador:

> It was here that I composed for you my first letter of love and trivia, away back last October, when I came here newly and madly in love. How long ago that seems, so many miles and so many feelings and so many capitals. And what changes in my life, my ways of living it, my perceptions of myself and where I stand in time and place—and all because of you. Sometimes I wonder: could I ever go back to being that old me? Now that I've gotten back to feeling, to really caring, I don't think I could ever return to my old ways. To measuring myself out in coffeespoons and two-week increments, to pleasant-enough times with friends who never learned that when I tell the truth, my eyes tear over.

Dial started carrying his divorce papers around with him wherever we went—he had been divorced for several years—on the off chance that I would agree to marry him in one of the tropical capitals we frequented. He became downright insistent when we were both sent to Argentina in the spring of 1982 to cover the Falklands War. I refused; I didn't want to embark on a life of conjugal bliss in a country engaged in a thoroughly idiotic armed conflict. But I promised to marry him before my next birthday.

I was in Tegucigalpa, Honduras, on 23 August, when Dial called from his home in Mexico. 'Lynda, I cannot not be married to you any longer,' he announced. 'Your birthday is in three days, and if you are a woman of honour, you must marry me. I'm flying down tomorrow with Jordy [his daughter] and two rings, and we're going to get married.'

'But I have interviews all day,' I said.

'You can still do your interviews. Just be back at the hotel by five.'

I set out early the next morning. There was a dreamy quality to the city that defied the knife-edge atmosphere in the region: the cotton-wool clouds sailing low across the horizon; the tiny, pastel-painted houses that dot the hillsides; the plodding *burros*. I raced from interview to interview with no time to think until, during a break at noon, it occurred to me that I had nothing to wear to my wedding. After making inquiries, I was directed across the main plaza, its phlegmatic fountain dribbling forth a rivulet of greenish water, to what was probably Tegucigalpa's only boutique. There I bought a white blouse, a white skirt and a knitted white belt.

For my last meeting of the day, a man I didn't know, but whose car had been described to me, picked me up at an appointed street corner and drove a circuitous route to a house on the outskirts of the city. The rendezvous was with representatives of the Contras, the guerrilla group trying to overthrow the Sandinista government in Nicaragua. It was an astonishing interview at a time when the US government was refusing to admit the Contras' existence, let alone the fact that it was providing them with aid. Suddenly I looked at my watch; it was 4.50. 'Gentlemen, I'm very sorry but I have to go,' I said. 'I'm getting married in ten minutes.'

I dashed back to the hotel to find Dial sitting on the edge of the bed in my room—he had somehow coaxed the key from the receptionist—dressed entirely in white, with matching knuckles. 'I didn't think you were going to show up,' he said tersely. I changed into my wedding outfit. Dial, Jordy and I then crowded into a taxi, along with a journalist friend who had been enlisted as a witness, and drove downtown to the four-hundred-year-old City Hall. The toothless old registrar, whom Dial had bribed to perform the ceremony—one could get the certificate only on Thursdays, and it was Tuesday—was waiting for us outside. He looked at Jordy, then at me, and said in a spray of Spanish, 'Which one of you is getting married? Ha ha!'

We trooped inside the building, an elaborate colonial relic

with beamed ceilings, gilded mouldings and wood-framed windows. The registrar mumbled something entirely unintelligible, to which Dial and I answered, '*Sí, quiero*,' the equivalent of 'I do.' My knees were shaking, and Dial had to steady me as I signed the register. Then he signed; when he looked up, his eyes were filled with tears. It was such an overwhelming moment that we almost forgot the rings he had brought from Mexico: delicate bands of twisted, burnished gold. We laughed and kissed and posed for Jordy to take pictures. Only one photograph came out, and even that is strangely overexposed. Dial stares steadfastly into the camera with an ebullient smile, while I demurely avert my face; behind us, the room is suffused with a pinkish aura that gives the scene an ethereal, fragile feeling.

Back at the hotel, we bought the only bottles of champagne to be found and shared them with a colonel in the Honduran air force who happened to be in the bar. He regaled us with an anecdote of how his helicopters had made a wrong turn that day into Nicaraguan air space and come under fire from Sandinista soldiers. We laughed (Dial taking notes all the while), finished off the bottles and retired to our room to call our families in the States. 'Hi Mom,' I shouted into the phone over what sounded like chattering rodents. 'I'm calling from Honduras. How are you?'

'I'm just fine, dear. How are you?'

'I'm married, Mom.'

Dead silence. Not surprisingly, this sudden telephonic announcement evoked virtually the same response from all my relatives; Ida, a younger sister, sobbed, 'But I don't even *know* him.' Dial had better luck: informed of our nuptials, his son Chris was positively ecstatic.

I quickly discovered that a journalistic marriage differs little from a journalistic romance: everything is dictated by the story. Our honeymoon was a reporting trip to the country's interior during which we became hopelessly lost and ended up at the Gulf of Fonseca, staring across the inlet at Nicaragua. Dial hurried back to Mexico two days later because the president nationalized the banking system, and we returned to our frenzied attempts at togetherness.

Then I got what seemed to be another break: the *Journal*'s Mexico correspondent asked to be transferred to New York—his pregnant wife couldn't tolerate the smog—and I was chosen to replace him. My beat now comprised only Mexico, a story of great importance to the *Journal* because of the country's huge foreign debt. It was also a sedate story, and I soon found myself missing the adventure of Central America's wars. Worst of all, I actually saw less of Dial than before, because he had to stay in El Salvador and Honduras much of the time. But we did, at last, have a home together: a spacious, airy apartment in the downtown district of Colonia Juarez. And, as Dial liked to say, what really counted was that we could keep our underwear in the same chest of drawers.

Dial managed to come home the last weekend of his life. We had two days together. In a raggedy salmon-coloured T-shirt and baseball cap emblazoned with the word BEETHOVEN, he assembled and painted bookshelves we had ordered from the States; I brought him cold beers and planted kisses on the back of his neck. Dial and I talked a lot that weekend about when I might become pregnant. He adored Chris and Jordy and yearned to have more children; I was worried about taking time off from my career; we talked without resolution. I left first; I had to file a story on Mexican labour unions from my office. He set off for Tegucigalpa later that afternoon. It was the only time that I didn't walk him to his taxi.

I might have been one of the last people on the planet to learn of Dial's death. By the time I found out, evening television programmes in the States had been interrupted; my Aunt Blanche in Chicago had called my mother in Detroit; Dial's kids had heard it on the radio.

All this happened while I was in a hideously touristic nightclub, sitting through two performances of Mexico's oldest mariachi performer so I could interview him afterwards. I didn't get back to the apartment until about 12.30 a.m.; as was our custom, I called Dial to say goodnight. The hotel receptionist in Tegucigalpa let the telephone in his room ring several times, then came on the line to say that Señor Torgerson must be out. I was not concerned: the previous night, Dial had said he was going down to the Nicaraguan border for a day or two and would leave his things at the hotel. I asked the receptionist to put a message in his box saying I had called.

Then I poured myself a glass of grape juice and settled down to read a relatively recent *New York Times*, a real luxury. The telephone rang: it was Eloy Aguilar, the bureau chief of the Associated Press; his voice was choked almost beyond recognition. It prompted an odd reaction in me. In a freeze-framed instant, my brain said: Hang up the phone. It's one o'clock in the morning, the AP bureau chief is on the line and he's crying. You know exactly what he's going to tell you. But if you don't hear it, nothing will have happened. So hang up.

'Hi, Eloy,' I said.

'Lynda, has anyone phoned you this evening?'

'No—I've been out.'

'You need to call the *Los Angeles Times*.'

'What's happened?'

'Just call them.'

'Eloy, you know how hard it is to make overseas calls from here. What's happened?'

'It's Dial.' Eloy was practically weeping. 'He's had an accident.'

'Is he alive?'

'No. Lynda, he's dead.'

Four words, and the earth shifts ninety degrees beneath your feet. Had Eloy said, 'Yes, Lynda, but he's hurt,' my world would have remained essentially intact, my life continuing on the same trajectory. But he didn't, and everything was changed.

I somehow reached the *Los Angeles Times* and was connected with the managing editor, who read me the paper's press release—something about a rocket-propelled grenade being fired from the Nicaraguan side of the border (the Honduran government's initial explanation of what happened), killing Dial and the photographer. He was startlingly laconic. After reciting the statement, he told me that the foreign editor was trying to get to Honduras, then he hung up. I was left in the stillness of a

Mexico City night, not knowing what to do.

The telephone rang again: it was the duty officer from the State Department in Washington, informing me of Dial's death. He said that the Honduran government was intending to bury him in Tegucigalpa if the body had not been claimed by three o'clock that afternoon. This was too much. 'But there are no commercial flights to Honduras today!' I screamed at the man. 'I can't get there by three o'clock! Stop them! You must stop them!'

The rest of the night was a delirium of telephoning. I called every foreign correspondent I knew in Mexico to see if anyone had a way down to Honduras. I called the television correspondents based in Miami to try to hitch a ride on one of their small planes, but no one could land in Mexico. One reporter paged through several US directories, reading off the telephone numbers of air charter services in Miami, Dallas, Houston and Los Angeles; I called them all and finally found one open at that abandoned hour, to hear that the company didn't have permission to land in Mexico. I called the press attaché from the US embassy and insisted that he wake up the ambassador to get me landing rights. I called the *Los Angeles Times* again to demand—from a junior copy editor, the only person still on duty—the use of the corporate jet. I called the US consular officer in Tegucigalpa to beg her not to let Dial be buried there. I called Jordy and Chris, who were very sweet and brave—no easy thing; their mother had died of cancer two months earlier. I called my parents. I called my sisters. I called and called, unable to stop the mad frenzy of dialling, afraid of being alone in my silent apartment.

The weird grey-green light of a Mexico City dawn began to filter through the windows. On that first morning of Dial's death, I realized I would never again see a sunrise with him; from now on, my life would be a series of small subtractions from what had amounted to a glorious fullness. It was an unbearable epiphany. I went outside to look for a taxi; I needed to talk to Lilia, my secretary, who didn't have a telephone. The cab driver shuddered when he saw my swollen face.

At Lilia's house, I pounded on the door, softly sobbing. Workers glanced at me curiously as they passed on the street. Finally Lilia answered, and I fell into her arms; from then on, she was in charge. She drove us back to my apartment and within a couple of hours had found a Mexican air charter company to fly me to Honduras. With some difficulty, she procured the landing rights for Tegucigalpa and Los Angeles, where Dial's children lived and where I wanted to bury him. By now the flat was filled with journalists come to help: Eloy Aguilar brought dollars to pay for the aircraft's refuelling; Chris Dickey of the *Washington Post* offered himself as an escort on the journey; his wife Carole followed me around with a spoonful of scrambled egg, murmuring, 'Eat, you must eat.' I was in the bedroom trying to find black clothes when Lilia yelled that it was time to go. The reason for the haste, besides the three o'clock deadline, was that Tegucigalpa's airport had no runway lights; we needed to be airborne, on our way to Los Angeles with the body, before dusk. I made a last call to the US embassy in Honduras to request that the body be waiting for me on the tarmac, and that the press be kept away.

There was less room inside the jet than I had imagined. Chris and I sat on opposite sides of the aisle, facing the cockpit; nevertheless our arms were practically touching. I'm usually uneasy about flying, especially on small planes, but this time I didn't even bother to fasten my seatbelt. It was, I think, the only time in my life I have understood the desire for suicide. To obliterate memory, to slip free of the relentless, crushing pain, to feel nothing, all seemed irresistibly alluring. I couldn't even watch the stewardess serve Chris a beer without recalling the way Dial gripped his glass with both hands, thumbs tapping a little tattoo on the sides. So I secretly welcomed every bump, every sudden, stomach-tightening dip the airplane took.

My longing for oblivion intensified as we approached Tegucigalpa. The plane passed over the familiar, squat houses clustered on the hills, banked hard and landed on a runway flanked by lines of drying laundry. It was well before three, but the place seemed deserted: no hearse, no body, only shimmery undulations of heat rising from the tarmac. Then I noticed the phalanx of television cameramen on the airport's observation deck, the deck where, on a similar afternoon a few months before, Dial had caught a strand of my hair between his fingers and kissed it, murmuring, 'See how it glows golden-red in this light.' I looked away.

Al Shuster, the *Los Angeles Times*'s foreign editor, was suddenly walking towards us across the tarmac. He looked ghastly: he too had been up all night. The US ambassador to Honduras was with him. The ambassador and I were not on good terms; he had flown to New York to complain to my editors about the Contra story, not because he disputed its accuracy but because he believed that it should never have been written. He explained the hearse's absence: to enter California, Dial's body had to be in a hermetically sealed casket; such a box wouldn't fit in our little plane, so we would have to spend the night here and take a commercial flight to Los Angeles the next day.

I could not spend the night there. I could not stay in the city where Dial and I were so lately married. I could not sleep in the hotel where, on our wedding night, we had turned off the lamps and opened the curtains and gazed at the hills aglitter with thousands of little lights. I furiously communicated this to Chris in whispers, trying not to cry; I didn't want to break down in front of the ambassador.

The embassy's consular officer appeared, asking for our passports. Chris walked to the terminal with her and the ambassador. She returned a few minutes later, saying that the ambassador would try to arrange something. In the meantime, we needed to go to the embassy to collect Dial's belongings and sign documents. The consular officer directed her driver to a back entrance, knowing that I didn't want to talk to the press. What, after all, could I say to them? True, they were colleagues; some of them were friends. But now, seen from the other side, they were contemptible. Our common profession made me no better-disposed towards them.

The consular officer brought me the worn leather carry-on that Dial had left in his hotel room; alone, I buried my nose in every shirt, every pullover, trying to detect his scent, so precious to me. She returned a while later to say that the ambassador had managed to get the rule about the casket waived; I could take Dial home in a body bag. I signed papers, stuffed Dial's clothes back into his carry-on and joined Al and Chris in the consular officer's car. When we reached the aircraft, the sun was already casting long shadows across the runway.

A hearse drew up, and two men pulled something out of the back that looked like a sleeping bag; the realization that Dial—or what remained of him—was in there caused me to break down, my face in my hands. 'The TV crews are filming you,' Al whispered, gently leading me round to the other side of the plane, out of sight. After a few minutes, when the hearse had gone, and I had regained my composure, we walked back round. A producer I knew and her cameraman pursued us across the tarmac. This was beyond my tolerance. 'Jesus Christ, he was your friend too, Viviana,' I exploded. 'Can't you be human for once?' She motioned to the cameraman, who snapped off his equipment.

The pilot helped me on to the plane. The body bag was on the floor in the aisle, and I virtually had to step over it to get to my seat. I was dazed by the sight: to behold your husband stowed on the floor is a shocking thing. The pilot started the engines and taxied to the end of the airstrip. I stared out the window at the fast-fading light, blinking hard to hold back the tears. The plane gathered power, then raced down the runway and rose, leaving behind the hovels, the swaying clothes lines, the children wildly waving goodbye.

Once we were airborne, the stewardess filled enormous tumblers with vodka and a splash of tonic for Chris and Al, which they gulped like soda. I couldn't stop looking at the bag; every curve, every projection, was outlined under the thin material. I was astonished at how little there seemed to be inside. And it took all the restraint I could muster to keep from getting down on the floor, putting my arms around whatever remained of Dial and holding him one last time.

After a while my companions fell into an intoxicated sleep. The sun hung just below the port window, the sky smeared an incandescent purple-pink. Al stirred suddenly, opened his eyes and said, 'My God, it's my thirty-first wedding anniversary,' then went back to sleep. On and on we flew, hurtling through a dusk of matchless beauty: the glory of the heavens at my elbow, the pieces of my husband at my feet.

I don't remember much of Dial's funeral. An exhaustion, a kind of emotional numbness, set in after we reached Los Angeles, as if all my strength were spent in that single act of retrieving his body. I do recall one thing vividly: on the morning of the funeral, I awoke to find I had my period. Oddly, this seemed more real than Dial's death. Here was something palpable, concrete, conclusive: I would never have a child with him.

I received hundreds of letters, telegrams and telexes of condolence. They came from journalists in Atlanta, Beijing, Bonn, Boston, Buenos Aires, Cairo, Chicago, Dallas, Houston, Jerusalem, Johannesburg, Los Angeles, London, Manila, Moscow, Nairobi, New York, Rio de Janeiro, Rome, Tokyo, Washington; from the Foreign Correspondents' Associations in Hong Kong, Israel, El Salvador, Florida; from the US ambassadors in Mexico and Honduras, the US embassies in Nicaragua and Panama, the consulates of Australia, Britain, France, Israel in Los Angeles; from senators, congressmen and the vice-president of Honduras; from bankers, businessmen and the Anti-Defamation League of B'nai Brith; from complete strangers who felt compelled to write. I read every one and cried over them all.

The comfort these rituals provided was tempered by the emerging political implications of Dial's death. The coroner in Los Angeles concluded that Dial's injuries could have been caused only by a massive upward explosion—despite the Honduran government's claim, supposedly backed up by three witnesses, that Nicaraguan soldiers had fired a rocket from across the border. An American reporter and photographer went to the site of the attack, where they saw the landmines embedded in the road, the demolished car, the crater. They took pictures of everything and showed them to officials at the US embassy in Tegucigalpa. Subsequently the Honduran government and the embassy decided the occupants of the white Toyota were indeed killed by an exploding landmine—planted by Nicaraguan soldiers. But other military analysts, who saw the photographs, believe the charges were of a type used only by the Contras, the US-supported guerrillas. I will probably never know the truth.

Not long after the funeral, Dial's death ceased to be news. Benigno Aquino, the Filipino political dissident, was shot dead on the tarmac at Manila airport by government soldiers. Two hundred and forty-three US Marines were blown up in Beirut. American troops invaded the Caribbean island of Grenada. The world, in other words, moved on. And so, eventually, would I.

Through the years, I've been sustained by the belief that Dial wouldn't have wanted his life any other way. He had been a desk man, an editor, before becoming a foreign correspondent and got out because, as he described it, the walls of the city room seemed to close in on him a bit more every year. Dial delighted in the challenges of foreign reportage: the hostile governments, impossible terrain, poor telecommunications. Surmounting those difficulties required the summoning up of what he called 'Greek excellence'. Given the choice, Dial would surely have preferred to live, but the security of the newsroom would, for him, have been no life at all.

For my part, I came to feel differently about the profession. I continued to work as a foreign correspondent in the Middle East, South America, Southern Africa. But it was never the same. The sense of glamour, of boundless expectation, had vanished; something in me had changed. Perhaps it was because I would never be twenty-five years old again and not have had the person I loved most in the world blown to bits. Perhaps I just outgrew it. I eventually left daily journalism to write about the world in a more measured way, bequeathing the coverage of coups and earthquakes to others. Only one such story, Dial's story, I carry in my heart always.

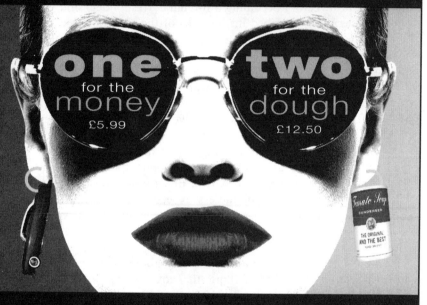

Janet Evanovich

one for the money £5.99

two for the dough £12.50

'Stone brilliant, the best crime fiction debut of the decade so far. More please, soon' - *GQ*

'The comic timing that turns tough set-ups into ironic put-downs is criminally original. Plum is the genuine, softboiled article' - *Vogue*

One for the Money marked the debut of Stephanie Plum, fugitive apprehension agent extraordinaire and crime fiction's feistiest and most original heroine in years. *Two for the Dough* elevates her from auspicious debutante to pop legend.

It takes balls to be a bounty hunter ... and she doesn't care whose

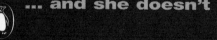

WRITING FOR NOBODY

On the other hand, however,
the President's intervention
will be seen as too little, too
late. There is justice to this
view. We believe that he has
no other course but to resign.
He should quit now, before
this country's international
reputation is further sullied by

ERIC JACOBS

My first proper job was writing leaders—unsigned editorials—for a broadsheet newspaper in Scotland, the *Glasgow Herald*. My last was writing leaders for a national tabloid called *Today*. I have often wondered whether anybody ever read what I wrote.

The first hint that they might not came one day in the late 1950s when a friend of my father's asked how I was getting on at the *Herald*. Fine, I said, adding snootily that the paper was a bit right-wing for my taste. A vacant look glazed his face. Right-wing? Left-wing? A native Glaswegian, he had read the paper all his life as a matter of habit and civic obligation and never noticed which way it leaned.

Much more recently, soon after *Today* began publication in 1986, its market researchers set up a series of tests. Selected groups of a dozen people—male, female, young, old—were paid to read an issue of the paper and then interrogated about their reaction while we studied them through a two-way mirror. I watched a group of youngish women as they were taken through the news pages towards the leaders. They had all read at least something on every page until they came to mine. Now there was utter silence. Not one of them had read a single word.

This is the slenderest of anecdotal evidence, but I suspect reflects a real state of affairs. Politicians and other self-publicists may like to gaze at their musings in print, but ordinary readers, people who pay for their newspapers, hardly care what those papers' opinions are. Even I don't read leaders now that I no longer write them.

When I told my father's friend that I was getting on fine at the *Herald* I unknowingly lied. After three weeks I was removed from the job. The task of leader-writing was often given to young graduates like me, then still fairly rare in the provincial press. This was not, I am sure, because of the brilliant edge our finely polished intellects might bring to matters of the day. It was because as novices we could do little mischief on the leader page. There the editor might keep a close eye on us while the serious business of bringing out the newspaper proper was left to experienced people. I particularly remember the sub-editors, middle-aged men of gravity and substance who wore green eye-shades, rarely loosened their ties or unbuttoned their collars, kept their shirt cuffs clear of their busy hands by means of elasticated silver bands placed around the upper arm and drank briefly but at prodigious speed in the pub between first and second editions. These were men who could spell, punctuate and adhere to the *Herald* style book as closely as a Guards sergeant to his drill manual. Where have they gone?

The offence for which I was sacked from leader-writing was not reckless deviation from *Herald* orthodoxy. I did not propose the abolition of the monarchy, independence for Scotland or that readers vote Labour. It was much worse than any of those. I failed to observe the inflexible rule that all *Herald* leaders must be divided into three paragraphs of roughly equal length. In the first you stated the problem ('The nation is divided over the Government's policy on . . . '). In the second you kicked the problem around a bit ('On the one hand it can be said that . . . On the other it might be argued . . . '). And in the third you produced a solution ('Men and women of good will must therefore hope . . . '). But I let my leaders sprawl, like my thoughts, in as many paragraphs of whatever length I thought fit. This was an appalling breach of form for which I was exiled to the letters-to-the-editor desk. There I made a further dreadful blunder. I misspelt a Gaelic place name and was exiled to the sports desk where I edited the daily racecard. After a couple of years I made my escape to the *Guardian* in London where spelling mistakes, like other errors, could always be explained away as part of the paper's homespun charm.

For some reason the *Guardian* did not make use of my leader-writing talents. Not that it mattered. I could always insinuate my views into the news columns by deploying the facts to suit my version of the truth. When I became deputy to the labour correspondent—first John Cole, later Peter Jenkins—I was able to depict the unions and the Labour Party as almost invariably in the right, and the bosses and the Tory government in the wrong, as in: 'The Transport and General Workers' Union made a mockery of government policy last night when . . . ' I came to think of these as little scoops of interpretation, and besides they were more dramatic, more cosmic, more fun than just saying, 'The Transport and General Workers' Union called a strike in Britain's docks last night.' Nobody ever took me to task, probably because they were all as pro-union as I was and so assumed that my glosses were no more than edifying clarification.

If nobody else reads leaders, they are at least useful to a paper's journalists. With leading articles as signposts, reporters know which stories are likely to find favour with the editorial hierarchy. Whenever Europe was discussed at a trade-union conference in the 1960s the man from the *Daily Express* would lay down his pencil, even nod off, until roused into frenzied note-taking by an attack on the Common Market. The wilder, the more comprehensive the denunciation the more the speaker would have the *Express* man's full attention, no matter how obscure or untypical that speaker might be. Lord Beaverbrook, the *Express*'s owner, greatly disapproved of Europe, and nothing in its favour found its way into the *Express*'s pages, whereas criticism of any kind was practically guaranteed space. Learning from the leaders how the wind blew, the *Express* reporter knew exactly where to look for the story that would earn him his precious quota of column inches. I suspect that this is how leaders exercise their greatest influence, by setting the broad agenda for the rest of the newspaper, the bits people actually read.

Soon after I moved from the *Guardian* to the *Sunday Times* I became part of the team that discussed at length every Friday morning what should be in the following Sunday's leader column. This was an agreeable way to pass the time, discussion being conducted in civilized, senior-common-room style. Disagreements were politely resolved. For instance, the editor, Harold Evans, was pro-abortion and had been active in the campaign to legalize it, while Hugo Young, who wrote most of the leaders, was a Catholic and thoroughly disapproved of it. Young stated his case, and Evans his. Evans naturally prevailed, regardless of the merits of his argument, but deferred to Young's feelings insofar as he did not ask him to write pro-abortion leaders. Evans prevailed because that is what editors are there to do. Under the circumstances those long and amiable discussions were rather pointless, however enjoyable, since the newspaper's line was always what Evans wanted it to be. Although perhaps those conferences did put into his head ideas which had not previously occurred to him and which he could adopt as his own.

My leaders were usually about trade-union affairs, then very much the centre of attention, now almost wholly ignored. By the late 1960s I was less sympathetic to the unions than I had been earlier. The *Sunday Times* had union troubles of its own. We could never be certain that the newspaper for which we had worked all week would actually get printed on Saturday night or, if it did, whether the full run of a million-plus copies would come off the presses. Vain and egotistical, journalists are apt to take a dim view of actions that deprive millions of people of the chance to read their highly perishable words. Even the most left-wing among us found their loyalties strained by the contrast between the unions' pious class-war rhetoric and the crude selfishness of their behaviour.

Harry Evans, the son of a railway worker, was surely an instinctive Labour man. But the *Sunday Times* was Conservative by tradition, so when it came to elections we mostly backed the Tories. Once I happened to pass Evans's office when he had just finished writing a leader endorsing the Tories at the following week's election. Being wise enough to know that no journalist, however exalted, should send his copy to be printed without at least one other person reading it through, he called me in and asked me to take a look at what he had written. 'Well, Harry,' I said, 'I personally don't disagree with a word. But where do you say "Vote Tory"?' He pointed to a subordinate clause which indicated a mild preference for some or other aspect of Conservative policy. 'Yes,' I said, 'but that's hardly a ringing endorsement. Shouldn't we say "Vote Tory" out loud if that's what we mean?' Evans harrumphed irritably and went off to make some changes.

I tell this story not to discredit him but as a reminder that leader writers, even when they are editors, are rarely masters of the opinions they peddle. They are advocates, like barristers, bought and paid for by their clients. An editor, a tradition, a proprietor or some combination of the three is always looking over the leader writer's shoulder. Of the thousands of leaders I must have written, not many have come from my heart. It is in any case difficult to have heartfelt opinions about fifteen different subjects a week, the number of leaders I was required to churn out at the peak of my *Today* days. The most I can say is that I

117

have never written a leader that I could not defend, however half-heartedly, or that was repugnant to my conscience. A leader writer can hardly expect more.

Nearly thirty years after my three weeks as a leader writer on the Glasgow *Herald* I became a full-time leader writer for the second time. I had left the *Sunday Times* following a row with its then editor, Andrew Neil. It was a propitious moment for the cruising pundit. Eddie Shah, fresh from his hard-won victories over the unions that printed his free sheets in the north of England and eager for new challenges, was about to start a new national newspaper called *Today*, and Brian MacArthur, his editor, had advertised for a leader writer. He suggested I apply for the job. I was happy to do so, but wondered why he didn't just sign me up on the spot. MacArthur knew my form from his own days on the *Sunday Times*; what more could he need to know? But he had asked all the applicants for the job to write a specimen leader, so I had to do the same. For the first and only time I entered an open competition for a job. It was like being back at school. Never has a leader been so sweated over as the one I submitted. For hours and hours I wrote and rewrote, cut and added, tuned and fine-tuned. At the speed I produced it I would have been able to turn out about two leaders a week for a normally functioning newspaper. But it did the trick and was judged the best leader submitted.

There remained one more hurdle, Eddie Shah. He wanted to approve personally the man who was going to be the voice of *Today*. I prepared myself for a thorough grilling on the issues of the moment. There were, I was ready to tell him, three great problems in the world for which any imaginable solution would be worse than the problem it was supposed to solve: the Middle East, Northern Ireland and South Africa. I foresaw bloodbaths in each, since any settlement could only be at the expense of one or another well-armed group which wouldn't accept it. How wrong I seem to have been.

Shah did not want to hear my opinions on anything at all. What he did want to know was whether I would be willing to leave London six times a year to take the pulse of the provinces. He was very wary, almost paranoid, about what he perceived as a mafia of London chatterers who controlled all opinion-forming channels and were totally out of touch with what was going on in the minds of people outside their circle. Certainly, I said, I'd be only too happy to get about the country. With that the job was mine. But I never did find time to go anywhere except once to Dublin where I sat all day in my hotel bedroom writing leaders—a much more exhaustingly complicated activity in a distant hotel than back at base in the office—instead of getting out among the people.

The trouble with *Today* was that it did not have enough money. Shah wanted everything to be new and different, from the computers on our desks to the colour presses and the franchised distribution system. Innovation on such a broad front needs much rehearsal if it is to succeed. But we had no time to rehearse. There were no proper dummy runs. The first issue to go on sale was the first we produced. Shah had a payroll to meet and he needed revenue. He couldn't afford to wait. The result was a dismal flop, and even the huge resources of Lonrho and Rupert Murdoch who took over the paper successively from Shah could not make *Today* profitable.

The practical effect on me of *Today*'s multiple defects was that I had to get out of bed extremely early. Production was so slow that the leader page had to be ready by ten in the morning. I drove to Pimlico ahead of the rush hour so as to read the papers and drum up some ideas in time to speak to Brian MacArthur on his car phone as he drove in to work at a more conventional time. We decided between us what I should write about, and I got on with it. By the time the rest of the staff arrived for work I had finished mine. This was nice for me, but it meant that the leaders lagged a day behind the rest of the newspaper, since I didn't know what the stories in the next day's paper would be. So far as I know, no reader complained (further evidence that nobody reads leaders?), but it was yet one more minor defect among many. A tabloid cannot afford to lurk behind events, even on its leader page.

As for *Today*'s political stance, this was not easy to define. Shah wanted us to be different here too; in particular he did not

want the paper to support any one political party. *Today* was to
be independent. This sounds bold but it all too easily leads to a
sort of nagging anti-everythingism. I have heard it argued on
more than one newspaper that it should stand magnificently
aloof and not declare for any party at election time. But my
response has always been that you cannot dish out advice on
every imaginable subject for five years and then have no opinion
at all on the one issue on which every adult in the country has to
make up his or her mind and might actually welcome some of
that advice. At the general election of 1987 we decided to plump
for the Social Democratic Party as the best available compromise
between having and not having an opinion. By this time Lonrho
had bought the paper, and the editor was Dennis Hackett. I
wrote the leader and then, much to my annoyance, he rewrote it.
He did this on Wednesday, recommending readers to vote SDP
'tomorrow', which meant that when it appeared on Thursday it
was advising people to vote on Friday, the day after the actual
ballot. I got much malicious satisfaction out of this. Hackett's
arguments were a rehash of my own, though in my view less
eloquently expressed. But his was also the only leader which I can
claim with certainty to have had a decisive effect on a reader, for
it struck me that if my arguments couldn't persuade anybody
else, at least they should sometimes convince me. So I voted SDP.

At subsequent elections for the European Parliament, I
advised readers to have 'a flutter' on the Greens, who then
clocked up their best-ever vote: fifteen per cent or thereabouts. It
is tempting to believe that this was the consequence of my leader,
but I resist the temptation. There was a mood at the time, a
feeling of disaffection, a plague-on-all-your-houses attitude
towards the main parties, and when better to take it out on them
than at a boring old Euro-election? Greenery was in the air too.
In place of labour experts like me, newspapers were busily hiring
environment correspondents. Much of this interest, curiously
enough, had been stimulated by Margaret Thatcher in a speech
endorsing concern about green issues, making them respectable—
not that she took much action to follow up her speech. Such are
the vague, intangible ingredients that make up a moment of
political flux. My leader belongs among these intangibles, an

unquantifiable factor in a complex equation, but likely to be slight if not negligible.

Taking a flutter on the Greens was not, in fact, my idea but David Montgomery's, the new editor put in by Rupert Murdoch when he bought *Today* from Lonrho. Why Murdoch bought the paper in the first place I have never understood. When asked at a dinner party he gave soon after the takeover he said that it was because Montgomery wanted him to, meaning, I suppose, that it made sense to put together an editor who had proved himself—at the *News of the World* in Montgomery's case—with a newspaper that the editor thought he could make a success.

Montgomery at once tried to put a new stamp on the paper. At his first morning conference he announced that henceforth *Today* would appeal to greedy people. He was all energy and go. But where were we going? Who were these greedy people? Yuppies, presumably. But whatever else you think about yuppies, they are not stupid. Printing endless pictures of girls in shoulder-padded red jackets, the then-current symbol of a young woman on the make, was not enough to persuade them that *Today* was their paper.

In some ways Montgomery was a progressive—solidly against hanging, greatly in favour of women getting ahead, deeply hostile to all forms of race discrimination. This was congenial enough to his leader writer. But there was an authoritarian, Thatcherite edge to his liberalism too. His remedies were peremptory: sack that man, change that law. Everyone should be free to do exactly what they liked except when Montgomery, like Thatcher, thought that, in their own interests of course, they shouldn't be free because if they were they would mess things up. He was a great one for regulating whatever seemed to him out of control: guns, dogs, food.

He seemed at his happiest when there was a queue of six people waiting for his decisions. Outside my cubby hole of an office, in the reception area, three men from Saatchi & Saatchi appeared to be forever expecting an audience.

Printing arrangements had by now been sorted out so that the deadline for my leaders was nearer ten at night than ten in the morning. Montgomery made full use of the extra time, never reading my copy until the last possible minute. This might have made sense to him but it was extremely boring for me. Thumping out five or six hundred words of tabloid advice and abuse takes, let's face it, not more than an hour or so. But the way Montgomery ran things, the process stretched out over ten or eleven hours. I took longer lunches than ever and started writing a novel (unfinished) on my screen.

In January 1991 I was put out of my misery. I was fired, along with forty others, in one of those cost-cutting campaigns that hit newspapers so often these days. The style of firing was very 1990s, very Murdoch. Montgomery summoned me to his office: We need to lose your job. Nothing personal. References will be provided. Kindly clear your desk, pick up your redundancy cheque on the way out and do not return. Four years later Murdoch closed *Today*, and most of the rest of the staff went the same way.

Do I miss writing leaders? No. There was some fun to be had in rearranging the world from the anonymity of an unsigned column. The risk is that you will come to believe you are rearranging the real world. The most I can claim to have done is to have made a bit of it wobble now and then.

HERE COME THE TANKS

Daily Mirror, 1 August 1917

PATRICK WRIGHT

FIRST PICTURES OF THE TANKS IN ACTION

The Daily Mirror

CERTIFIED CIRCULATION LARGER THAN THAT OF ANY OTHER DAILY PICTURE PAPER

No. 4,082   Registered at the G.P.O. as a Newspaper.   WEDNESDAY, NOVEMBER 22, 1916   One Halfpenny.

"HUSH, HUSH"—A TANK GOES "GALUMPHANT" INTO ACTION ON THE WESTERN FRONT.

At last! To-day we are able to publish the first photograph of one of his Majesty's land ships, which have been making such successful cruises on the sea of mud off the Somme. They are the first to be published in any British newspaper, and two others will be found on pages 6 and 7. This "juggernaut," this "Diplodocus," to give it but two of the hundred and one names which have been conferred upon it, was seen "galumphing" into action, its progress being best described in the immortal language of Lewis Carroll. The tanks have been at Flers—one "led" the men down the High-street—and many of the important battles of the great "push" in France. Before them barbed wire becomes as limp as macaroni, while they mow down trees and pass casually over trenches, dealing out death as they go.—(Exclusive to The Daily Mirror.)

The first picture of a tank to appear in the British press

Out of the civil disturbances of the twentieth century—protests, riots, rebellions—have come two sentences that ring bells of alarm and excitement among the people who are paid to gather and spread the news. The first is: 'They are sending in the tanks!' The second: 'The tanks are on the streets!' The reports will then move on to what the tanks are there to do, and usually the same verb will occur: to crush. Sometimes the crushing is effective—Budapest in 1956, Prague in 1968, Tiananmen Square in 1989—and the protest is ended; sometimes it achieves only a temporary lull; sometimes it escalates protest into deeper conflict. But in its narrow and purely physical sense, the word is always appropriate. Crushing is the way with tanks. Their steel tracks grind forward, bricks turn to powder, tramlines get crazily bent, human bodies that happen to be in the way are flattened to bloody tissue and splintered bone. In these civilian circumstances, unhampered by any opposition from aircraft, landmines, artillery or other tanks, the tank seems unstoppable.

This view of the tank has made it one of the century's most potent global symbols, the pride of emperors, dictators and juntas, and of more popular governments when the going gets rough or when politicians seek to present themselves as men and women of resolve. Margaret Thatcher passed the tank test triumphantly when she was photographed kitted out like Lawrence of Arabia, riding a British tank across the military training grounds of Germany, the Iron Lady on an ironclad. Michael Dukakis, on the other hand, failed the same test when he clambered on board a tank during the presidential elections of 1988 and allowed George Bush's campaign managers to exploit what they saw as his fake militarism; Bush was the real thing, the true vet.

For many soldiers and military historians, the symbolism of the tank is only a sideshow, a reflection of its power as an instrument of war. Yet, as civilians may be better placed to grasp, the *idea* of the tank has been part of its effectiveness from the beginning. As a machine, a collection of parts, it had modest origins. In 1915 Winston Churchill, who as First Lord of the Admiralty had already sponsored the pioneering Landships Committee, commissioned William Foster and Company, a manufacturer of agricultural implements in Lincoln, to set aside its ploughshares and make experimental 'landships' which could break the unexpected deadlock of trench warfare on the Western Front. But the tank had been imagined long before then, not in military academies still planning the strategies of cavalry charges, but by popular authors such as H. G. Wells who evoked future wars conducted by intimidating, inhuman, tank-like things. Some of the tank's technical innovators later suggested that it was not so much a military invention as a hastily-engineered precipitate of the Zeitgeist, which meant that it could be acclaimed as an awesome, almost magical weapon before it had a single military achievement to its credit. In fact, the new war machine was a clumsy, motorized metal box that had still to be turned into a useful weapon, but its rampant image, so easily turned into myth and publicity, was hardly to be contained by this limited practical reality.

The tank became an unstable amalgam of fact and fantasy; in other words, news.

Early in the morning of 15 September 1916, the British army went into action in the Battle of the Somme with a scattering of thirty-six tanks. Many broke down as they crawled forward, or got stuck in the mud, or were wrecked by shellfire. Others went off course and, in their crews' confusion, attacked the wrong trenches or fired at their own infantry. But tanks had never been used before, and there was great interest in their limited successes. A tank nicknamed 'Crème de Menthe' took a heavily defended sugar factory at Courcelette, but greater triumph belonged to Lieutenant Hastie's 'Dinnaken'—the Scotticization of 'don't know'—which reached the village of Flers. As an airman reported in a famous wireless message: 'Tank seen in main street Flers going on with a large number of troops following it.' Improved by the press, this soon read: 'A tank is walking up the High Street of Flers with the British Army cheering behind.' The tank was also said to be flying a piece of paper proclaiming: GREAT HUN DEFEAT: SPECIAL!

Several soldiers wrote down their impressions of this new war machine before the newspapers took over. 'In evening saw a new horror of war arrive—an armoured "caterpillar",' wrote Captain Foxell of the Royal Engineers on 11 September 1916. To him, the tank seemed 'a fearful-looking article manned by desperadoes'. He added that 'hopes are built upon its action. It seems to move slowly with considerable noise and smoke.' J. H. Price of the Shropshire Light Infantry described how a general had briefed the troops before their advance. When the general remarked that the soldiers would 'have the help of three tanks', Price had asked, 'Did the General think we would be running short of water?'

He was not to know that the name 'tank' had been adopted for security reasons when the previous designation, 'landship', threatened to give too much away. 'Tank' was chosen as less clumsy than alternatives such as 'reservoir', 'cistern', 'container' or 'receptacle', and the diversionary story was put about that they were actually mobile water tanks built to a bizarre Russian design and intended for export.

Captain D. H. Pegler of the artillery called them 'land crabs' in his diary and noted on 18 September that 'some are lying on their backs, mangled masses of twisted and broken iron, others are back in their repairing yards, all are more or less crocked, but Gad, the execution they did was awful.' It struck him, he wrote, how symbolic of all war they were. 'One saw them creeping along at about four miles an hour, taking all obstacles as they came, spluttering death with all their guns, enfilading each trench as they came to it—and crushing beneath them our own dead and dying as they passed. I saw one body on a concrete parapet over which one had passed. This body was just a splash of blood and clothing about two feet wide and perhaps an inch thick. An hour before, this thing had been a thinking, breathing man, with life before him and loved ones awaiting him, probably somewhere in Scotland, for he was a kiltie. Nothing stops these cars, trees bend and break, boulders are pressed into the earth.'

Astonishment, awe, disbelief, hope: all these feelings were mingled when British troops first saw these large lozenge-shaped objects on the front. But there was another and, in the circumstances, odder reaction: laughter. As one tank soldier later wrote, 'The predominant emotion excited in anyone seeing them for the first time was a feeling of hilarity. One wanted to laugh.' They reminded soldiers of pantomime animals and were dubbed 'Old Mother Hubbard' to guffaws of vengeance as well as glee.

127

According to Major Clough Williams-Ellis, an architect and tank veteran who wrote one of the first books on this new weapon, British troops liked to imagine their German enemy quaking and crying out *'Kamerad! Kamerad!'* as the tanks bore down on them.

Philip Gibbs, the Liberal journalist and novelist who reported from the front for the *Daily Chronicle* and *Daily Telegraph*, noticed this frantic laughter in his account of the exploits of the tank known as 'Crème de Menthe'. British infantrymen, wrote Gibbs, were laughing 'even when bullets caught them in the throat'. Out of this strange comedy came fantasy enriched by the irony of trench humour, in which the tanks became mechanical miracles. C. E. Dukes, a private in the Bedfordshire Regiment, wrote home to his fiancée in England:

They can do up prisoners in bundles like straw-binders, and, in addition, have an adaptation of a printing machine which enables them to catch the Huns, fold, count and deliver them in quires, every thirteenth man being thrown out a little further than the others. The Tanks can truss refractory prisoners like fowls prepared for cooking, while their equipment renders it possible for them to charge into a crowd of Huns, and by shooting out spokes like porcupine quills, carry off an opponent on each. Though 'stuck up', the prisoners are, needless to say, by no means proud of their position. They can chew up barbed wire and turn it into munitions. As they run they slash their tails and clear away trees, horses, howitzers and anything else in the vicinity. They turn over on their backs and catch live shells in their caterpillar feet, and they can easily be adapted as submarines; in fact, most of them crossed the Channel in this guise. They loop the loop, travel forwards, sideways and backwards, not only with equal speed, but at the same time. They spin round like a top, only far more quickly, dig themselves in, bury themselves, scoop out a tunnel and come out again ten miles away in half an hour.

Don't miss out on major issues.

GRANTA

'With each new issue, *Granta* enhances its reputation for presenting, in unequalled range and depth, the best contemporary writers in journalism and fiction.' *Sunday Times*

'More than an excellent taster, it's the finest prose anthology for years.' *New Statesman & Society*

'A magazine absolutely charged with life and risk.' George Steiner

Subscribe and save up to 40%.

Why not take advantage of these substantial discounts on the £7.99 bookshop price by subscribing, and ensure a regular supply of writing that matters and that endures is delivered right to your door.

- **1 YEAR (4 ISSUES): £21.95**
  You save £10.

- **2 YEARS (8 ISSUES): £41.00**
  You save £23.

- **3 YEARS (12 ISSUES): £57.50**
  You save £38.

The order form is overleaf.

YES I would like to subscribe:
❏ new order
❏ renewal

Subscribe for yourself

❏ 1 year £21.95 ❏ 2 years £41.00 ❏ 3 years £57.50

Please start my subscription with issue number:_____

NAME AND ADDRESS *(please complete even if ordering a gift subscription)*

_____

_____

_____

POSTCODE _____

Total* £_____

96C5S53B

❏ Cheque (to 'Granta') ❏ Visa, Mastercard/Access, AmEx

Card no:

Expire date:_____ Signature:_____

* POSTAGE: FREE IN THE UK. PLEASE ADD £8 PER YEAR FOR SUBSCRIPTIONS IN EUROPE, AND £15 PER YEAR FOR OVERSEAS SUBSCRIPTIONS.

Please tick this box if you would prefer *not* to receive promotional offers from other approved organizations ❏

or for a friend.

I would like to give a subscription to the following. My name, address and payment details are above.

NAME AND ADDRESS: Mr/Mrs/Ms/Miss

_____

_____

_____

Postcode _____

Return, free of charge if posted in the UK, to:
Granta, Freepost,
2-3 Hanover Yard, Noel Road, London N1 8BR

NAME AND ADDRESS: Mr/Mrs/Ms/Miss

_____

Or use our
CREDIT CARD LINES:
UK (free phone and fax):
FreeCall 0500 004 033
OUTSIDE THE UK:
Tel: 44 171 704 0470
Fax: 44 171 704 0474

_____

_____

Postcode _____

Don't miss out on major issues (or on major savings).

GRANTA

A milder version of this kind of fantasy had inspired the tank's first designers. In 1903, H. G. Wells published a short story, 'The Land Ironclads', in which a horrified war correspondent described the unstoppable advance of new armoured weapons over a previously immobilized battlefield. Wells's story was known to Churchill and other tank pioneers, and the author was invited to attend trials at which he confirmed that the machines were, with some minor discrepancies, just what he'd had in mind. In 1914, after the First World War began, another storyteller, Colonel Ernest Swinton, was appointed Official Observer or 'Eyewitness' to the British expeditionary force in France, where his literary skills were deployed writing uplifting reports, known by sceptics as 'Eyewash', for the newspapers. Before the war, Swinton had specialized in military adventure stories in which 'blasted anarchists' got a 'proper biffing'. The idea of caterpillar-tracked 'machine-gun destroyers' came to him in France, as he watched the development of a new kind of siege warfare. He submitted a proposal to the War Office and by 1916 was installed as the first commander of the emerging tank corps, then still known as the Heavy Section of the Machine Gun Corps.

As a literary apparition, the tank should not have survived (and today, with instant television pictures, probably would not have survived) the reality of its ponderous appearance at the Somme. But in 1916 there were only five British newspaper correspondents covering this bit of the war, all of whom were based, with their censors, at a small chateau near General Headquarters at St Omer. They projected the romance of the new war machine back across the English Channel, dragging the tank into the realms of imagination as they did so. They called the tanks Behemoths, Juggernauts, Elephantine Tractors. As Clough Williams-Ellis recalled, they 'ransacked their dictionaries for octosyllables in which to describe the new "All British" destroyer of Germans. It was "diplodocus galumphant", it was "polychromatic toad". It was a "flat-footed monster" which performed the most astonishing feats of agility as it advanced, spouting flames from every side.'

The reports had started to appear in newspapers immediately after the tanks first went into action on 15 September, and the confusion between the practical reality of the tanks and their burgeoning myth is still there to be read in the newspapers of that time. On 16 September, a dispatch from GHQ mentioned 'a new type of heavily armoured car' which had proved of 'considerable utility' in battle. Two days later, *The Times*' special correspondent was offering a more vivid account of the story. The new 'fortresses on wheels'—which the correspondent, Percy Robinson, claimed to have seen—were of an 'extraordinary and ungainly shape', and readers were asked to imagine them 'thrusting themselves with all their spines out, like . . . hedgehogs into a nest of snakes'. On 21 September, in another dispatch, Robinson changed metaphors. He had seen tanks 'sitting down' on enemy trenches like 'huge tame pachyderms' after trundling across previously impassable terrain. 'It is difficult to speak of the things quite seriously,' he wrote, 'because they are so preposterous, so unlike anything that ever was on earth before.'

Lord Northcliffe's *Times* may have felt obliged to hide its amusement behind this respectable sigh of wonder, but the *Daily Mail* knew no such inhibition. William Beach Thomas's report on the camouflaged tanks he had seen gathering for the attack on the night of 14 September was considerably less restrained:

> A gibbous moon and brilliant stars, shining in an almost frosty night, lit with fantastic shadows and crescent patches of light the earth craters and parapet ridges of the bare highland; and as the night yielded to the dawn, the colours on the backs of the monsters shifted like a chameleon's . . .
>
> They looked like blind creatures emerging from the primeval slime. To watch one crawling round a battered wood in the half-light was to think of 'the Jabberwock with eyes of flame' who *Came whiffling round the tulgey wood /And burbled as it came . . .*
>
> With ludicrous serenity they wobbled across the gridiron fields and shook themselves as if the bullets were flies that bit just deep enough to deserve a flick. Those who had inspected these *saurias* in their alfresco stalls beforehand or followed their lethargic course over impossible roads in the moonlight gasped with humorous

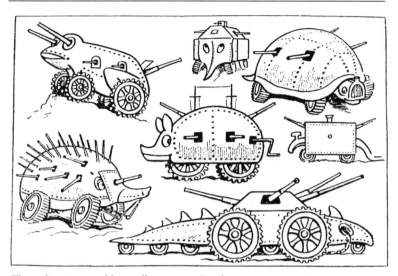

The tank as imagined by an illustrator at Punch

wonder at the prodigy. Munchausen never approached the stories imagined for them by soldiers. But their pet name will always be 'Tanks', and they were chiefly regarded as a practical joke. Whales, boojums, dreadnoughts, slugs, snarks—never were creatures that so tempted the gift of nicknaming. They were said to live on trees and houses and jump like grass hoppers or kangaroos.

Thomas didn't hesitate to surrender the tank soldier to his sense of humour as well. Like their machines, the tank men were a comic species apart: 'it is a pity the tanks were not invented in the time of the little Picts. They are made for tough little men, who can stow themselves away anywhere.' He felt honoured to have been inside one of these 'humorous juggernauts', to 'enter their cribbed cabin and talk with the little men, wearing their padded leather helmets, who inhabited them'. Since the tanks were whales as well as 'jaundiced batrachians', it followed that their crews were 'Jonahs', cramped up inside their monster and 'seeking the obscurity of the latest camouflage'.

The metaphorical exuberance of the special correspondents

131

owed at least as much to the demands of official secrecy as to the inherently monstrous qualities of the tank. The five correspondents lived and worked with their censors, and while the most whimsical flights of fancy would get through, neither the tanks nor their crews could be reported in their actual detail. The fantastic imagery was built up around a silent core of things that could not be said, and their impact on the reader at home was increased by the absence of realistic images. No photographs or accurate drawings of the 'wonder weapon' were published until 22 November—two months after the first written reports—when the *Daily Mirror*, having paid one thousand pounds for the privilege, was able to print a front-page photograph of a camouflaged tank apparently going into action. Until then, magazines such as *Punch* and the *Illustrated London News* had subsisted on drawings inspired by the war correspondents' prose, with equally unlikely results.

Soon the tank was launched into a spectacular advance on the home front—rolling its way across the cinema screen, through art galleries (where the modernism of this 'Cubist slug' would be observed) and into boys adventure stories with titles such as 'Tommy of the Tanks'. By Christmas 1916, it had become the star of popular songs, music-hall jokes and pantomimes. In early November, still two weeks before the first photograph was published, the new 'Vanity Fair' revue at the Gaiety Theatre in London included a sequence in which the sixteen chorus girls wound their way on to the stage disguised as 'His Majesty's Landship "Tanko"', a caterpillar-like thing, which bristled with guns and was 'commanded' by the twenty-two-year-old French singer Mademoiselle Régine Flory, who sang:

> *I will teach the Kaiser & Co, we know how to win*
> *When they see us dance the Tanko right into Berlin . . .*

It was this sort of stuff that offended Siegfried Sassoon, who in February 1917, wrote in his poem 'Blighters':

> *I'd like to see a Tank come down the stalls,*
> *Lurching to rag-time tunes, or 'Home, Sweet Home'*
> *And there'd be no more jokes in Music-halls*
> *To mock the riddled corpses round Bapaume.*

There certainly were corpses to be mocked. While London audiences were invited to laugh at the thought of the 'dear old tank', the men of the Heavy Section were discovering the reality of their machines. Crouching inside the 'behemoth', they endured awful extremes of noise, fumes and heat. Enemy machine-gun fire sent molten splinters of 'bullet-splash' flying about inside; in the earliest models there was also the distinct danger that flaming petrol would pour in from the storage tanks on top of the machine and incinerate the men. Communication with other tanks or with any other part of the world outside was difficult at the best of times and almost impossible under fire; messages were sent by carrier pigeons, or by waving coloured discs in the air. So how were the tanks to be guided to their destination? Sometimes white tapes would be laid on the ground for the tanks to follow the next morning, but often the tank's commander would have to jump from his tank in the heat of battle and give hand signals—to the right, to the left—that would be obeyed by the driver.

The tank men grew despondent and bitter over the mockery of the infantry and the unrealizable expectations that the burgeoning cult of the tank had created. They were inclined to blame the press. As a tank captain, D. G. Browne MC, later complained: 'An immense amount of nonsense was talked and written about the first appearance of the tanks in the field. The newspapers, as was to be expected, excelled themselves in absurdity. Any lie was good enough for them.'

Browne dismissed the correspondents as purveyors of 'ignorant flapdoodle' which humiliated tank crews. Few troops had seen the new machines in successful action, but 'tens of thousands had seen tanks lying derelict in the Somme mud or holding up traffic through mechanical breakdowns on important thoroughfares.' Exaggerated claims made in ill-informed newspaper reports may have inspired readers in Britain, but on the front they only brought down ridicule upon 'men who had done wonders in circumstances inconceivable to the writers . . . People at home, who believe anything they read in print and have the press they deserve, naturally expected miracles of machines which pushed down houses on battlefields, where, in fact, no house had been standing for months.' Clough Williams-Ellis made a similar point about the press commentary: 'This lavish praise had spread a gloom over the Tank Corps: they had been unmercifully twitted by unfeeling gunners and infantrymen who knew the real facts. The newspapers had succeeded in making their intercourse with any but battalions fresh from England an unbearable round of facile jest.'

But in Britain, the idea of the tank as wonder weapon was not to be halted. In November 1917, a few days before three hundred tanks went into battle successfully over firm chalk ground at Cambrai, the tank was sent into a new kind of action at home. The public's growing desire to see the new machines for itself had been noticed by the National War Savings Committee, which arranged for a tank to be displayed in Trafalgar Square. In the words of the Committee's publicity director, tanks 'had captured the imagination of the man in the street like no other device of modern warfare'. Members of the public could, of course, see the outside of the tank for free, but anyone who wanted to see the interior had to buy War Bonds. The tank, attended by military bands, comedians and chorus girls, sat in Trafalgar Square for two weeks, and its appeal so far outstripped expectations that rather than be sent to its originally intended destination, the Western Front, it was dispatched to Sheffield for more fund-raising. Two other damaged tanks were brought back from France and sent on similar service to Liverpool and Cardiff; a third, a blasted veteran of the battle of Cambrai, was introduced later in Portsmouth. By the end of the war a series of provincial 'tank bank' campaigns had visited 168 British towns and, according to some claims, raised more than three hundred million pounds.

The National War Savings Committee was told in an internal report that it was impossible 'verbally to reproduce the extraordinary atmosphere of enthusiasm' created by the travelling tanks. They were usually accompanied by a band of itinerant hawkers, some of whom were said to have amassed 'quite appreciable fortunes' from the sale of tank souvenirs. Sham fights would be staged when a tank arrived. The town would be 'thrown into a state of defence' with sandbag entrenchments from which members of the local Volunteer Regiment would 'fire' at the approaching tank. Once the tank had 'won' its way into the town,

The tank bank, 1917

it was barricaded into an enclosure that would usually also include a travelling office and a bandstand. The mayor and other civic dignitaries would preside over the official opening ceremony, which was 'invariably attended by a huge crowd'. Enthusiasm rose through the week, inflamed by rousing speeches delivered from the top of the tank and also by the local journalists, who were happy to come up with their own variations on the monster vocabulary used by the special correspondents in France. 'Saturday at the Tank usually resembled the scene at a pre-war cup final.'

Many large corporate investments came in through the tank banks, but the campaign also proved spectacularly successful with ordinary wage earners who were its main target. After the first week of the Trafalgar Square tank bank, *The Times* declared that an 'altogether new public' had been reached: 'the large majority of those who have come from a distance have been unacquainted

135

with the value of the investment and have known nothing about filling up the forms.' *The Times*, which supported this campaign, singled out a soldier who attended the Trafalgar Square tank with two little children and a bag of halfpennies and old farthings with which he bought them a certificate each. The tank that visited Southwark, in working-class south London, was reported to have made its first sale—two five-pound bonds—to 'a rat-catcher named Dalton'. Another patriotic investor is said to have turned up soon after in odd boots and an old cap: 'To the inspector of police on duty he said, "Do you think I haven't got any 'dough'?" He at once produced sixty pounds in gold and bought war bonds to that amount.' Succeeding where previous government appeals had failed, the travelling tanks flushed out so much working-class money and valuables that the National War Savings Committee described them as 'vacuum cleaners' for gathering gold.

And so, by the end of the war, the tank had become many things other than a problematic weapon: it was a behemoth, a bank, a song, a theatrical act, a symbol of uncompromising patriotism, an advertisement, a vacuum cleaner and (not least) a soapbox. People—civilians as well as military men—liked to stand on tanks to make speeches. As it travelled the country for the National War Savings Committee, the tank became a platform from which bishops, politicians, music-hall artistes and popular novelists would denounce not just the Kaiser and his Huns, but those Britons who were losing their appetite for the war. One of the first to be targeted from the top of a tank was Lord Lansdowne, a former foreign secretary, who had written to the *Daily Telegraph* in November 1917 arguing against 'wanton prolongation' of the war and suggesting that a compromise peace should be negotiated with Germany. As the popular entertainer George Robey promised from a tank in St Pancras, London: 'We will put those who talk about peace in the front line to dig trenches for old gentlemen like me to shoot from.' Havelock Wilson, president of the National Union of Sailors and Firemen came to the Trafalgar Square tank with some amputee sailors and roared that 'Lord Lansdowne must not for a moment believe that British seamen would ever forget German crimes on the high seas.' Martin Harvey, a well-known singer, mounted the same tank a couple of days later to say: 'There is a certain class among us who want a German peace just as before the war they wanted German articles because they were cheap and nasty. We want a well-made peace, hallowed and cemented by the blood of our heroes.'

Such was the success of the tanks on the domestic front that the Chancellor of the Exchequer, Andrew Bonar Law, felt he could say to a dinner of the National War Savings Committee that 'appearance is reality'; that the tank had confirmed something he had always suspected, namely that credit depended 'not merely on what things are, but on what people think they are'.

After the war ended, 265 tanks were brought back from France by the War Savings Committee and presented to towns that had made the largest contributions to the war-bonds campaign. Carefully disarmed and demobilized to prevent any future use by insurrectionists, they were mounted as war memorials in squares and municipal parks, where public figures would inaugurate them with speeches about the message that the tank held for those post-war times.

In the military, however, there was much less certainty about the future of the tank as a weapon. The old cavalrymen in the command structure hoped that the tank could now be forgotten, or at least remembered only as a military freak made necessary by the exceptional and unrepeatable circumstance of trench warfare. The future of the Tank Corps looked insecure for a time, until it was guaranteed by the notorious 'moral effect' of the tank's appearance on civilian crowds. Tanks were used to intimidate militant crowds in Glasgow, to terrorize opposition in Ireland during the last years before independence and by the British Army on the Rhine. They survived difficult years—until the Second World War, when the rusting hulks in Britain's parks and squares were carted away and melted down to make the next round of weapons: tanks in which myth and military power were altogether more effectively combined.

Today there are very few men left alive who fought inside a tank during the First World War. One of them is W. L. M. 'Mac' Francis, who manned a Lewis gun when the Fifth Battalion of the

Tank Corps went into action at the Third Battle of Ypres in July 1917. In the winter of 1995, when I went to see him in his bungalow in Oswestry, Shropshire, he was nearing his ninety-ninth birthday. He could remember his experience clearly, though he found it difficult to believe that it had happened to him. As he sat beside his gas fire, he would stop in the middle of a story which had been dredged from the mud and fear of nearly eighty years before, and ask himself: 'Can that be true?'

It was not what newspaper correspondents had described. On the night of 30 July 1917, Mr Francis's battalion had been shown a battle plan mapped out in sand on the ground. He could remember the names of farms and villages, such as St Julien, and the German pillboxes that were identified as the target. It had, he said, 'sounded so easy', but this impression had disintegrated by the time he and his driver had manoeuvred their tank, named 'Enchantress', to the point where the attack was to start next morning. Mr Francis had been in France for some months by then and had seen a lot that horrified him: lice, prostitutes and unremitting foul language (he was a grocer's son from a small country town and twenty years old), and the terrible slaughter of a company of exhausted troops, who were encamped behind the lines at Oosthoek Wood, where a German plane saw their lights and bombed them. Nothing, however, had prepared him for the shock of driving in a tank at two miles an hour across no man's land in Flanders. There had been torrential rain, and constant artillery bombardment had churned earth into mud and broken the water courses. The dead were everywhere: pulverized corpses of mules and horses, soldiers fragmented or half-buried with putrefying limbs sticking out of the mess. Mr Francis and his tank ploughed on through 'bodies, horses, machine-guns, barbed wire, duckboards . . . everything mucked up, like a big farm churn had come and churned it up'. They found their target villages already in 'total ruin', and then their tank got stuck in a deep shell crater. Mr Francis climbed out and was immediately splattered from head to foot in putrid slime by an exploding shell.

The enemy bombardment did not let up all that day, and it was not until five in the evening that Mr Francis and the five other members of his tank crew decided to abandon their sinking

'Enchantress' and struggle back on foot to the British lines.
Later that year he was wounded in the head. At the battle of
Cambrai in November he won the Military Medal for shooting
down a plane with his Lewis gun—reputedly, the first time a tank
gunner had accomplished such a feat. The infantry had stopped
laughing at tanks by then, though not because they were
impressed by their usefulness. 'They cursed them,' Mr Francis
said. Tanks broke down, blocked roads, cut signal wires and
made perfect targets for German artillery. Infantrymen quickly
learned the disadvantages of going anywhere near them.

Recently, the descendant of a victim of the battle of Cambrai
had asked Mr Francis if he knew how his ancestor had died. Mr
Francis would not tell him, and he told me only reluctantly, his
Edwardian sense of discretion offended: there were some things
that should not be spoken of. The truth was that the man had
been, in Mr Francis's phrase, 'roasted alive' after his tank was hit
by a shell. 'There's nothing worse than a tank going on fire, I tell
you. Hopeless, hopeless.'

TV IS GOOD FOR YOU

Gerry Adams   TODAY/REX

DAN JACOBSON

Television is constantly accused of encouraging apathy, sloth, passivity, illiteracy, mindlessness and docility among those who are addicted to watching it. But no one seems to have noticed the effects of television on those who have been denied access to it, in all its global variety and vulgarity. Debarred from participating as viewers and actors in the global electronic carnival, they can be roused first to disappointment and anger and then to action. Once they have won their battle, it is true that they are likely to become just like the rest of us. In fact one of the symptoms of their condition is their extreme longing to become like the rest of us.

The inhabitants of the former Soviet bloc used to manifest this condition in its simplest and severest form. So did the South Africans during the apartheid years. Every now and again, as if through a wall grown momentarily transparent, they would find themselves gazing at crowds of wealthy, licentious, fashionably dressed people—movie stars and pop singers, international models, top sportsmen, the super-rich, the super-smart, the super-brazen, even a handful of politicians who had somehow managed to make their trade glamorous—doing the wicked, attention-getting things that they alone were permitted to do and being paid large sums in consequence. Around them were phalanxes of lesser celebrities and hangers-on, without whom the show would have looked frail and denuded. Around them, in turn, were the indispensable, uncounted millions who were free to watch it or not, as their inclination took them.

And there, effectively locked out of it all, were the wretched inhabitants of Russia or South Africa, just as deserving of a good time as anyone else, but carefully excluded from it by their governments. Their reward was to be told repeatedly that it was much better for them to be kept outside; that to sit there patiently was proof of their moral and cultural superiority.

But how could they believe this story when a choice in the matter had never been given to them? Why should they be grateful to their political masters for officiously pre-empting their judgement of what might suit them best? It is no fun to feel yourself condemned forever to the status of the untrustworthy child, the outsider, the perpetual provincial or colonial. It is more painful still when this has happened to you not because of some implacable historical or geographical fact, or because of a limitation in the technology which you know to be available, but simply by virtue of a jealous government's decree.

The intensity of the resentment felt by the populations involved first came home to me on my visits to the 'old' South Africa. The whites there were, if anything, even more angrily conscious of what they were missing than the blacks. After all, it was their own government, the one they had elected, that had imposed from within its forms of censorship on what they were allowed to see, and that had brought down on the country a stifling array of external bans and boycotts. As for the blacks, they may well have supported the boycotts politically—with their heads, as it were—but in their hearts they too yearned for all they were missing. These mixed emotions showed especially, I thought, in the kind of wistful cockiness with which they spoke of such figures as Margaret Thatcher, or Sylvester Stallone, or the Princess of Wales. They were eager to show that they knew exactly who these people were and why they were important. Yet their expressions and tones of voice as they spoke revealed also how distant they felt themselves to be from the universe inhabited by such glistening creatures.

It was of scant comfort to them, in those days, to know that they were not nearly as badly off as viewers in the Soviet Union. The first time I looked at Soviet television was during the Brezhnev era. The programme switched on for my benefit opened with an interminable sequence of combine harvesters harvesting, while a voice-over gabbled lies about production figures. My host turned off the set. Later, when we tried it again, a troupe of folk dancers was to be seen folk dancing.

We switched to another channel. This one carried a more welcome offering: a football game. Placarded around the West German stadium in which the match was being played were advertisements for the kinds of consumer goods which Soviet citizens had no hope of obtaining—unless, as many of them tried to do, they begged or bought them from western visitors. So even while the brave Soviet footballers were scoring goals on their behalf, the viewers back home were being reminded yet again of all they were missing.

A year later I sat in a bar in Prague along with several sombre natives of the city. We were watching an unsavoury, run-of-the-mill Hollywood thriller. Possibly it had been allowed on the screen with the notion (or under the pretence) of showing up western decadence. What was most striking about the occasion, however, was the intense concentration of the audience. They followed the movie like people preparing for an examination. No one in the West would have taken it so seriously. But the clues these spectators were searching for in it had nothing whatever to do with the solution to its plot.

It came as no surprise, after several such experiences on other visits, to learn that workers in the German Democratic Republic were refusing to accept jobs in regions beyond the range of West German television transmissions. That was how widespread the ravages of 'television hunger' had become in the years preceding the collapse of the Soviet empire. Obviously I am not suggesting that the collapse took place because of it, but I have no doubt that it helped the process along. The best evidence of this could be seen on the faces of former servants of the regime who had contrived to shed the guilt of past misdeeds and who were now being welcomed on to the talk shows from which they had been excluded previously.

They were like children out on a treat. No longer compelled to defend the indefensible, to wear permanently the mask of the official liar, to fear their friends at home more than their countries' supposed enemies, they had suddenly begun to smile, to argue, to shrug, to say hitherto forbidden things, to acknowledge past errors. The same was true of the spokesmen of the apartheid government in South Africa. The pleasure they took in being treated like real people, not as freaks and outcasts, was manifest. At last they had been readmitted, in their own eyes, to the human race.

A different strain of television hunger has played its part in the abatement of protracted and exhausting conflicts such as those between Arabs and Israelis in the Middle East, and Protestants and Catholics in Northern Ireland. People trapped in such situations have to pay an extra, adventitious penalty for the violence and uncertainty they are compelled to endure, year after year. On the one hand, they are able to watch on their television sets the non-stop fun and games that appear to be taking place in more fortunate areas of the world. On the other hand, the only part they themselves can play in the feast is that of the grisly counter-example, the horrible warning to others.

Some groups and individuals obviously take a perverse pride in having this status conferred on them; in their eyes it marks them out as serious, dangerous people. But many others eventually begin to feel it as a humiliation. In comparison with everything else they have to suffer, this particular source of unease may seem little more than trivial. Yet trivialities also wear people down and make them long more intensely for a different dispensation—especially when the television constantly presents them with images of what that different dispensation looks like.

A good example is President Sadat's visit to Jerusalem almost twenty years ago: a visit that began the movement towards peace between Israel and its Arab neighbours which is still proceeding, despite the wars and acts of terror that have punctuated it. Sadat went to Jerusalem for many reasons. He had restored Egyptian military self-esteem in the half-victory of the Yom Kippur War of 1973. He knew Egypt's economy to be in desperate need of relief. Long before anyone else, he had the insight and courage to conclude that his great Soviet ally and supplier was a broken reed.

All that said, I am convinced that he also went to Jerusalem because he wanted to be a star. He wanted to be invited to the White House, to appear on its lawn in front of the whole world, to cut a figure in the global carnival, to be recognized and saluted everywhere. Just as he was smart enough to see through the Soviet Union's superpower pretensions, so too did he have the capacity to understand that he could never realize these aims as long as he was trapped in the wretched, hole-in-corner existence to which the Israel–Arab struggle had condemned him.

Well, he achieved international stardom and got his peace; and in the end paid dearly for both. Since then others, each in his own fashion, but all driven by a similar combination of weariness and ambition, have followed in his path. For Anwar Sadat one might read F. W. de Klerk of South Africa, or Yasser Arafat of the Palestine Liberation Organization, or Yitzhak Rabin of

Israel. (The last of these differed from the others in joining the circus with a patent degree of reluctance; but that did not save him from paying with his life for doing so, as Sadat had before him.) Gerry Adams of Sinn Fein and David Trimble of the Ulster Unionists have also found themselves nudged and pulled in the same direction. They too want to be among those people—on the *Larry King Show* and on first-name terms with David Frost, embracing and embraced by all and sundry, endowed with the prestige and glamour that only television can bestow.

Of course these leaders had loftier ends in mind: the ones they avowed in their speeches and in the documents they signed. But the prospect of being taken into the embrace of television and put on universal display—not as a villain or a suffering creature but as a star—can for them become an important political end. The ambition they nourish is not just their own. The people they represent have gone through a parallel experience of exclusion, of being regarded by the world at large as one of its special, no-hope cases. They too have suffered too long from the hunger their leaders are trying to satisfy on their behalf.

If the white South Africans have surprised everyone, themselves included, by the readiness with which they accepted the actuality of a black president ruling over them, it is partly because they know Nelson Mandela to have been an international superstar for decades. What is more, since his accession to office he has shown that he has the magnetism to attract to the country innumerable other stars, from the Queen of England to Whoopi Goldberg, who would never have set foot in it previously. Rabin's funeral on television, with its array of mourning dignitaries from all over the world, was in itself a crushing defeat for those who had opposed the treaty he had made with Arafat.

All kinds of obstacles may block the road to a permanent peace in Northern Ireland. Gerry Adams, on the other hand, will not find it easy to give up his entrée to the White House; nor will his people find it easy to forgive him if he makes it impossible for Bill and Hillary Clinton ever to return to Belfast, and to smile and wave at them, right there, where they live.

THE TRIAL

Sun, 23 November 1995

GORDON BURN

PHOTOGRAPHS BY TOM PILSTON

There are constants in the media landscape, the images that, even half-seen, alert us to another excitingly dire occurrence. Police divers emerging from a local lake or culvert.

The ragged wave of police, friends, neighbours and tourist volunteers lapping slowly across woodland or wasteland, scouring the thickets popular with local courting couples, poking into long grass with sticks.

The distraught father or mother at the centre of the formal disposition of the police press conference, and the home video or snapshot of the missing person enlarged from a copy negative and pushed until it lacks precision and definition.

The feeding-time noises of electric shutters as they are directed at arm's length into the inky glass of the accelerating prison van, in the remote chance that something behind the glass—something syndicable—might stick to the film.

Women with children placing flowers and teddy bears and fluffy bunnies on the impromptu pavement shrine marking the site of the latest atrocity.

'News, darker and darker news, may be the only narrative people need, and the shapers of this narrative are authors in their own right,' Don DeLillo has written. 'To a certain extent their world has become our world, a place of extreme anger and danger.'

Community is partly built on members sharing stories, and the stories we tell ourselves increasingly seem to have death as their theme. There are now so many of these stories that only the most sensational or brutal or those which contain unusual elements stand any chance at all of making it on to the news agenda.

The murder of a sixteen-year-old by her parents was a story that would have made any news editor reach for the phone. Heather West had last been seen in June 1987. Her remains were discovered on 26 February 1994 in the garden of a house at 25 Cromwell Street in the cathedral city of Gloucester where she had lived with her seven brothers and sisters, her mother, Rosemary, and her father, Frederick. Two days later the remains of two other young women, Shirley Robinson and Alison Chambers, were excavated from below the patio area. Four days after that the police search moved into the interior of the house where, during the course of forty-eight hours, the remains of five more women, Therese Sieganthaler, Shirley Hubbard, Lucy Partington, Juanita Mott and Carol Ann Cooper, were discovered buried in a roughly circular pattern in the cellar. The remains of a ninth woman, Lynda Gough, were discovered under a bathroom floor.

Familiarity with the Wests ('dumpy mum Rose', 'Gloucester builder Fred') seemed to increase as the body count rose. Most of the women had disappeared in the 1970s. They had been dead for more than twenty years. The time lag accelerated the process of objectifying them as 'victims', of divesting them of their identity. 'Fred and Rose', meanwhile, were soon bloated into myth. There were Fred-and-Rose jokes, as there had been Haigh ('the acid-bath murderer') and Reginald Christie ('Reggie-No-Dick') jokes forty years earlier: the comedian Jimmy Tarbuck told them in magazine profiles; Billy Connolly told them in a video which was eventually taken off the market. Schoolchildren photocopied and circulated a spoof flier decorated with skulls and spades: 'Fred West Home Improvements. Don't have grave doubts. Most of Fred's family have been in patios, bathrooms, fireplaces etc for years.'

West hanged himself in his cell in Winson Green Prison in Birmingham on New Year's Day 1995. By then the bodies of his first wife, Rena Costello, and her friend Anne McFall had been recovered from fields near the village of Much Marcle on the Herefordshire–Gloucestershire border. The remains of Charmaine, Rena Costello's daughter, who had last been seen in 1971, aged eight, had been found under the bathroom of a house at 25 Midland Road in Gloucester where Frederick and Rosemary West lived when they were first married.

In February 1995, a year after she was arrested, Rosemary West faced committal proceedings alone in a small country court in Dursley, a few miles south of Gloucester. A committal is a preliminary hearing of the evidence by a magistrate, who then decides whether the case should be heard in front of a judge in a higher court. Rosemary West was charged with the murder of her daughter Heather and of the eight other young women and girls whose remains were found in and around the house where she and her husband had lived for twenty-three years; she was also accused of murdering her stepdaughter Charmaine.

Twelve seats in the courtroom's public gallery were allocated to the media. The overspill, about a hundred and fifty journalists, listened via an audio link in another part of the building. No witnesses were called; their statements were read aloud in a deep, above-stairs accent by the pink, Micawberish junior prosecution counsel, Mr Chubb, who frequently attempted the underclass vernacular. Several newspapers by then had bought up witnesses, so some of the journalists at Dursley might have been expected to be prepared for what was coming, but nobody remained unshocked by the accounts of child rape, sadomasochism, sexual abuse and torture that Mr Chubb gave in his brown, classic-radio-serial voice. Frederick West had been twenty-seven when he met Rosemary Letts, as she then was, in 1968. She was fifteen and had been physically abused by her father in childhood: she was sexually obsessed with both men and women. He was a psychopath with sadistic-paedophiliac tendencies, and an obsessive voyeur. They worked in tandem, cruising the streets for female hitch-hikers, runaways and girls from broken homes. They trussed them and gagged them with masking tape and kept them hanging from beams in the basement until the pair's lust had burnt itself out. Then the victims' bodies were decapitated and dismembered and dumped in pits in the ground. The West children were forced to have sex with their parents and their mother's 'visitors' from the age of eight. Their father videoed what went on in Rosemary West's 'special room' through a hole in the door.

Mr Chubb read this catalogue of fantastical and barbaric obscenities at slightly faster than dictation speed; in the audio annexes our hands moved urgently in unison, ashamed and hot-eyed and driven, hungry to get it all down.

By law, nothing could be printed until the trial itself had begun and the evidence heard before a judge and jury. But every night the journalists working for daily papers transmitted an account of the day's proceedings back to the London office. And every night the reaction from the London office was the same: disbelief, revulsion, excitement and a fear that, even when the law permitted publication of the evidence from the higher court, it could not be published on grounds of taste.

Sensational murder cases are usually regarded by newspaper

editors as a way of putting on readers. Not as reliable a way, perhaps, as in the days when the death penalty still existed in Britain (the last meal, the last wish, the possibility of a last-minute reprieve; the pre-dawn vigil, the posting of the typed notice on the prison gate). Scotland Yard's murder squads would go out around the country, and a sort of travelling circus of crime reporters would go with them. On really big stories a paper such as the *Daily Express* would send four cars—three of them to block the road while the lead car got away with the quarry. Crime reporters saw themselves as a kind of journalistic elite. Their lifestyle was lavish, their expenses legendary. The death penalty was abolished in Britain in 1965, and the years since then have seen a gradual shift in serious resources from reporting crime to reporting the royals.

R osemary West's trial opened in the first week of October at the Crown Court in Winchester and lasted until late November. Many of the photographers who staked out the area around the court in the early days of the trial had been pulled off the Diana beat. Their presence was in many ways symbolic: with the picture opportunity limited every day to five or six seconds of a speeding police vehicle, they had nothing to shoot but each other. At Dursley on one occasion they had handed out eggs and encouraged local schoolchildren to throw them at West's transporter. But Winchester is a prosperous, reserved, conservative town with historic links to Keats and Jane Austen. Lacking a spectacle and unable to invent one, the media had to become its own. The television footage of Rosemary West's high-speed, precision-timed comings and goings became a ritual. There was nothing much to see and it was always much the same, but the heavy media presence was in itself justification for having the story high in the running order.

Independent Television News chartered a helicopter on the first day, and there was something immediately familiar about the sequence that ran in ITN's bulletins that evening: the white vehicle with the police outriders; the path cleared through the commuter traffic; the implacable helicopter dipping and tracking. It was the visual vocabulary of O.J. and the Bronco, borrowed, presumably, partly in the hope of inheriting some of the same

Anne Marie Davis, Rosemary West's stepdaughter, arriving at court for the verdict

audience. The timing was impeccable: Simpson was acquitted on Rosemary West's first day in the dock.

The French artist Christian Boltanski once spent a year clipping images of criminals and their victims from *Détective*, a weekly tabloid that focuses on grisly tragedies. What attracted him to these images was the fact that, once a photograph was separated from its caption, it was impossible to distinguish victim from criminal. 'He has the face of a Nobel Peace Prize winner,' Boltanski has said of the Nazi war criminal, Klaus Barbie. 'It would be easier if a terrible person had a terrible face.'

Searching for the terribleness of her 'inner being', reporters and court artists scrutinized Mrs West compulsively, hoping to catch the intimate and unintended. She showed signs of agitation sometimes: her tongue would flick out, a finger would wipe behind her enormous glasses. She appeared to cry in earnest, although reflexively, whenever her daughter Heather's name was mentioned.

153

Her clothes attracted constant attention. 'I've done a piece to camera for the six [o'clock news] but I'm going to redo it for the nine,' a television reporter told me one day. 'The green thing, I've seen it up close and it's not a waistcoat, it's a tailored dress.'

With her notepad and balled tissues and beakers of water, Rosemary West came to occupy the dock like a long-distance railway traveller laying claim to a whole compartment. Then, called to the witness stand for her evidence, she proved lumpen, intractable, as uncommunicative as the walls and bricked-up windows of the house at 25 Cromwell Street. (She did reveal herself as a tabloid reader. Asked for her reaction to various atrocities, she several times replied: 'Shock-horror.')

It seemed appropriate at the end of the trial that, rather than using a picture of 'the most depraved woman on Earth' as an identifying logo for their 'Fred and Rose' features, television and the newspapers went unanimously for a picture of the wrought-iron nameplate—all Fred's own work—that hung outside 25 Cromwell Street until the police removed it to keep it out of the hands of souvenir hunters. (More than thirteen hundred household items were destroyed 'under controlled conditions' for the same reason.)

As an example of suburban kitsch, the plaque was a suitable symbol for the ersatz gentility that Rosemary West displayed in court every day: the bows of exaggerated deference towards the judge; the protestations about being 'too proud a woman' to wear another woman's clothes when it was put to her under cross-examination that she had dressed in the garments taken from the victims; the wearing of a poppy in the week before Armistice Day.

In the third week of the trial the court travelled in convoy from Winchester to Gloucester to make a site visit to Cromwell Street. I made the trip in the same car as a woman reporter on one of the broadsheet papers who apologized for her appearance and said she had been unable to sleep because of nightmares. She had seen what in the darkness looked like the ghost of a woman, standing with arms outstretched at the foot of the bed. She had sat up until dawn drinking tea.

But when the Royal College of Nursing offered a free counselling service for journalists attending the West trial in Winchester, nobody applied.

R osemary West's first day of evidence made all the front pages. The playing of the police's tape-recorded interviews with Frederick West—'a confession from beyond the grave'—was another page-one splash. Journalists covering the trial were gratified by the amount of coverage the story was getting. Long 'backgrounders' on the Wests were being written in expectation of a guilty verdict; some tabloids were planning pull-out supplements. But then word started to spread about an interview that the Princess of Wales had given to a reporter from the BBC: it was rumoured to be explosive; pages of space were being cleared.

At 11.44 a.m. on Monday 20 November, ten hours before the interview was due to be broadcast, the judge sent the West jury out. If they arrived at a verdict quickly, news of it would be swamped by the Diana coverage in the papers the following day. When they hadn't agreed by 4.30 p.m., the judge sent them to a hotel, and the journalists tried to disguise their relief. The Diana story was still dominating the headlines forty-eight hours later when Rosemary West was found guilty on all ten counts of murder and jailed for the rest of her life.

The parallels between a major trial and a theatrical production are frequently drawn. They apply to the supporting cast no less than to the featured players; at the end of eight weeks, the reporters who had covered the case felt as though they were a repertory company breaking up and going their separate ways.

Fittingly, the first reunion dinner took place less than a fortnight later at the Garrick Club in London, which was founded in 1831 as a place in which 'actors and men of education and refinement might meet on equal terms'. The club motto is 'All the world's a stage.'

The cover of the special menu announced the occasion as the 'Westologist's Dinner'. It comprised Garrick Smokies, mignons of veal with Parma ham and nut butter, chocolate soufflé with white chocolate sauce. Coffee was followed by Churchill's Vintage Character Port. A printed slip—'It is expected that no mention of Mr or Mrs West will be made after the first ten minutes'—was briefly acknowledged and then, in the draughty, unclubby silences, quickly ignored.

TO SEE JUSTICE DONE
Scenes from the West trial. Previous pages: a TV reporter prepares to deliver his piece to camera. Above: a protester. Opposite: a cameraman and crowds outside the court. Overleaf: members of the public sit in the early morning queue for the public gallery

Above: cameramen take up positions. Opposite: top, the judge arrives on the day of the verdict; bottom, an artist's sketch of Mrs West in the dock—photography is not permitted inside British courts

BEST OF YOUNG AMERICAN NOVELISTS
the regional winners

mid-atlantic

Madison Smartt Bell
David Bowman
Edwidge Danticat
Michael Drinkard
Jeffrey Eugenides
Jonathan Franzen
Indira Ganesan
Randall Kenan
Binnie Kirshenbaum
Allen Kurzweil
Jim Lewis
Fae Myenne Ng
Robert O'Connor
Agnes Rossi
Paul Russell
Joanna Scott
Katharine Weber
Jacqueline Woodson

[JUDGES: FREDERICK BUSCH,
MAUREEN HOWARD, STEPHEN WRIGHT]

west

Sherman Alexie
Rick Bass
Ethan Canin
Cristina Garcia
David Guterson
Chang-rae Lee
Renée Manfredi
Antonya Nelson
Ann Packer
Charlotte Watson Sherman
Mona Simpson
Steve Yarbrough

[JUDGES: LEONARD MICHAELS,
MARILYNNE ROBINSON, JAMES WELCH]

midwest

Brian Kiteley
David Haynes
Lorrie Moore
Chris Offutt
Daniel Lyons
J. S. Marcus

[JUDGES: CHARLES BAXTER,
STUART DYBEK, THOM JONES]

new england

Gish Jen
Tom Drury
Elizabeth McCracken
Stewart O'Nan
Connie Porter
Patricia Powell
Melanie Sumner
Melanie Rae Thon
Kate Wheeler

[JUDGES: ROSELLEN BROWN,
HOWARD FRANK MOSHER, JAYNE ANNE PHILLIPS]

south

John Gregory Brown
Tony Earley
Louis Edwards
Kaye Gibbons
Jill McCorkle
Michael Parker
Ann Patchett

[JUDGES: RICHARD BAUSCH,
BEVERLY LOWRY, PADGETT POWELL]

Who are the best young novelists in the USA?

Discover their names and read their new work in the next issue of  **GRANTA**

Who are the finest new writers in the United States? Who is demonstrating outstanding talent and promise? Which young novelists are best at telling the stories that illuminate, examine and enrich our lives? *Granta* decided to find out.

We asked for nominations from large publishers, small publishers, university presses, librarians and booksellers. Then we sent their submissions – several hundred novels and short-story collections by published authors under the age of forty – to fifteen of America's most distinguished writers for their opinion. The fifteen were enrolled as judges in five regional panels, spent five months reading the books and eventually decided on a shortlist of fifty-two regional winners (opposite), from which the twenty finalists will be chosen by *Granta*'s national judges: Henry Louis Gates, Jr, Robert Stone, Anne Tyler, Tobias Wolff and *Granta*'s editor, Ian Jack.

Read the final, finest twenty in the next (and rather special) issue of *Granta*, published in June and devoted to the best new American fiction.

the national judges

Anne Tyler

Tobias Wolff

Henry Louis Gates

Robert Stone

Let These Go To Your Head

AN INTOXICATING BREW OF WRITERS AND IDEAS.
IT'S ENOUGH TO DRIVE YOU TO THINK.

WRITING AND BEING
NADINE GORDIMER

In this resonant book Nadine Gordimer tries to unravel the mysterious process that breathes "real" life into fiction by exploring the writings of revolutionaries in South Africa and the works of Naguib Mahfouz, Chinua Achebe, and Amos Oz.
Charles Eliot Norton Lectures

THE DUSTBIN OF HISTORY
GREIL MARCUS

Cultural critic Greil Marcus—author of *Mystery Train* and *Lipstick Traces*—reveals the history embedded in cultural happenstance.

"The virtues Greil Marcus demands of those he writes about he embodies himself: truth, authenticity, and passion." —ARTHUR DANTO
Not for sale in the Commonwealth except for Canada

THE ROOSTER'S EGG
PATRICIA J. WILLIAMS

"Written in a personal and anecdotal style from the author's perspective as a professor, a single black mother and (much less important) a lawyer...Many [of Williams' essays] are inspired by a popular event or personality, which becomes the springboard for her hyper-intelligent musings."
—Saul B. Shapiro, NEW YORK TIMES BOOK REVIEW

WRITING WAS EVERYTHING
ALFRED KAZIN

New York Times Notable Book of 1995
"An impressionistic, unashamedly subjective tour of the most important writers of this century. Kazin...writes engagingly and provocatively."
—Guy Lawson, TORONTO GLOBE AND MAIL
William E. Massey Sr. Lectures in the History of American Civilization

ENIGMA VARIATIONS
RICHARD PRICE AND SALLY PRICE

"A fabulous and unique artifact, an art-historical whodunit told with great flair, intelligence and sensitivity. Like the art it tells us so much about, [it] is a hybrid work that keeps tempting you to read it as fact although it is officially labeled fiction."
—Raymond Sokolov, WALL STREET JOURNAL

At bookstores now

Harvard University Press
US: 800-448-2242
UK: 0171-306-0603
http://www.hup.harvard.edu

TAKEN OUT OF CONTEXT

Evening Standard, 30 April 1992

PAUL BEATTY

ABBAS/MAGNUM

Unlike the typical bluesy, earthy, folksy, denim-overalls, noble-in-the-face-of-cracker-racism, aw-shucks Pulitzer Prize-winning protagonist mojo magic black man, I am not the seventh son of a seventh son of a seventh son. I wish I was, but fate shorted me by six brothers and three uncles.

My name is Kaufman, Gunnar Kaufman. Preordained by a set of weak-kneed DNA to shuffle in the footsteps of a long, cowardly queue of coons, Uncle Toms and faithful boogedy-boogedy retainers. I am the number-one son of a spineless colorstruck son of a bitch who was the third son of an ass-kissing, sell-out house Negro. From my birth until their divorce, my parents indoctrinated me with the idea that the surreal escapades and 'I'z a-comin'' watermelon chicanery of my forefathers was stuff for hero-worship.

What's a few nigger jokes among friends? We Kaufmans have always been the type of niggers who can take a joke. I used to visit my father, the sketch artist at the Wilshire Los Angeles Police Department precinct. His fellow officers would stand around cluttered desks breaking themselves up by telling 'how-many-niggers-does-it-take' jokes, pounding each other on the back and looking over their broad shoulders to see if me and Daddy was laughing. Dad always was. The epaulettes on his shoulders raising up like inch worms as he giggled. I never laughed until my father slapped me hard between the shoulder blades. The heavy-handed blow bringing my weight to my tiptoes, raising my chin from my chest, and I'd burp out a couple of titters of self-defilement. Even if I didn't get the joke. 'What they mean, "Lick their lips and stick 'em to the wall?"' Later I'd watch my father draw composite sketches for victimized citizens who used his face as a reference point. 'He was thick-lipped, nose a tad bit bigger than yours, with your nostril flare though.' Daddy would bring some felon to still life and without looking up from his measured strokes admonish me that my face better not appear on any police officer's sketchpad. He'd send me home in a patrol car, black charcoal smudged all over my face, and his patriotic wisdom ringing in my ears.

'Remember, Gunnar: God, country and laughter; the world's best medicine.'

I remember one day he came home drunk from the LAPD's unofficial legal defense fund-raiser for officers accused of brutality. (Dad later told me they showed *Birth of a Nation* followed by two straight hours of Watts Riot highlights.) He sat me on his lap and slurred war stories—Dad had joined the army three hours after graduating from high school in 1968 and served two tours in Vietnam. How his crazy Black-is-Beautiful platoon of citified troublemakers used to ditch him in the middle of patrols, leaving him alone in some rice paddy having to face the entire communist threat on his lonesome. Once he stumbled on his men behind the DMZ cooling with the enemy. The sight of the slant-eyed niggers and nigger niggers sharing K-rations and rice, enjoying a crackling fire and the quiet Southeast Asian night flipped Pops the fuck out. He berated his rebellious troops, shouting, 'Ain't this a bitch, the gorillas snacking with the guerrillas. Hello! Don't you baboons know that this is the goddamn enemy? The fucking yellow peril and you fucking Benedict Leroy Robinson Jefferson Arnolds are traitors to the democracy that weaned you apes from primitivism. You know you're probably eating dog.' The VC saw the disconcerted looks on the faces of the black American men, and a good colored boy from Detroit raised his rifle and put a M-16 slug inches from my pop's crotch. My father's men just sat there waiting for him to bleed to death. The Vietnamese had to beg them to take my dad back to base.

My father ended this confession with the non-sequitur wisdom that ended all our conversations: 'Son, don't ever mess with no white women.'

On our custody outings to the drag races in Pomona my father would tell me how he came back from the war and met my mother at a stock-car race. They fell immediately in love—the only two black folks in the world who knew the past five winners of the Daytona 500 and would recognize Big Daddy Don Garlits in the street. Then he'd put his arm around me and say, 'Don't you think black women are exotic?'

Mom raised my sisters and me as the hard-won spoils of a vicious custody battle that left the porcelain shrapnel of supper-dish grenades embedded in my father's neck. The divorce made Mama, Ms Brenda W. Kaufman, more determined to make sure that her children knew their forebears. As a Brooklyn orphan who never saw her parents or her birth certificate, Mom adopted my father's patriarchal family history for her misbegotten origins.

Kaufman lore plays out like a self-pollinating men's club. There are no comely Kaufman black superwomen. No poetic heroines caped in kinte cloth stretching welfare cheques from here to the moon. No nubile black women who could set a wayward Negro straight with the snap of the head and stinging 'niggah puh-leaze'. The women who allied themselves to the Kaufman legacy are invisible. Every once in a while a woman's name tangentially floated from my mother's lips as a footnote to some fool's parable only to dissipate with the vegetable steam. Aunt Joni's mean banana daiquiri. Meredith's game-winning touchdown run versus Colin Powell High. Giuseppe's second wife Amy's Perry Como record collection. Cousin Madge who was the complexion of pound cake dipped in milk. These historical cameos were always followed by my mother's teeth-sucking disclaimers 'but that's not important' or 'let's not go there.' I wondered where did my male predecessors find black women with names like Joni, Meredith and Amy? Who were these women? Were they weaker than their men or were they proverbial black family lynchpins? I spent hours thumbing through photo albums fearful that I was destined to marry a black Mormon Brigham Young University graduate named Mary Jo while I became the spokesperson for the Coors Brewing Company. They say the fruit never falls far from the tree, but I've tried to roll down the hill at least a little bit.

My earliest memories bodysurf the warm, comforting timelessness of the Santa Ana winds, whipping me in and around the palm-tree-lined streets of Santa Monica. Me and white boys sharing secrets and bubblegum. We were friends, but we didn't see ourselves as a unit. We had no enemies, no long-standing rivalries with the feared Hermosa Beach Sand Castle Hellions or the Exclusive Brentwood Spoiled Brat Millionaire Tycoon Killers. Our conflicts limited themselves to fighting with our sisters and running from the Santa Monica Shore Patrol. I was an ashy-legged black beach bum sporting a lopsided trapezoidal natural and living in a hilltop two-storey townhouse on Sixth and

Bay. After an exhausting morning of bodysurfing and watching seagulls hover over the ocean expertly catching french fries, I would spend the afternoon lounging on the rosewood balcony. Sitting in a lawn chair, my spindly legs crossed at the ankles, I'd leaf through the newest Time-Life mail-order installments to the family's coffee-table reference library: *Predators of the Insect World, Air War Over Europe, Gunfighters of the Old West*. The baseball game would crackle and spit from the cheap white transistor radio my father gave me for my seventh birthday.

I was the funny, cool black guy. In Santa Monica, like in most predominantly white sanctuaries from urban blight, 'cool black guy' is a versatile identifier used to distinguish the harmless male black from the Caucasian juvenile while maintaining politically correct semiotics. I was the only 'cool black guy' at Mestizo Mulatto Mongrel Elementary, Santa Monica's all-white multicultural school. My early education consisted of two types of multiculturalism: classroom multiculturalism, which reduced race, sexual orientation and gender to inconsequence; and schoolyard multiculturalism, where the kids who knew the most polack, queer and farmer's daughter jokes ruled.

Black was hating fried chicken even before I knew I was supposed to like it. Black was being a nigger who didn't know any other niggers. Black was trying to figure out 'how black' Tony Grimes, the local skate pro was. Tony, a freestyle hero with a signature-model Dogtown board, was a hellacious skater and somehow disembodied from blackness, even though he was darker than a lunar eclipse in the Congo. Black was a suffocating bully that tied my mind behind my back and shoved me into a walk-in closet. Black was my father on a weekend custody drunken binge one summer, pushing me around as if I were a twelve-year-old, seventy-five-pound bell-clapper clanging hard against the door, the wall, the shoe tree.

That same summer my sister Christina returned from a YMCA day camp field trip in tears. My mother asked what was wrong, and between breathless wails Christina replied that on the way home from the Museum of Natural History the campers cheered, 'Yeah, white camp! Yeah, white camp!' and she felt left out. I tried to console her by explaining that the cheer was, 'Yeah Y camp! Yeah Y camp!', and that no one was trying to leave her out of anything. Expressing unusual concern in our affairs, Mom asked if we would feel better about going to an all-black camp. We gave an insistent 'Nooooo.' She asked why, and we answered in three-part sibling harmony, 'Because they're different from us.' The way Mom arched her left eyebrow at us we knew immediately we were in for a change. Sunday I was hitching a U-Haul trailer to the back of the Volvo, and under the cover of darkness we left halcyon Santa Monica for parts unknown.

I don't remember helping my mother unload the trailer but the next morning I awoke on the floor of a strange house amid boxes and piles of heavy-duty garbage bags jammed with clothes. The blinds were drawn, and although the sunlight peeked between the slats, the house was dark. My mother let out a yell in that distinct from-somewhere-in-the-kitchen timbre, 'Gunnar, go into my purse and buy some breakfast for everybody.' Rummaging through my personal garbage bag I found my blue Quicksilver shorts, a pair of worn-out dark grey Vans sneakers, a long-sleeved clay-colored old school Santa Cruz shirt and, just in case the morning chill was still happening, I wrapped a thick plaid flannel shirt around my bony waist. I found the front door and like some lost intergalactic B-movie spaceman who has crash-landed on a mysterious planet and is unsure about the atmospheric content, I opened it slowly, contemplating the possibility of encountering intelligent life. I stepped into a world that was a bustling Italian intersection without Italians. Instead of little sheet-metal sedans racing around the Fontana di Trevi, little kids on beat-up Big Wheels, and bigger kids on creaky ten-speeds wove in and out of the water spray from a sprinkler set in the middle of the street. It seemed there must have been a fire drill at the hair salon because males and females in curlers and shower caps crammed the sidewalks. I ventured forth into my new environs and approached a boy about my age who wore an immaculately pressed, sparkling white T-shirt and khakis and was slowly pacing one slew-footed black croker-sack shoe in front of the other. I stopped him and asked for directions to the nearest

173

store. He squinted and leaned back and stifled a laugh. 'What the fuck did you say?'

I repeated my request, and the laugh he had suppressed came out gently. 'Damn, cuz. You talk proper like a motherfucker.'

Cuz? Proper like a motherfucker?

My guide's bafflement turned to judgmental indignation at my appearance. 'Damn, fool, what's up with your loud ass gear? Nigger got on so many colours look like a walking paint sampler. Did you find the pot of gold at the end of that rainbow? You not even close to matching. Take your jambalaya wardrobe down to Cadillac Street make a right and the store is at the light.'

I walked to the store, not believing some guy who ironed the sleeves on his T-shirt and belted his pants somewhere near his testicles had the nerve to insult how I dressed. I returned to the house, dropped the bag of groceries on the table and shouted, 'Ma, you done fucked up and moved to the 'hood!'

My black magical mystery tour had ground to a halt in a West Los Angeles neighborhood the locals call Hillside. Shaped like a giant cul-de-sac, Hillside is less a community than a quarry of stucco homes built directly into the foothills of the San Borrachos Mountains. Unlike most Californian communities that border mountain ranges, in Hillside there are no gently sloping hillsides upon which children climb trees, and overly friendly park rangers lead weekend flora and fauna tours.

In the late 1960s after the bloody but little-known I'm-Tired-of-the-White-Man-Fuckin'-With-Us-and-What-Not Riots, the city decided to pave over the neighboring mountainside, surrounding the community with a great concrete wall that spans its entire curved perimeter save for an arched gateway at the south-west entrance. At the bottom of this great wall live hordes of impoverished American Mongols, hardrock niggers, Latinos and Asians who, because of the wall's immenseness, get only fifteen minutes of precious sunshine in summer and a burst of solstice sunlight in the winter. If it wasn't always so hot it would be like living in a refrigerator.

After a week in our new home—a pueblo-style house with a cracked and fissuring plaster exterior—a black-and-white

Welcome Wagon pulled up to help the newcomers settle into the neighborhood. Two mustachioed officers got out of the patrol car and knocked on our front door with well-practiced leather-gloved authority. Tossing courtesy smiles at my mother, the cops shouldered their way past the threshold and presented her with a pamphlet entitled *How to Report Crime and Suspicious Activity Whether the Suspects are Related to You or Not.*

Mom was not the kind of matriarch to let her brood hide up under her skirt, clutching her knees, sheltered from the mean old Negroes outside. I walked the streets comfortable in the knowledge that I was a freak. 'Hurry! Hurry! Step right up! All the way from the drifting sands of whitest Santa Monica, the whitest Negro in captivity, Gunnar the Persnickety Zulu! He says "whom", plays parchisi and, folks, you won't believe it, but he has absolutely no ass what-so-ever.'

In a world where body and spoken language were currency, I was broke as hell. Corporeally mute, I couldn't saunter or bojangle my limbs with rubbery nonchalance. I stiffly parade-marched around town with an embalmed soul, a rheumatic heart and Frankenstein's autonomic nervous system.

I learned the hard way that social norms in Santa Monica were unforgivable breaches of proper Hillside etiquette. I'd been taught to look people in the eye when speaking to them. On the streets of Hillside even the briefest eye contact wasn't a simple faux pas, but an interpersonal trespass that merited retaliation. Spotting a potential comrade I'd catch his eye with a raised eyebrow that said, 'Hey guy, what's up?', a glance I hoped would open the lines of communication. These silent greetings were often returned in spades accompanied by an angry rejoinder, 'Nigger, what the fuck you looking at?' and a pimp slap that echoed in my ears for a week.

The people of Hillside treat society the way society treats them. Strangers and friends are suspect and guilty until proven innocent. Instant camaraderie past familial ties doesn't exist. It takes more than wearing the same uniform to be accepted among one's ghetto peers. I couldn't just roll up on some folks and say, 'I know the Black National Anthem, a killer sweet-potato-pie

175

recipe and how to double-dutch blindfolded. Will you be my nigger?' Dues had to be paid, or you wasn't joining the union. I walked the dark streets of Hillside with my head down looking for loose change and signs that would place me on the path to right-on soul-brother righteousness.

I arrived forty-five minutes early for my first day of school at Manischewitz Junior High. I walked through the metal detector and found a receptionist in the dean's office, who directed me to homeroom. I slunk over, imagining I was wearing dark glasses and a trench coat. Pressing my back against the walls and peeking coolly around corners, I managed to avoid detection and made it there twenty minutes early.

Eventually the hallways stopped echoing with the footsteps of the Oxford wing-tipped and high-heeled administration. In their place was the sound of brand-new sneakers squeaking on the waxed floors and the heavy clomp of unlaced hiking boots. Steadily the students entered the classroom and slid into the empty seats around me. First to arrive were the marsupial mama's boys and girls. The reformed and borderline students followed. Creeping into class carefully trying to avoid last year's repercussive behaviours, they sat upright at their desks, face front and hands folded, mumbling their September resolutions to themselves: 'This year will be different. I will do my homework. I will only bring *my* gun to school.' Two minutes before nine signalled the grand entrance of the fly guys and starlets. Dressed in designer silk suits and dresses, accessorized in ascots, feather boas and gold, the aloof adolescent pimps and dispassionate divas strolled into homeroom smoking tiparillos and with a retinue of admirers who carried their books and pulled chairs from tables with maître d' suave.

I'd never been in a room full of black people unrelated to me before. As my classmates yelled out their schedules and passed contraband across the room I couldn't classify anyone by their dress or behaviour. The boisterous were just as likely to be in the academically enriched classes as the silent. The clothes horses stood as much chance of being on a remedial track as the bummy kids with brown-bag lunches.

At nine o'clock the bell rang, and Ms Schaefer stormed into the room. Dishevelled and visibly nervous, she never bothered to introduce herself or say good morning. She wrote her name on the board in shaky, wavering strokes and took attendance. The class instantly interpreted her behaviour as a display of lack of trust and concern. That day I learned another ghetto lesson: never let on that you don't trust someone. Even if he has bad intentions toward you, he will take offense at your lack of trust. I've seen people stalk a victim, and when the victim takes evasive measures—quickening his pace, pretending to tie his shoes, crossing the street—the thief forgets the robbery motive and reacts to the distrustful behaviour. 'What? You think I'm going to mug you or some shit? You better run, 'cause now I'm really going to kick your ass.'

'Wardell Adams?'

'Here.'

'Varnell Alvarez?'

'*Aqui.*'

'Pellmell Atkinson?'

'*Presentemente.*'

'Praise-the-Lord Benson?'

'Yupper.'

'Lakeesha Caldwell?'

'What?'

'Ayesha Dunwiddy?'

'Who wants to know?'

'Chocolate Fondue Egerton?'

'That's my name, ask me again and you'll be walking with a cane.'

'I don't know how to pronounce the next one.'

'You pronounce it like it sounds, bitch. Maritza Shakaleema Esperanza the goddess Tlazotéotl Eladio.'

'So you're here.'

'Do crack pipes get hot?'

Then the gangsters trickled in, ten minutes late, tattooed and feisty. 'Say man, woman, teacher, whatever you call yourself. You better mark Hope-to-Die Ranford AKA Pythagoras here and in the house. Nobody better be sitting at my desk. I had the

shit last year and I want it back for good luck.'
'Mr Pythagoras, take any available seat for now, OK? Who's
that with you?'
'Why you ask him? I can speak for my damn self. This is
Velma the Ludicrous Mistress Triple Bitch of Mischief Vinson.'
I sat like a tiny bubble in a boiling cauldron of teenage
blackness, wondering where all the heat came from. I realized I
was a cultural alloy, a mixture of tin-hearted whiteness wrapped
in blackened copperplating.

2

By high school I was no longer the seaside bumpkin, clueless to
the Byzantine ways of the inner city. But I hadn't completely
assimilated into Hillside's culture. I still said 'ant' instead of
'awwwnt', 'you guys' rather than 'y'all' and wore my pants a bit
too tight, but these shortcomings were forgiven because I had
managed to attain 'a look'. My sinewy basketball physique drew
scads of attention.
'You play ball? Don't say no, you got that look. I can tell by
your calves. Skinny, powerful legs. And the way you walk.
Pigeon-toed, small ass'n all. You ain't nothing but a ball player.'
In the past three years, I had become part of a heroic trio of
sorts: me, Nicholas Scoby and Psycho Loco.
Scoby was a thuggish ball player who never missed. I mean
never. He sat in the back of the class, ears sealed in a pair of top-
of-the-line Stennhausen stereo headphones and each of his
twiggish limbs parked in a chair of its own. Rocking back and
forth in his seat, Nicholas Scoby seemed like an autistic hoodlum.
His pea-head lolled precariously on his wiry neck like a
gyroscope, he snapped his fingers in some haphazard pattern and
muttered to himself in a beatnik word-salad gibberish, 'Dig it.
This nigger's tonality is wow. Like hep. It's a contrapuntal
glissando phraseology to bopnetic postmodernism. Blow man
blow. Crazy.' Much to the dismay of those who paid attention to
the burnt-out teachers, Scoby was a straight-A student.
Psycho Loco's real name was Juan Julio Sanchez. I knew all

about him before I met him. His mother used to tell me how Juan Julio's voice was the best missionary religion ever had. On Sundays he'd sing with the choir, and his baritone would make the babies stop crying and the deacons start. Ms Sanchez would hold a crucifix up to the sky and swear that drunks, bums, prostitutes, hoodlums, even police officers would walk into the original First Ethiop Aztlan Catholic–Baptist Church and Casa de Sanctified Holy Rolling Ecumenical Sanctification, kneel at Juan Julio's feet pleading forgiveness, renounce sin, accept the Lord Jesus Christ as their saviour and put all the money they had in the collection plate. When the service ended, the plate would be filled with car keys, crack vials and stolen credit cards.

On the street the angelic Juan Julio was Psycho Loco, leader of the local gang Gun Totin' Hooligans. I'd heard how as a strong-arm man-child for a loan shark, when he tired of a debtor's sob story on why that week's payment was late, he'd heat his crucifix with a nickel-plated lighter and press the makeshift branding iron into the victim's cheek and scream, 'Now you really have a cross to bear, motherfucker!'

Psycho Loco was my next-door neighbor and he decided he liked me. As Scoby said, 'If Psycho Loco says you're his friend, there ain't nothing you can do about it. You're friends 'cause he says so. Oh yeah, nigger, thirteen years old and you involved now.'

At Phillis Wheatley High the message was always the same. Stay in school. Don't do drugs. Treat our black queens with respect. I made decent money taking bets on whether the distinguished speaker at our monthly 'Young Black and Latino Men: Endangered Species' assembly would say, 'Each one, teach one' first or 'There's an old African saying, "It takes an entire village to raise one child."' I suppose I could afford to be snide. I had a personal motivational speaker, Coach Motome Chijiwa Shimimoto. The stereotype is that most successful black men raised by single mothers have a surrogate father who turn their lives around. A man who 'saw their potential', looked after them, taught them the value of virtuous living and set them out on the path to glory with a resounding slap on the butt. Coach Shimimoto didn't do any of those things. He just paid attention to me. The only time he ever told me what to do with my life was during basketball practice. I can't say that I learned any valuable lessons from Coach Shimimoto. He never gave me any clichéd phrases to be repeated in times of need, never showed me pictures of crippled kids to remind me how lucky I was. The only thing I remember him teaching me was that as a left-hander I'd have to draw from right to left to keep my charcoals from streaking— Coach Shimimoto was also my art teacher.

I often think the real reason Coach Shimimoto fêted me was to get inside Nicholas's head through me. Nicholas was his prized student, his ticket to high-school coaching fame. Shimimoto knew that in thirty years reporters would call him at home and ask what it was like to coach—if not the greatest, the most unusual basketball player in the world. Coach had his answers all prepared; he would tell them, 'Nicholas doesn't understand the game, but the game understands him.'

Both Nicholas and I entered tenth grade with solid basketball reputations. Nick was the wizard and I the sorcerer's apprentice. My duty was to get Scoby the ball so he could score, play tough defense so the other team wouldn't score and bow reverentially after each dazzling feat. A collective self-esteem was at stake. People who didn't give a fuck about anything other than keeping their new shoes unscuffed all of a sudden had meaning to their lives. They yelled at the referees, sang fight songs, razzed the efforts of the other team.

Everywhere Scoby and I went, we were Wheatley High's main attraction. Teachers and students treated us with unwanted reverence. The murmur of everyone clamoring for our attention rang in my ears like a worshipping tinnitus. Girls slipped phone numbers into my pockets and rubbed the tips of their angora nipples on my shoulders. Boys bear-hugged us and enthusiastically replayed entire games for our benefit.

To avoid the incessant adulation the day before a game against South Erebus High, we spent the lunch period in Coach Shimimoto's art room. I doodled in Indian ink, and Nicholas sat at the pottery wheel, shaping amorphous clay blobs. Toward the end of the period Nicholas was pumping the pedal so fast he couldn't get the clay to stay on the spinning disc. 'Fuck arts and crafts!' he yelled as wet slabs of clay flew across the room, flattening themselves on the walls and windows. I'd never seen Scoby mad about anything. He was always the one who dispensed advice and remained in control. Whenever the crew got stopped for unjustified or justified police shakedowns, it was Scoby whispering, 'Maintain, maintain.' I looked to Coach Shimimoto, but he was removing clay pancakes from his face and motioning with his eyes for me to say something first.

'Yo, nigger, why you so upset? We got a game tomorrow, just cool out.'

'Man, I'm tired of these fanatics rubbing on me, pulling on my arms, wishing me luck. I can't take it. People have buttons with my face on 'em. They paint their faces and stencil my number on their foreheads. One idiot showed me a tattoo on his chest that said NICK SCOBY IS GOD.'

'They're just trying to say how much they appreciate what you do. It'll get better man, they'll get used to us winning.'

'But they'll never get used to Scoby making every shot he takes,' Coach Shimimoto interrupted us. 'Nicholas, you're right, it'll only get worse. You've got to figure out how you can live with it.'

'It's not fair. I wasn't born to make them happy. What I look like, motherfucking Charlie Chaplin?'

'So miss once in a while.'

'I can't. I can't even try. Something won't let me.'

Scoby's eyes reddened and he started to sniffle. He was cracking under the pressure. Watching Nicholas's hands shake I realized that sometimes the worst thing a nigger can do is perform well. Because then there is no turning back. We have no place to hide, no Superman Fortresses of Solitude, no reclusive New England hermitages for xenophobic geniuses like Bobby Fischer and J. D. Salinger. Successful niggers can't go back home and blithely disappear into the local populace. American society reels you back into the fold: 'Tote that barge, shoot that basketball, lift that bale, nigger ain't you ever heard of Dred Scott?'

Nicholas didn't shoot much for the rest of the year. For us to win basketball games I had to play like hell. Gradually I realized the decision Nicholas made was to remove temporarily the burden of success from his shoulders and place it solely on mine. The classroom, locker room and bathroom acclaim fell on me. When Scoby's name came up they all said, 'Oh, that fool can shoot, but Gunnar has to carry us.' Nicholas loved the shift in fame and willingly played his part in the role reversal, calling me 'the Deity' and asking me to forgive him his sins.

There are certain demands on a star athlete that I didn't anticipate or enjoy. The most arduous was having to participate in the social scene. Every weekend Scoby and Psycho Loco pressured me to use my star status to get them retinue privileges at the Paradise, La Cebolla Roja or the Black Lagoon. When a club manager balked at admitting the volatile Psycho Loco into his establishment, I had to agree to take complete responsibility for his actions, which was like asking a dog collar to be responsible for a Rottweiler. Wringing their hands like mad scientists they'd thank me for my kindness, ignoring the fact that I suffered from what the American Psychiatric Association *Manual of Mental Disorders* lists as Social Arrhythmia and Courtship Paralysis, meaning I couldn't dance and was deathly afraid of women.

I wasn't completely lacking in social skills. With practice I learned to serpentine cool-as-hell through a crowded dance floor with the best of the high-school snakes. I could hiss at young women but not much else. When the opening strains of the latest jam crescendoed through the house, I would shout a perfunctory 'Heeeyyy!' showing the club-goers I was up for the downstroke and that any moment there might be a 'par-tay ovah heah'. Scoby and Psycho Loco would soon abandon my hepster front for the chase; melding into the swirling mass of bodies and leaving me to fend for myself.

Even Psycho Loco could dance. He did this little gangster jig where he leaned back into the cushy rhythms like he was reclining in an easy chair, kicking one foot into the air, then the other, sipping from a bottle of contraband gin and lemonade during the funky breakdown. Girls interested in dancing with me propped themselves in front of me, a little closer than necessary, swayed to the music and tried to catch my eye. I stared off in the opposite direction pretending to be engrossed in an intricately woven bar napkin and praying she wouldn't be bold enough to ask for a dance. As an athlete I had a ready-made excuse for the nervy women who did ask. 'I can't baby. Twisted my ankle dunking on the Rogers brothers in last night's game.' I'd get a funny look in return, and the rebuffed co-ed would return to her circle of friends. The whispers and over-the-shoulder looks followed by phony smiles set off my social paranoia. My auditory hallucinations cleared their throats: 'Something wrong with that nigger, he don't never dance. Maybe he just shy. Maybe he's shy? He ain't shy with Coach Shimimoto. That's why Coach be sweating so much. Boy got some big ol' feets and hands that's a waste of some good young nigger dick. Fucking an old man.' Soon Scoby and Psycho Loco would interrupt my neurotic musings. 'Why you ain't dancing homes? Crazy honeys is checking you out.'

'I don't feel like dancing.'

'Are you crazy? There some fine ladies in here. You just scared of women. Scared of pussy.'

As the evening wound down, the house lights dimmed to deep red haze, and the DJ began to play the latest slow jams. I'd pray Psycho Loco would start a fight so I could leave without having to support someone's head on my shoulder and listen to them warble inane love lyrics in my ear. Invariably Psycho Loco came through, slugging some fool for stepping on his shadow or some equally petty infraction. As the bouncers escorted us out, Psycho Loco and Scoby compared the night's harvest.

'So Gunnar, how'd you do?'

'Do people be staring at me when I'm out there dancing? It feels like everybody is looking at me.'

'First off, you ain't out there dancing. You out there having a brain aneurysm. You move so crazy it looks like you caught the holy ghost. Second off, nobody is paying any attention to your rhythmless behind 'cause they trying to get they own mack on.'

'Gunnar, do you even like girls?'

'Yes.' Which was true, I just had yet to meet one who didn't intimidate me into a state of catatonia.

'When you gonna get a girlfriend?'

'I had one once in Santa Monica.'

'What some pasty white girl named Eileen? Please. That don't count. Nigger, have you ever seen any parts of the pussy?'
'Of course man. I've fucked . . . er, been fucked . . . um been fucking . . . I is fucking.'
'Does the line go up and down or from side to side?'

During the ride home one evening Psycho Loco was leafing through a copy of *Bow and Arrow Outdoorsman*, heading straight to the classified ads in the back.
'Gunnar, we're gonna find you a wife.'
Somehow I knew that Psycho Loco was right; I'd never start a romance on my own accord. But it was difficult to accept sexual counsel from a pugnacious male who had to be drunk to fuck and whose first rule of courtship was 'Always make sure your dick is out. That way no matter what happens you can say, "Well, I had my dick out."'
Changing the subject, I snatched the magazine from Psycho Loco's hands and said, 'My pops said Rodney King deserved that ass-kicking for resisting arrest and having a Jehri Curl. He said some curl activator got into Officer Koon's eyes and he thought he'd been maced so he had to defend himself.'
I asked Psycho Loco if the rumours about a gangland truce if the jury found the cops innocent were true. He said that there already had been a big armistice at the Tryst N' Shout Motel. Bangers who had killed each other's best friends shook hands and hugged with unspoken apologies in their watery eyes.
'Damn, I hope they find those motherfuckers guilty,' I said with surprising conviction.
'Not me,' said Psycho Loco. 'I hope those boys get off scot-free. One it'll be good to have a little peace in the streets, and besides, me and the fellas planning a huge job. Going to take advantage of the civic unrest, know what I'm saying?'
I pictured Rodney King staggering in the Foothill Freeway's breakdown lane like a black Frankenstein; two Taser wires running fifty thousand volts of electric democracy through his body. I wondered if the battery of the American nigger was being recharged or drained.

3

For some reason Coach Shimimoto was reluctant to end practice. Usually these post-season workouts were light affairs, mostly intra-squad scrimmages followed by a dunking contest. This one he kept prolonging with wind sprints and full-court defensive drills. Shimimoto finally blew his whistle and motioned for the team to gather around him. Exhausted, we flopped to the floor, sucking wind and hoping that Coach Shimimoto would take pity on our fatigued bodies.

'What does concatenate mean? Tell me and you can go.'

Harriet Montoya, the only person with strength enough to speak, raised her hand. I didn't have much faith she'd know the answer—yesterday she had defined 'repeal' as putting the skin back on an orange and peeling again, and we had to run thirty laps backward. 'Concatenate means together. Not like all-in-the-same-boat together, but like connected, like a bicycle chain.'

'Close enough. Remember that definition, you soon-to-be revolutionaries.'

With that, Coach dismissed us into a cool late-April afternoon.

On the way home I was wondering what Coach meant by 'soon-to-be revolutionaries' when I noticed a distant column of black smoke billowing into the dusk like a tornado too tired to move.

'What's that?' I asked Scoby.

'Eric Dolphy,' he replied, referring to the stop-and-go shrieking that was escaping from his boom box.

'No, I mean that,' I said, pointing to the noxious-looking cloud.

Scoby didn't know but he was more than willing to make up for his ignorance in smoke formations by lecturing me on the relevance of Dolphy's sonic turmoil to teenage Negromites like ourselves. Midway through his seminar another silo of smoke twisted into the dusk, this one closer. The driver of a run-down Nova sped down Sawyer Drive leaning on her high-pitched horn for no apparent reason. Scoby turned up the volume on the tape deck just a bit. Another car flew through a stop sign then reversed. When the car drew parallel with us, the driver flashed a gap-toothed smile, then shot a raised fist out of the window and raced away. Soon every driver that passed was joyriding through the streets, honking their horns and violating the traffic laws like Hollywood stunt drivers in the big chase scene.

People began spilling from their homes. They paced up and down the sidewalks looking tense and unaware they'd left their front doors open. Something was wrong: no Los Angeleno ever leaves his door open. I caught the eye of a middle-aged man wearing white patent-leather shoes, ochre-coloured polyester pants and a Panama hat who was standing on his front porch looking desperate for someone to talk to.

'What's happening?' I asked.

'Them cracker motherfuckers did it again.'

The Rodney King verdict; I'd completely forgotten.

'They let them racists go. I'm surprised the judge didn't reprimand the peckerwood so-called peace officers for not finishing the job.'

Let go? What did that mean? The officers had to have been found guilty of something—obstruction of traffic at least. Maybe if it was the maid's day off in Simi Valley, and the jury was in a bad mood, the most sadistic officer, Stacy Koon, would be found guilty of all charges. I doubted the man in the patent-leather shoes. I could hear the TV in his living room and I peeped into his doorway. The smirk on the reporter's face told me the man was right, even before I heard her say, 'Not guilty on all charges.'

I never felt so worthless in my life. Uninvited, we walked into the man's living room, set our book bags on his coffee table and sat on the couch. I looked out the window and saw a store-owner spray-paint BLACK OWNED across her boarded-up beauty salon. I wanted to dig out my heart and have her do the same to it, certifying my identity in big block letters across both ventricles. I suddenly understood why my father wore his badge so proudly. The badge protected him; in uniform he was safe.

Sitting on that couch watching the announcer gloat, the anger that resided in my pacifist Negro chrysalis shed its innocuousness. I felt a glistening animosity testing its wings. Right then I envied Psycho Loco. Psycho Loco dealt with his rage by blaming and lashing out; there was no pretense of fairness and justice; due process was his mood, or if he ran out of bullets while shooting at you. Watching the acquitted officers shake hands with their attorneys and stroll triumphantly into the April sun, I saw his brutality as a powerful, vitriolic stimulant. I wanted to sip this effervescent bromo that cleared one's head and numbed the aches and pains of oppression. Psycho Loco had the satisfaction of standing up to his enemies and listening to them scream, watching them close their eyes for the last time. Psycho Loco had a semblance of closure and accomplishment. He was a threat. I wanted to taste immediate vindication, experience the rush of spitting in somebody's, anybody's face.

I looked at Scoby and said, 'Let's break.' We gathered our things, thanked the man for his kindness and prepared to leave. We spent an awkward moment in silence, till the man asked, 'Is that Dolphy?' Scoby nodded yes, and we made our way toward the commotion listening to Dolphy play his horn like he was wringing a wash rag. I couldn't decide whether the music sounded like a death knell or the cavalry charge for a ragtag army. We'd turned the corner on to Hoover and Alvarado and walked into Carnival poor-people's style. The niggers and spics had decided to secede from the Union, armed with rifles, slingshots, bottles, camcorders and songs of freedom. Problem was nobody knew where Fort Sumter was.

The next afternoon Scoby and I sat in his basement watching the rest of the city burn on television. A parade of relatives marched through his house hawking their wares. 'Look what I came up on.' Holding up sweaters and jackets that smelt of smoke for our perusal. 'Gunnar you'd look good in this. Got a lamé collar. Bill Cosby would wear this jammie. You Nick's man, two dollars.'

'Nigger move, you in front of the TV.'

It was hard not to be envious of anybody who had some free shit and a little crumb of the California dream. I too wanted to 'come up' but I didn't think I was a thief. The television stations were airing live feeds from hot spots around the city showing looters entering stores empty-handed and exiting carrying furniture on their backs like worker ants carrying ten times their weight.

'Hey isn't that the Montgomery Ward Plaza?' The mall was about ten minutes away, just outside the wall.

'Yeah, there go Technology Town.'

'Oh shit, fools coming up on free computers and shit.'

Scoby and I looked each other in the eye for about a nanosecond then stormed out of the house. Running down the streets we argued over the virtues of IBM-compatible and Apple. 'Dude, I'm looking for a Wizard Protean.'

'What? You can't carry out a desktop. Go for a laptop. You get all the qualities of a Protean, plus mobility. Your dumbass is trying to steal a whole mainframe.'

Coach Shimimoto's arduous workouts had served their purpose. We reached Technology Town fresh and ready to celebrate Christmas in April. Leaping through the broken windows we tumbled over a stack of plastic shopping baskets and landed in a snowbank of styrofoam package filler. We were too late. All the presents had been opened. The showroom was stripped bare. Broken shelving dangled from the walls; overturned showcases spilt over on to the floor, serving as caskets for dead batteries and the shells of busted stereo equipment. Unraveled cassette tape hung from the overhead pipes like brown riot tinsel. Even the ceiling fans and service phones were gone.

'What happens to a dream deferred?' I said in my best classical recitation voice. Scoby cursed and threw a nine-volt battery at my head.

'Fuck Langston Hughes. I bet when they rioted in Harlem, Langston got his.'

Kicking our way through the piles of cardboard we left the store and stood in the parking lot thinking of our next target. People were still ransacking Cribs N' Bibs, the toddler shop, but rattles, powdered milk and designer diapers didn't interest us. Scoby snapped his fingers, shouted 'What Did You Say?' and sprinted down toward the alley that ran behind the mall.

What Did You Say? was a car-accessory emporium that specialized in deafeningly loud car stereos and equally loud seat covers. I couldn't figure out how Scoby planned to get in the place;

it was known to be impenetrable. A solid metal garage door that had foiled the attempts of a Who's Who of burglary specialists sealed the front entrance. The famed barrier had withstood ramming from hijacked semi-trucks, dynamite and every solvent from Paul Newman's salad dressing to 150-proof rum mixed with corrosive black-hair products.

When we got to What Did You Say? the steel door was still in place. Scoby and I put our ears against it and heard what sounded like mice scurrying around inside. We zipped around the back and found a small opening smashed into the cinder-block wall, a guilty-looking sledgehammer lay atop a pile of rubble. Every ten seconds or so a contortionist would squeeze through the hole bearing some sort of electronic gadgetry. Standing nearby in tears was fat Reece Clinksdale. Reece was bemoaning his girth because he was too big to fit in the hole and was missing out on the rebellion. He wiped his eyes and stopped blubbering for a bit.

'You guys going in?'

'I guess so,' we answered.

'Well you better hurry up. I think most of the good stuff is gone.'

Reece was right. The crawl space was starting to give birth to zoo animals. Guys were popping head first through the hole wrapped in sheepskin and leopardskin seat covers and looking like cuddly animals. I helped deliver a breech baby alligator seat cover who'd decided to exit feet-first and had to be pulled through the cement birth canal.

When the traffic was light enough to make an entrance, Scoby and I slid through the hole. The absolute lack of chaos was amazing. Instead of a horde of one-eyed brigands pillaging and setting fires, the looters were very courteous, and the plundering was orderly. Everyone waited patiently in a line that wound through the aisles and into the storeroom. Once in the storeroom, a philanthropic soul handed you a box off the shelf. You didn't get your choice of goods, but no one complained. If you wanted something else you just got in line again.

Looting wasn't as exciting as Scoby and I hoped it would be. Nicholas came up on a car alarm, and I on a box of pine-tree-

189

shaped air-fresheners. On the way back to his neighborhood we saw Pookie Hamilton drive by in his convertible bug. I whistled, and Pookie pulled over, waving for us to get in the back seat.

'Where you headed, Pook?'

'I just got a page from Psycho Loco. He needs some help.'

I hadn't forgotten about Psycho Loco's planned big score, but the greedy look in his eyes whenever he had talked about The Heist had told me that I didn't want to be involved.

'Drop me and Scoby off at my house.'

'No time, G.'

'Well where we going?'

'Montgomery Ward.'

When we pulled into the parking lot there was Psycho Loco and his friends No M. O. Clark and Joe Shenanigans. They were standing behind Psycho Loco's van next to a huge iron safe. Grimy, covered with sweat, the boys were overjoyed to see us. This was The Heist.

'What the fuck? Are you motherfuckers crazy?'

'Chill, homes. We just want help lifting this thing in the van.'

'How did you get it out?'

'Look,' Scoby said, pointing to a set of rubber wheels attached to the bottom of the strongbox.

I had two thoughts. Why are all safes painted beige? And would my mother come visit me in prison?

'Dude, I can't be wearing no stonewashed prison outfit for the rest of my life. That shit makes me itch.'

Scoby tried to comfort me. 'You can wear any kind of shirt you want, just no rhinestones or metal buttons. Besides, I haven't seen one police car the whole day.'

He was right. I hadn't even noticed. The entire day had been an undeclared public holiday. Los Angeles was a theme park, and we were spending the day in Anarchyland. I calmed down. The safe was unbelievably heavy, which everyone but me took as a positive sign. I thought the thing could just as easily be empty or filled with employee time cards as stuffed with valuables.

On our third try we almost had the safe inside the back of the van when we all heard an extremely disheartening sound. 'What's that?' everyone asked.

'Uh, the Doppler effect,' I said.

'Shit, it's the cops.'

With a final strain we edged the safe on to the bumper of the van, but our knees buckled under the weight, and the safe dropped to the ground with a heavy thud. The sirens were getting closer. No one had the energy for another lift, but we couldn't leave the safe in the middle of the parking lot, not with visions of Spanish gold doubloons dancing in our heads. I looked in the van and saw a length of rope. How stupid we'd been. All we needed to do was tie one end to the safe's handle and the other end to the van's bumper and we could drive away, pulling the safe along behind us. I heard the cop car pull into the parking lot. My back tightened in anticipation of hearing a gunshot or a threatening, 'Get your hands up and step away from the vehicle.' What I did hear was something I hadn't heard in years, my father's voice. 'Gunnar!' I told the boys to keep going, that I'd distract him. I turned around to see my father step out the car gripping a shotgun in one hand.

'Dad. Long time no see. Things must really be hectic if you're out on the streets.'

I heard the van slowly pull off, and I looked back to see the safe trailing behind it, like a tin can tied to a car of newly-weds. When I turned to face my father, the hard rubber butt of the shotgun crashed into my jaw. I saw a flash of white and dropped to the pavement. His partner stepped on my ear, muffling my father's words. 'You are not a Kaufman. I refuse to let you embarrass me with your niggerish ways. And where did you get all these damn air-fresheners?'

Something hard smacked the side of my neck, sending my tongue rolling out of my mouth like a party favor. I could taste the salty ash on the pavement. Ash that had drifted from fires set in anger from around the city. I remembered learning in third grade that snakes 'see' and 'hear' with their sensitive tongues. I imagined my tongue, almost bitten through, hearing the polyrhythms of my father's nightstick on my body. Through my tongue I saw my father transform into a master Senegalese drummer beating a surrender code on a hollow log on the banks of the muddy Gambia. A flash of white—the night of my conception, my father twisting mama's arm behind her back and ordering her to 'assume the position'. A flash of white—my father potty-training me with a slap across the face and sticking my hand in my mushy excrement. Soon my body stopped bucking with every blow; there was only white: no memories, no visions, only the sound of voices.

4

Gunnar, my young revolutionary, while you were in a coma, you got a letter from the Nike Basketball Camp. You've been chosen as one of the hundred best ball players in the nation. Actually you're number one hundred. Coach Shimimoto

Son, your father and I both think it's best for you to transfer to another school. We're sending you to El Campesino Real in the Valley. Mom

Dude, you got fucked up. Nicholas Scoby

You gots to get better, cuz. We can't figure out how to open the safe. Psycho Loco

The safe sat in the middle of Psycho Loco's den. Old Abuela Gloria, reportedly an expert safecracker in Havana during Batista's glory days, was wearing a stethoscope and listening to the tumblers click as she spun the combination dial back and forth.

'Isn't Abuela Gloria deaf?' I asked Ms Sanchez.

Abuela removed the stethoscope from her ears and pulled on the latch. Nothing happened.

Scoby was calculating possible permutations of a combination lock numbered from zero to a hundred. He'd already tried thirty-two thousand combinations while I was in hospital. He knelt beside the safe flipping the dial from number to number and shaking his cramped hands in frustration as his magic failed him.

'Gunnar, look at the safe, maybe you can figure out a way to open it.'

'What I know about opening a safe? That thing almost got me killed. I don't give a fuck if you never get it open.'

I was lying, and Psycho Loco knew it. I hadn't taken my eyes off the box since I'd been there. I couldn't shake the word 'treasure' from my head: rubies and gold lanterns, ancient scrolls and taboo vestiges. I wanted to free the genie and fuck up my three wishes.

I ran my hands over the safe's tapered edges, then stood back, waved my fingers and said in a slow, spooky voice, 'Open, sesame.'

'We did that shit already,' said Psycho Loco. 'Ala-kazam, hocus-pocus—we even paid that voodoo lady on Normandie fifty dollars to open it with some of that ol' time Yoruba religion.'

'What happened?'

'She got chicken blood and pixie dust all over the fucking place. Damn near burnt the house down with all the candles.'

I looked closely at the safe. The tag dangling from the handle flapped in the current of a draught. The tag read, MONTGOMERY WARD DURO-SAFE. THIS SAFE IS SOLID TUNGSTEN. AIRTIGHT, FIREPROOF, AND GUARANTEED TO WITHSTAND PRESSURE UP TO 3500 POUNDS PER SQUARE INCH.

I knew there had to be a way to open it; this was a Montgomery Ward product. Nothing they made worked. Their television sets came with wire hangers and a pair of pliers to turn the channel after the knobs fell off.

I had an idea. I asked Abuela Gloria for her safe-cracking kit. I set the small metal box about three feet behind the safe and asked Scoby, Ms Sanchez and Psycho Loco to help it on to its back. There, on the bottom, on a dirty white label, was written:

4 turns to the right to 67
3 turns to the left to 23
2 turns to the right to 55
1 turn to the left to 63

The best thing about treasure is the assortment. I didn't think gold bars really existed. I thought they were a movie prop used to speed up the plot. Yet there was a shoebox full of domino-sized ingots stamped MONTGOMERY WARD 24K. Stacks of dusty paper money sat in the back. Silver and platinum rings and brooches, and tiaras inlaid with rubies, emeralds and diamonds glittered under the lamplight.

It was surreal to watch Psycho Loco divide the bounty. Tossing stacks of money and gold bars around the room like so many paperweights. We played *The Price is Right* for the jewelry. Whoever was closest to guessing the stickered price won the bauble.

For a while living in Hillside was like living in the Old West in a thriving goldmining town's bubble economy. Psycho Loco customized his van. Scoby bought a car and every jazz CD on his extensive list. Joe Shenanigans moved to Brooklyn and tried to join the Mafia. Ms Sanchez went door-to-door selling jewelry at discount prices. No M. O. Clark got plastic surgery to remove his fingerprints. His hands looked like they'd been steamrolled, sanded down then varnished. He got a kick out of harassing the palm readers on Hollywood Boulevard.

I refused any payment for my part in The Heist. I had wanted only to satisfy my curiosity, not fence gold bars and pray that the money I was spending was untraceable.

I spent the last two weeks of my sixteenth summer away at camp, not shooting rapids and learning Indian folk songs, but shooting baskets and learning when to double-down and give weak-side help.

GRANTA

HOME IS HERE NOW

Los Angeles Times, 17 January 1995

DAVID XIAO

Kobe after the earthquake, January 1995   HARUYOSHI YAMAGUCHI/SYGMA

My wife and I were lying in bed, watching a CNN update on the Kobe earthquake. The newscaster, Bernard Shaw, said that the body of an American woman had just been found. June gasped, then quickly covered her mouth.

'It's not her,' I whispered, but June held up her hand and pointed to the screen, which was showing the same footage it had been showing for the past few days: the freeway that had tipped on to its side; houses everywhere going up in flames; women wandering through the debris-filled streets, screaming into the rubble of what had once been their homes.

I was not trying to put on a brave face when I told June that the woman they uncovered was not our daughter. I meant it. I truly believed that Bernard Shaw couldn't possibly be talking about Angela, in part because I foolishly assumed that the Japanese authorities would have contacted us before they talked to CNN. But mostly it was because I just had a feeling that Angela and her room-mate had escaped the worst of the quake and were safe in their tiny apartment overlooking Osaka Bay.

'She's probably trying to reach us right now to tell us everything's OK,' I said. But June had picked up our phone and was trying, for the hundredth time that day, to get through to our daughter. I watched her frantically hitting the redial button. 'I tell you she's fine,' I said. Then I leaned across the bed and whispered, 'Hasn't Angela always been lucky?'

'I'm on the phone!' June shouted. But of course she wasn't getting through. No one was getting through.

It was just after eleven o'clock. I switched over to the local news. The anchorperson, Marsha Runyon, was grimly announcing what CNN had already reported—that the body of an American had just been found—adding that her station's on-the-ground reporters were looking into this late-breaking story and would provide us with more details as soon as they could. Marsha was my favourite Seattle newscaster. She was less effusive than the others, and at times seemed almost reluctant to appear on the screen. While the other anchors were yapping away like tiresome little dogs, Marsha would keep her chin down and stare intently at the sheets of paper gripped tightly in her hands. Her face was long and bony, as if the news of the world was eating her up inside.

Marsha was, I thought, a steel-eyed professional with a heart of glass, and I found this combination attractive. But as I watched her talking about my daughter (although at the time I did not know she was talking about my daughter), I suddenly felt a terrible rage boiling up inside me. Marsha looked different—her pursed lips and grim eyes, which I had once found so alluring, now seemed like an act. I even detected a hint of glee running under her deliberately pained expression, as if she was saying: 'This story has become more important now; it is no longer just about the Japanese.'

June had given up on trying to get through to Kobe. Frustrated, she slammed the phone down, hit her pillow a few times, then slumped back and jerked the blankets over her face. 'Turn off the lights,' she said curtly.

The bedroom lights weren't even on. I assumed she must have meant the light from the television. But I couldn't bring myself to switch off the set. Perhaps I was hoping that Marsha would tell me something new, or perhaps I was waiting for her to apologize for thinking that a dead American was nothing more than a local angle on a foreign disaster story. I don't know why I couldn't switch off the television.

'Why did we let her go?' my wife said, her voice muffled by the blankets. I hit the mute button on the remote. 'This wouldn't have happened if she was here,' she added.

But this wasn't true, I thought. The local news had been reporting that Seattle might be hit by its own devastating quake any day now, pointing out the fault lines running through Puget Sound, suggesting it could have just as easily been our highways toppling over, our houses burning, our women screaming.

I could hear June sobbing underneath the blankets. I reached out to try and comfort her, but pulled my hand back at the last moment. What I really wanted was for her to reach out and touch me.

I clicked the sound back on and heard Marsha Runyon reminding us that Kobe was Seattle's sister city. I turned off the set. But I couldn't lie down and cover my eyes like June. Instead I stared at the afterglow of the screen and suddenly thought of another reason why the body they had found could not be our daughter's. If it had been Angela, CNN and Marsha wouldn't have said: 'An American was found dead.' They would have said: 'The body of a Chinese-American was found.' It still makes me sick when I think about this. On the worst night of my life, I was still listening for those superficial identifications, the way I always have.

Marsha Runyon came to our house the following morning. By then we had already been told about Angela. The call came in the middle of the night. It was Linda, Angela's room-mate, who told us that our daughter was dead.

Marsha and her news crew piled out of their big white van and sauntered across our lawn. Through the screen door, Marsha asked me if I could say a few words about our daughter. 'Mr Tam, why did Angela go to Japan?' But I did not answer her and tried as hard as I could not to look at the camera. 'Get a translator over here,' Marsha shouted to one of her crew, and then she began gesturing to me with her hands. I slammed the door in her face and did not open it when she rang our doorbell again, twenty minutes later, with a young Asian-American woman standing behind her.

Our daughter, as I had told June, had always been lucky. By that I don't mean that Angela was merely fortunate—that she lived in a nice house in an exclusive suburban neighbourhood and had parents who could afford to send her to Cornell and buy her a Toyota Celica for her seventeenth birthday. No, Angela was truly lucky. Back when she was just thirteen months old, our daughter fell out of a second-storey window and landed face down on the narrow concrete pathway surrounding our house. She wasn't even bruised. I was there. I saw it. I had parked my car on the street in front of the house and was changing the radiator coolant and engine oil, as I always did at that time of the year. Angela was watching me from her bedroom window. The only word my baby knew how to say at the time was 'Ba', and she repeated it over and over again as I worked on the Buick. 'Ba ba ba ba ba ba ba,' she squealed, and whenever I stuck my head out from underneath the car, she would raise her arms and wave to me.

I remember thinking that this was as happy as I would ever be, that my life had become almost too good to be true. But as I was waiting for the last few drops of oil to drain from the crankcase, I had a sudden premonition that she was going to fall out of the window. In my mind, as clearly as if I had seen it with my own eyes, I saw Angela tumble to the ground and lie there like a broken doll. But the worst part was: I felt that there was nothing I could do to prevent it from happening. I did not scoot out from under the car and dash towards the house like I should have done; instead, I froze, like an iceman caught in an ancient avalanche, staring mutely at the grimy black oil dripping into the catch pan.

Angela did not make any sound as she fell from the window, but I heard her hit the ground. Only then did I slide out from underneath the Buick. My baby was lying face down on the concrete path, silent and motionless. 'Stop!' I screamed, as I held my arms out and sprinted across the lawn. I was running as fast as I could, but it felt as if I was moving through water. And I remember thinking that it was already too late, that everything in the world was already too late.

But then Angela suddenly began to cry, wailing away at the top of her lungs. It was the most beautiful sound I have ever heard. My baby shrieked as loud as she could, just as she had done the night she was born.

I slid on the narrow pathway, cutting my palm on the edge of the concrete, then crawled over to my daughter's side and ran my hands over her little body, searching for broken bones. Angela tried to sit up, but I held her down. She screamed and screamed and screamed.

Nothing was broken as far as I could tell, but of course I still had to take her to the hospital to make sure. June was not at home, and the front wheels of my car were still resting on jack stands, so I carried Angela over to our neighbour's house and asked Mrs Gunderson to take us to the emergency ward at Harborview. As we were driving across the floating bridge out of Mercer Island, Angela suddenly stopped crying and buried her face in my chest. I could smell my blood on her dress. Mrs Gunderson honked her horn and began reciting the Lord's Prayer, but I knew that everything would be just fine—my girl was holding on to me almost as hard as I was holding on to her. I knew that we were going to be safe.

A gentle rain began to fall. The water on the south side of
the bridge was choppy and latticed; to our right it was completely
calm. And by the time we pulled into the hospital Angela was
smiling and cooing 'Ba ba ba ba' again. Mrs Gunderson turned
to me and said, 'The Lord certainly had His hand out today.' My
neighbour and I belong to the same church, although she attends
services regularly and I don't. 'Jesus knows when every sparrow
falls, doesn't He, Harry?'

June was not so easy on me. 'You left her alone in the house
with all the windows open!' she screamed. 'What kind of a father
are you?'

I promised June that I would never let anything like that happen
again, and so for the next twenty years I tried to give our
daughter all the protection a parent can. If being a good father
means keeping a close eye on your child, then I can honestly say
that I tried my best. By the time Angela was a teenager, young
suitors would show up at our house, and I would drive them
away, one by one. This was the sad pattern of her adolescence on
Mercer Island. I would not let any of those unsuitable boys, and
there were many, come anywhere near my daughter unless they
had gone through me first. Every how-to book I have ever read
says that this is not a wise thing for a parent to do.

Bart Roberts was the first boy I had to get rid of. He was
seventeen years old when he started coming after my daughter,
who was only fourteen at the time. Bart was a racist, I thought,
although his father would not have agreed. 'How can my son be
a racist if he wants to date your daughter?' he would have asked.

John and I both worked over at Boeing. John designed
guidance systems for fighter-bombers, while I worked on ways to
defeat them. We had dealt with each other for many years. I
thought we had an understanding.

'Boys just gotta be boys,' he said. I suppose men can afford
to feel this way about their sons.

'My girl's too young to be involved with anyone,' I replied.

'Come on, Tam, she's not a baby anymore. Angela's a smart
little lady; she can take care of herself.'

I think John was waiting for me to say something similar

about Bart, but I didn't. John had no idea how much I detested his son. One day, as I was walking home from the video store on Crest Drive, I saw Bart and three of his loutish friends cruise by in an old Mercedes. They zipped past me and then stopped at a red light a few yards ahead. All the car windows were rolled down, and the boys were playing loud music that I dimly recognized, probably because Angela played it too. The air seemed to shake. I had a feeling that they were either drunk or stoned. And although I knew who three of those four boys were, or at least I knew their names and what their fathers did for a living, I was trembling as I approached that battered Mercedes. It was the same kind of fear I had felt back when I was an engineering student and was walking past Greek Row on a Friday night with an armful of books and technical manuals, head bent to avoid the beer bottles the fraternity boys would have hurled down from their balconies if any of them had actually been sober enough to see me walking by.

The light turned just before I reached the intersection, and as the Mercedes started to peel off, Bart stuck his head out the rear side window and shouted, 'What about Sony?' It was the line RCA used in their commercial, urging Americans to buy their sets rather than ones made in Japan. And Bart said it in the same gruff, Japanese-prison-camp-commandant voice employed in the ad, as well as in a hundred Hollywood movies. Maybe he wouldn't have said it if he had recognized me; perhaps he thought that I was someone else, someone who didn't belong in this neighbourhood and therefore didn't warrant the considerations of normal etiquette. (Bart and his friends probably couldn't imagine that I, or anyone else living on Mercer Island, would actually go somewhere on foot rather than by car.) But that just made what Bart did seem even worse. The fact that he had said what he said to someone he thought was a stranger suggested things to me about his true nature. There wasn't some debased, written philosophy behind his gesture; he was merely repeating something he had heard on television. He said it casually, flippantly, as if he couldn't help himself. And it wasn't personal, either; it was just part of the ambience of America.

John probably wouldn't have made much of his son's

wisecrack, which is why I didn't bother to tell him about it. I knew he would dismiss it as some silly teenage prank, and might even suggest that I was being overly sensitive. Which I am, of course.

'They're kids, for Christ's sake,' John protested after I had pestered him for the tenth time about Bart and Angela. 'By this time next year the two of them probably will have forgotten each other.'

But I knew this wouldn't be true, at least not for Angela. My daughter would always remember the time she spent with Bart— if I had let her. I knew she would always remember that boy, even if she never saw him again after their first date. Angela was that kind of girl. In that way, she and I are very much alike. We both have a tendency to hold on to things, probably longer than we should. I knew Angela would remember her first love, just as I can still clearly remember mine.

I was only twelve years old, and so was she. (I know that sounds very young, but back then people in China got married a lot sooner than they do now. I knew boys who were only thirteen or fourteen, yet already had children of their own.) The girl I once loved would go down to the river every morning and scoop out two buckets of water for her family to use, and she would pass by our house on her way back home even though it was out of her way. I used to sit by my bedroom window and wait for her. And when I leaned out the window and asked her if she needed any help, she would wrinkle her nose at me and say, 'What good can you do, turnip head?'

I didn't even know her name. I thought the two of us could carry on like this forever, and that our little exchanges were something we would end up telling our children and grandchildren about. That girl, that sixty-four-year-old woman, is probably still in China. Maybe she's still living in Danpeng, with a man I can only imagine. I left China at the age of fourteen, when a Catholic missionary sponsored my passage to America. I haven't been back since. Home is here now.

I never saw any reason to tell June or Angela about this girl. It was such a long time ago, and it happened so far, far away. I never told my wife or daughter anything about China. Neither of them had ever been there; neither of them spoke the language; neither of them could really have understood what I was talking about. And yet, over the past fifty years, not a day has gone by when I haven't thought about that girl, even if just for a second. And there have been mornings when I have actually stood next to my bedroom window and imagined her passing by.

I didn't want to give Angela the chance to fall in love with a boy like Bart. I didn't want someone like him to loom in my daughter's mind for the rest of her life. So I took Angela out of Mercer Island High, where she and Bart both went to school, and enrolled her in a Catholic school in Seattle. I felt good knowing that the priests and nuns at St Joseph's Academy would be keeping an eye on my daughter by day, and I by night. This was perfect, I thought.

But Angela hated St Joseph's. And June didn't like it either. 'Those nuns give me the creeps,' she said, so I lied and told her that the admissions director at Princeton was a graduate of St Joe's. (These things do matter.)

'Isn't it a little early to be planning for college?' June asked.

'I'm just thinking about our girl's future,' I replied.

Bart, as it turned out, was a lot easier to deal with than some of the other boys who followed in his footsteps. Bart gave up on Angela shortly after she transferred to St Joseph's—like his father had said: there never was anything serious between them. Some of the other boys were much more persistent. One of them, Vincent Brown, managed to sneak a photograph of himself to Angela despite my repeated warnings to him to stay away from my daughter. I found his picture in Angela's drawer. It was disgusting. Vincent had pulled down his pants and was sticking his ass up in the air, mooning a stick-figure drawing of a man I knew was supposed to be me. Yet I have to admit that I was actually glad when I first saw this photograph—I figured Angela would never want to go out with Vincent now, not after he had insulted her own father like that. But this was not how my daughter thought. This is not how any sixteen-year-old American girl thinks.

June was always telling me that I behaved like an old-fashioned Chinese father—a priest and a policeman rolled into one. 'Why is this?' she asked. 'You didn't live in China that long.'

June thought that we should just let our daughter be herself—let the girl see whomever she wanted—but I just could not allow this to happen. Perhaps I am just like my father, who, so many years ago, forbade me to ever speak to that girl in Danpeng. 'Her family's beneath us,' he said. And I listened.

Angela would mope and sulk after I had extinguished another of her teenage romances, but in due course she would revert to her usual self. It was amazing how quickly she was able to regain her bearings and resume life with her old enthusiasm, with the same intense curiosity that would serve her so well during her years at Cornell (as it turned out, the admissions director at Cornell was an alumnus of St Joseph's) and inspired her to go off to Japan. It was probably these same qualities that had entranced Bart and Vincent and all the other boys, although at the time I thought they were interested in my daughter only because she was Chinese. I thought they saw my girl as some kind of trophy, an exotic creature who would employ the mysterious ways of the East to keep them up all night long and then get up and make them breakfast. I had my reasons for thinking this way. I had had Caucasian men wink at me after I showed them a photograph of June. 'How lucky you are!' I thought they were saying—in an obscene way. Perhaps I was just being paranoid, but perhaps I wasn't; I have seen the way middle-aged Caucasians gawk and drool at all the contestants in the annual Miss Chinatown Pageant, something unnatural in their eyes as they follow the girls down the runway. Those white men should never have been allowed in. They had no business being there.

Perhaps I am the racist here. But I had my reasons for thinking the way I did. It was not a casual feeling; I felt it in my bones.

Not once did I ask Angela how she felt about Bart Roberts, or Vincent Brown, or Jonathan Merck, or Raymond Harris, or all the other white boys she had tried to fall for. I was never good at talking about these things, although there was one night when the two of us came close. I had gone into Angela's room to ask her something. She was sitting on her bed, reading a book.

There were posters of rock singers and television stars

plastered all over the walls. I once thought about picking out some different posters for her, from Chinatown, but I couldn't think of anyone she would like. Bruce Lee was the only person who came to mind, but he was dead—buried right here in Seattle. And Bruce Lee never was a girl's kind of man; his steel-eyed glances were an expression of power and vengeance, there was nothing romantically inviting about them. It was boys, not girls, who dreamed about Bruce Lee's perfectly honed body. Besides, the Hollywood people who made *Enter the Dragon* had made sure that he remained celibate throughout the film. Bruce could take his shirt off—and he did it a lot—but his pants were another matter.

Angela was engrossed in her book. She lay on her bed, completely still, resting one long bare leg on top of the other. Angela was reading *Out of Africa*. And as I stood at the foot of her bed, watching her read about a woman who had transformed herself by leaving home, I finally saw why so many boys were interested in my daughter. It was quite simple, really: Angela was a beautiful young woman. I suppose I had always known, but this was the first time I had actually seen it.

'Why don't you ever go out with Chinese boys?' I blurted.

'What do you mean?'

I misheard her question. I thought she said 'Who do you mean,' so I replied, 'There's John Wang, Paul Chin, Yang Fung, and Joe and Ellie's son . . . '

'Please.'

'Why not?' I asked, and suddenly realized that my short list of names was the sum total of all the Chinese boys who lived on Mercer Island and that except for Yang, who never dated anyone, I had never seen any of those boys with Chinese girls.

'They're kind of ugly, Dad.'

'How can you say that?'

'Never mind.'

'No!' I shouted. 'Tell me what you mean!'

'Why are you doing this?' she shouted back.

'Answer me!'

Angela placed her book down on the night stand. 'Just forget I said anything, OK?' Then she got up and tried to walk past me. I was about to let her go, but then she said the words I had hoped she would never say, but which, deep down, I had always expected her to.

'If you wanted me to date Chinese boys,' Angela sneered, 'you should have just stayed in China with the rest of them.'

I grabbed my daughter's arm and began jerking her across the room, inflamed by the rage of someone who feels that everything has been taken away from him. And then, I swear, for the first and only time in my life, I hit my baby. I saw my fist move through the air but I could not stop it.

Angela landed face up on the bed. Her long straight hair cascaded across her face and fell through the crack of her lips. My daughter lay there and looked up at me for a second, her eyes filled with terror, and then she began to cry.

The regular telephone lines into Kobe opened up two days after Marsha Runyon had tried to tape our reaction to Angela's death. June called the shelter at Kobe University and spoke to Linda, our daughter's room-mate, for about half an hour. She asked Linda if she needed anything from us and invited her to stay at our home if she was ever in Seattle. My wife also asked Linda about the facilities in the shelter, and if there were a lot of men sleeping there. They sounded like mother and daughter. June offered me the receiver halfway through their conversation, but I shook my head and walked away.

It was night here when I finally picked up the phone and called the municipal office in Kobe. I wanted to make the arrangements for Angela's return.

'Sorry, cannot do this,' the man said to me in broken English.

'I'll pay for everything,' I said. 'Just put her on the next plane.'

'Sorry. Body cannot fly. Must first be burnt.'

'No!' I shouted. 'You put my daughter on a plane right now and send her back to me in one piece!'

'Must be burnt. Health reason.'

I wanted to tell him that I was someone important, that I once knew how to render entire air forces blind, but instead I said, 'You cannot cremate her. We are Christians; our religion does not allow that.' This was a lie, of course.

'It is to stop sickness we burn bodies,' the man replied.

'Then embalm my daughter—preserve her, you know—and send her back later, in one piece, when things return to normal.'

'No facility. Sorry.'

'No facilities!' I screamed, 'What are you talking about? This is Japan, not Africa!'

'No facility now.' I could tell he was getting increasingly exasperated with me—he was beginning to sound like that Japanese voice on the RCA commercial.

It was hopeless. There was nothing I could do to get him to change his mind. And the man in Kobe was just doing his job; he had probably spoken to thousands of fathers, but they would have talked in their own language, using words they knew intimately. 'Please,' I whispered, and then I suddenly began to cry.

There was a long pause. We listened to each other breathe. Finally, the man said, 'I am sorry.'

I telephoned the State Department, as well as the American embassy in Tokyo, to see if they could stop the cremation. I also called my senator and congresswoman, and even tried to reach President Clinton through the Internet, but they all said the same thing: they were sorry, but this was a Japanese matter.

'You're making things worse by carrying on like this,' June said. 'What difference does it make how she comes back now?'

But it would make a difference to me, I wanted to tell her. It didn't matter if Angela's body had been damaged in the earthquake; I wanted all of her right there in front of me. I wanted to see our daughter one more time. I just wanted to touch her. And I was petrified that Angela's ashes might get mixed up with someone else's. Dust is dust—who could tell?

My brother was killed during the war with Japan. His remains were never recovered. We never even got his ashes back. Ying-wai left Danpeng on 3 June 1944, and I never saw him again. Like most of the million-and-a-half teenage soldiers who died for China during those terrible years, my brother was left where he fell and has long since dissolved into the earth. Our family wasn't even notified of his death. It was that kind of war. We heard the news from a soldier who straggled back from the front and showed us a small piece of cloth which he said belonged to my brother. My father and I didn't know whether to believe him or not. But my mother shrieked as soon as she saw that blue rag.

Japanese soldiers arrived in Danpeng in the summer of 1945, just two months before the war ended. The Japanese army was on its last legs, but their defeat had come too late for us. The invaders, who, I later found out, were actually fleeing for their lives, showed up in our town without tanks or trucks or air cover. We did not hear them coming. The first soldiers to enter the town seemed more bewildered than anything else. Those young men did not look like the animals I imagined they would be; they looked just like us, like my brother and his comrades. But by mid-morning more and more Japanese soldiers began pouring into town. They stormed through the streets of Danpeng, kicking down doors and dragging young women and boys and furniture out of our homes. My mother lunged at them after they burst into our house and grabbed me, but my father quickly pulled her back and wrapped his arms around her, covering up her mouth. I understood perfectly well why my father did that—he was trying to protect the only thing he had left. But I thought that I would never be able to forgive him for not even pretending to try saving me.

The soldiers dragged me and seven other boys to the town square. They pointed at the ground and motioned for us to sit down. As we were sitting there, waiting, a platoon walked by, and the soldiers began sharpening their bayonets against the edge of a wall. The eight of us were crying the way thirteen-year-old boys cry: with clenched fists and through clenched teeth, a terrible mixture of fear, rage and embarrassment. All of a sudden, a Chinese man in a black uniform—a translator for the Japanese— walked over and told us that we would be sent to Yulaukok, a small village north of Danpeng. An important general was going to use the village as his command centre, and we were to go there and clean it up for him first. Two soldiers would accompany us to the village, the translator said. He warned us not to try to escape, and reminded us that the Japanese soldiers knew where our families lived.

It took us three hours to reach Yulaukok. We could smell

the village before we reached it. I can't even begin to describe the stench, but all of us knew what it was.

The entire village was filled with dead bodies, most of them dumped outside the houses. Most of the corpses had turned grey, some were brown and a few had exploded in the heat.

'Take them there,' a soldier said, pointing to a ravine cutting across a nearby field. 'Burn them all.'

So the eight of us began dragging these bodies out of the village and, one by one, rolled them down into the ravine. Then we went back and tore the thatch off people's roofs and used it to build a fire. And after the thatch ran out we found some kerosene stored inside a shed and poured that on to the pile. There were three thousand bodies in Yulaukok. It took us three days and three nights to burn them all. I thought the odour would never come off me.

On the fourth morning, two other boys and I escaped into the surrounding hills.

Japan did not mean the same thing to Angela as it did to me. And why should it? To her, Japan was the land of Sony and Toyota and random-access-memory chips—and she was absolutely right to think that way. The country has changed and is changing still. What I remember about the Japanese happened a long time ago, in a world that Angela and June and most people I know know nothing about.

'The future is being made there right now,' Angela told me, as she was filling out the forms that would enable her to live and work in Kobe. 'I want to be in the middle of it all, and see it with my own eyes.' Her enthusiasm was charming. 'It's the beginning of the Pacific Century, Dad; things are going to be different.' Then she lowered her voice and whispered, 'No one will ever call us gooks and get away with it.'

She was still young but perhaps she was right; I don't know. But as I was listening to her talk about her plans, I finally understood that it was the right place for her to be and that I should let her go. To Angela, Japan was a land of optimism. And who doesn't want his child to remain optimistic for as long as she can?

My biggest regret is that I never told Angela about anything that was really close to my heart. I never told her about my brother, or my father or my mother, or the girl who carried two buckets of water past my home every morning. I never told Angela about the time she fell from the bedroom window; or about the three days and nights I spent in Yukaukok; of how I ran away on the fourth morning and found, when I got home, that my parents had disappeared. I kept this all to myself, and through my silence thought that I could protect her from the things that I had wanted to forget, things that I had no use for any more. But maybe Angela would have found a way to talk about these things if I had been willing to give it to her. Unlike me, maybe she could have made something of it.

I am glad it was Linda, not Bernard Shaw or Marsha Runyon or some bureaucrat in Kobe, who told us that our daughter was dead. Linda is not a stranger. June and I had spoken to her on the phone several times. We have photographs of her and Angela together in Japan, sitting in their tiny apartment or smiling as they waved from the Awaji Island lookout. But when the phone rang at three o'clock that morning, I did not recognize Linda's voice. All I heard was a young woman whispering to me from the other side of the world, the signal bouncing off a satellite floating high above in space.

The other morning, June and I were leafing through our daughter's photo album.

'What was your happiest day of her life?' my wife asked.

I thought about this for a moment, and then told her about the time Angela fell out of her bedroom window. June remembers that day quite differently, of course, but she listened calmly to every word I said. And afterwards, she leaned her head against my shoulder and closed her eyes. I felt a strange sense of peace, the kind that comes from an unspoken forgiveness for things that could not have been avoided in the first place. I reached out and began stroking her hair. Neither of us looked at the porcelain urn resting on the mantel. The two of us just sat there on our living room sofa, quietly, like the comfortable old couple we have become.

211

**TRULY TINY
GARDENS**
Thomasina Tarling
£12.99

**QUAGLINO'S:
THE COOKBOOK**
*Richard Whittington
& Martin Webb*
£14.99

**COLIN SPENCER'S
VEGETABLE BOOK**
Colin Spencer
£20.00

**THE ESSENTIAL
HOUSE BOOK**
Terence Conran
£25.00

**NATURAL
DECORATING**
*Elizabeth Wilhide
& Joanna Copestick*
£16.99

**TRICIA GUILD
ON COLOUR**
Tricia Guild
£12.99

Conran Octopus

THE LAWYER'S STORY

AMANDA ALIC

PAUL THEROUX

Hoyt Maybry was calling aliens 'fruit pickers' again, though I could not imagine a better name than aliens. He was describing them with breathless, unsmiling praise in a tone that was a little too reasonable not to be sarcastic. Talkative people tend to be awful drivers. He was impulsive and distracted behind the wheel, gunning the engine and braking hard and muttering at other cars.

We were stuck in traffic in front of the old Harborfront Tower near the Maidan where our former offices were being gutted.

In the back seat, Kinglet Chee said, 'What's that wood panelling in there—teak?'

'Mahogany,' Hoyt said.

'Good for salvage,' Kinglet said.

'Insure it and burn it,' Hoyt said.

'How would you deal with the claim?'

'Mug them with a rusty razor,' Hoyt said. 'Give them paper in return for bureaucrap.'

Kinglet said, 'So what do you think, Mr Grillo?'

'Seems a little rash,' I said.

'This isn't the Peace Corps, Grillo,' Hoyt said. 'Be a lawyer.'

Bow tie, blue shirt, tight suit, cowboy boots—he was over-dressed for Singapore, but that was his image, corporate, with Santa Fe accessories: his watch on a silver bracelet, a turquoise stone on a silver ring, a silver bear-claw belt buckle, tooled boots, a racy monogram on the shirt. It was Hoyt's intention that when you saw him you did not think lawyer. He wore aviator glasses. He chewed gum. Hoyt's gum seemed more obnoxious than the cigarettes it replaced. He had a motorcycle too. When we skied, as we did each January in Telluride, Hoyt wore a black leather biker's jacket with a skull and crossbones airbrushed on the back. You did not notice all these things at once, but over time they became obvious and important. Another thing: today his thumb was bandaged.

'Just incredible,' Hoyt said, changing the subject back to the United States. 'You want to know the reason for this miracle of social engineering. Is it money?'

Hoyt had just returned to Singapore from San Diego, the run we called the shuttle. Kinglet was on his way there—same deal, the Southern Tech joint venture, the funding for the off-shore assembly of their third-generation memory chip, a very big deal; 'our blue chip,' Hoyt called it. From this chip and Kinglet Chee's confidence he expected to make almost eight hundred thousand dollars. But there was first the matter of Kinglet's American visa to attend to at the embassy.

'My parents were wealthy,' Hoyt said. 'What does that make me? Just a lucky sperm. I was a lucky sperm, weren't you?'

Kinglet Chee's silence was the Chinese answer to a leading question. He lowered his window to see the condemned building better, and into the car rushed a Singapore gust of fried noodles, the eggy stink of sweated chicken meat, the coal-tar tang of soy sauce and the grit of street dust, with yakking voices and hot steamy air. Singapore looked tidy but it stank of its wealth—car fumes, the reek of its busy harbour. Its gases were like complaints and errors. You could bottle them and give them to someone to snort and he would straightaway know the city intimately and see it as a failure.

Hoyt inhaled and made a face and said, 'The thing you have to remember about a tiny city state like Singapore is that it is something between a summer camp and a small town. In other words, a penal colony with superior facilities. Name another country where you actually get spanked for doing something wrong.'

He slammed on his brakes and cursed and hit his knee against the steering column. This impulsiveness and overreaction made him accident-prone. He fumbled things and dropped them. I had never known a lawyer who had sustained so many hard-to-explain stitches. That bandage on his thumb was typical. It was wrong to ask.

'Your fruit picker is always so small, so dark, so silent—so necessary,' Hoyt said.

Kinglet winced. 'I could send one of my men in to remove the panelling,' he said tentatively.

Ignoring him, Hoyt said, 'On my way to, um, Tom Bradley Airport in Los Angeles, I remembered how back in ninety-two I saw smoke rising from South Central—the LA riot. Oh, sorry, did I call it a riot? I meant to say a disturbance. At the time I got sad

215

and thought, "What is this place coming to that they're incinerating inner-city commercial space and tying up freeway traffic?" But if I witnessed something like that again I would feel that it was a legitimate expression of social discontent. It's a kind of eloquence. Gunfire from a high-calibre automatic is a statement with an American accent.'

'Or even remove it myself,' Kinglet said. 'I like to keep busy on the weekends. And that old detail is great. What do you call it? Urban archaeology?'

There is single-mindedness bordering on obsession in people who are able to ignore someone's interruptive questions as they are talking. Hoyt was like that. He could not be sidetracked. Yet he filed the question away. When he was finished with what he had to say he would reply to the question he had been asked ten minutes ago, with a verbal efficiency that bordered on rudeness.

Chewing for emphasis, as he used to puff smoke for emphasis, Hoyt was unstoppably monologuing about what he had seen in America: the teenagers with rings in their nose, the youths with their caps on backwards, the welfare mothers with their many children, the panhandlers, and more—the president, the politicians, the liberals, the guns, the traffic, the aliens.

'We have to do more for these unfortunate people,' Hoyt said.

He sounded forceful and indignant and a bit strident. His tone might have confused Kinglet, though it was impossible to tell what his silence meant.

I turned to Hoyt and asked, 'What's it like to be back?'

'I can't express it in words,' Hoyt said.

Hoyt could be pleasant but was not a naturally humorous man and so when he laughed, his laugh seemed whinnying and insincere, more like a loud gloating that matched his aggressive and unsmiling sarcasm.

Kinglet replied by suggesting he go to Harborfront Tower on Sunday. Just detach the panels from the walls and stack them for removal.

On this recent trip, Hoyt said, he had run into Indians—'dot Indians, not feather Indians'—in airports. You had to understand their patriotism, he said, in order to know why they cut in front of him and pushed and shoved. Their children had grown huge and clumsy on American food. They were happy in America.

'Hey, now and then you hear of a wealthy old widow who takes in a tramp, thinking that he will be grateful to her and that her kindness will do him some good. She takes pity on the unfortunate down-and-out. I think the word is "outreach". And the tramp rapes and kills her and goes on living in her house.'

The traffic had begun to move. Hoyt drove on, snapping his gum.

Kinglet stared at him, the smooth mask of his face a challenge to say more.

'If paying for ambitious social programmes is the price of progress, isn't the answer, "Pay"?' He was driving with a fixed grin and staring eyes. 'Surely "lots of money" is the meaning of the word "proactive".'

At last, stirred by this, Kinglet said, 'But it's your money.'

'I was wondering whether you were listening. Of course it's my money.'

'Maybe it's a waste,' Kinglet said, his tentative voice trailing off.

Hoyt found his client's face in the rear-view mirror and said, 'It's an investment in the future. Isn't it, Grillo?'

'Whatever you say.' I hated Hoyt in this mood.

'Oh, it shouldn't take more than a few hours to strip it off,' Kinglet said. I looked back and saw that he was smiling. 'I could go over with a crowbar and a claw hammer.'

At the American Embassy, Hoyt swerved into Visitors' Parking and, cursing an oncoming car, scraped a post. Hurrying to get out, his confusion rising, he opened his door too hard and dinged the next car. He was in a terrible mood when inside he asked for the consular officer, Victor Scavola.

'He will be out just now,' the Chinese receptionist said.

'He will be out shortly,' Hoyt said, correcting her by biting his words with white precise teeth. His hands were two fists which he held by his side like pistols.

There were other people waiting for visas or interviews— Indonesians, Chinese, Malays, Filipinos, Indians, Thais, Vietnamese. Hoyt said nothing. He sized them up. He winked at the portrait of the smiling American president.

He turned to Kinglet and said, 'Are you insured?'

Kinglet Chee smiled a bit carelessly, as though the question was ridiculous. Before Hoyt could say anything else, Victor Scavola appeared, pink-faced, in a tight white shirt and blue tie and plastic picture-ID badge pinned to his breast pocket. In his chubby hand he held Kinglet's file and ignored us while he looked through it.

'Before I issue this visa I want to remind you that as the holder of a Tongan passport you have one month, and when your time is up you must exit the United States. This is non-renewable. Do you understand, Mr Chee?'

Hoyt said, 'Given the present situation in the States it's easy to understand why he would want to stay a lot longer. Maybe get proactive.'

'No problem,' Kinglet said in a submissive, peace-making tone.

Scavola sighed and stamped the passport and scribbled on it. I sneaked a look at it. I had not realized Kinglet carried a Tongan passport. Tonga was—what? A little coconut kingdom somewhere in the vast Pacific?

'A lot of people do overstay,' Scavola said.

Hoyt laughed in his whinnying, gloating way.

On the way back to the office Hoyt said, 'There's a certain fragrance in the air. The sea. The sky. The flowers. There's a kind of energy. No, it is not hysteria.' He raised his eyes at Kinglet in the rear-view mirror. 'This is my home. Get some insurance, Mr Chee.'

Kinglet smiled the Chinese smile of bewilderment and uneasiness and incomprehension.

'Because if you get injured you might sue us.'

'I would never do that.'

Hoyt laughed; it was the instinctive reflex of a lawyer hearing the word 'never'.

'You might have to sue us,' he said.

'Help him with that,' I said, seeing Kinglet fidget, as though he had been insulted.

'It's a no-brainer.'

'Take him through it, Hoyt.'

'You trip, you fall, you sustain severe trauma to the base of the skull, you're paralysed from the neck down, you've got the reflexes of a beanbag, and there's a loophole in your policy big enough to drive a truck through. Plus, you're on a respirator. Round-the-clock nursing. Your medical bills hit seven figures. You're desperate. You don't want to sue me, but you have no choice. You take legal advice. You have no money. There is only one course of action. Sue.'

The logic of this was irrefutable.

'So put a rider on your policy and you're welcome to salvage anything you like from the old office.'

K inglet returned from San Diego just before Christmas, when Singapore was thick with Santa Clauses—sleighs, fake snow, reindeer on the walls and roofs of hotels and office buildings; lights were strung along Orchard Road and reflected in the Singapore River; carols were played as elevator music.

Hoyt said, 'I like Christmas this way,' and I could not tell whether it was more of his gloating sarcasm. He gave his annual party, and it was grander than usual. Alison, his eldest child, had returned from her college in Oregon. She said, 'Daddy bought me a new Jeep Cherokee!' When Hoyt and I talked about having had a good year and began to tot up our earnings, profit-sharing and bonuses, Hoyt said, 'There's more to come. We just need a few signatures.'

He meant Kinglet Chee's joint-venture contract, the memory-chip project. Just after New Year, Kinglet closed the deal. We held a partner's meeting and were told of our bonuses. Hoyt's share was a million-eight.

'You think that's a lot of money,' Hoyt said. We were in his office, the two of us. He scowled at me. 'That is not a lot of money. Not in my tax bracket.'

Was he being sarcastic again? A million-eight was much more than he had been expecting.

'But this is something else,' he said.

He eased the door shut. His scowl softened and became a smile.

'This is tax-free,' he said.

It seemed to me a fool's smile, and yet he was confident and happy—I had never seen him happier.

'I'm not American any more,' he said. He was very nearly tearful with gladness. 'I handed my passport back. I'm a free man.'

2

'Some lawyers flatly deny who they are,' Hoyt said to me once, 'like those Germans in Florida who claim to be Swedish when they meet Jews on the golf course.'

When I joined the firm, Hoyt told me, 'You know how much a person matters in your life when you realize you're constantly quoting him.' I was struck by the truth of that, and the fact that I have just quoted him shows how much Hoyt mattered to me.

'You might have to sue,' was a Hoyt line that seemed like a precept. I once confessed to Hoyt that I had originally wanted to become a writer.

'What are writers?' Hoyt said to me. 'Know what? Words for sale! That's a writer!'

Hoyt was my partner, my client, my friend. I was with him when two of the other partners, Elfman and Warfield, mentioned renunciation of citizenship as a possible solution for him, and it was I who explained in detail the risk factors and the total downside.

Everyone says lawyers are the lowest form of life. We are green bubbly scum. Something happens to people's eyes when they utter the word 'lawyer', and they usually swallow hard afterwards. It is more self-consciously subtle than just blinking and gulping; it is the sort of cold glaze you see in the eyes of a cornered animal, gagging with fear. 'Attorney' sounds somehow worse, and even I have hesitated at times, muttered 'corporate counsel' or 'jurisprudence' or 'litigation', but never within earshot of Hoyt Maybry, the enemy of equivocation.

This widespread public perception is not entirely without foundation, and yet what the public does not seem to understand is that the true haters of lawyers are other lawyers. Warfield? Personal injury? After he won the settlement of seventy million for the blind smoker who lit the wrong end of his filter-tip cigarette and suffered severe trauma he became a pariah among other lawyers in Chicago and joined us in Singapore.

Ours was a busy firm. The day after our embassy run with Kinglet Chee, Elfman spent the morning in conference with a pharmaceutical firm that wanted to sell asthma inhalers in China. I had a sandwich at my desk while taking a deposition from a woman who had experienced sensory loss in the fingers of one hand after removing a jam-filled Wacky Cracker from a toaster. 'Overheated jam acts like napalm,' I wrote. In the waiting room a woman renegotiating her pre-nuptial agreement was telling Hoyt, 'A divorce after ten years means I am no longer viable on the marriage market. Either that's reflected in the settlement with fifty per cent, or I'm not signing.' Our local partner, Loong, had found a case in the *Chinese Gazette* which stated that the unique fold of the fortune cookie had been invented by a particular individual in China and proposed patenting them. It was Loong—not Hoyt—who said, 'A patent on the fortune cookie could have worldwide implications,' and wanted to beat the bushes to find this Chinese man and sign him up as a client.

Some lawyers ask for trouble. Yet Hoyt did not drive a white Rolls like Burton Elfman, whose vanity licence plate was lettered SUE EM. Why all the jokes? Like Hoyt, I cannot stand them: the imagery of death and rape, disgusting acts, horrible creatures, sharks, wolves, snakes, the sort of jokes that are told about despised minorities. 'What do you call twenty lawyers in a cesspool?' sent one of his twins, Mallory, home from school in tears. Hoyt said, 'Mal, get used to it, they're just ignorant,' and she sniffed and said, 'I told them you're a dentist, please back me up, Dad.'

Hoyt told me: 'God Almighty, for that alone I would have slapped a personal injury suit on the school, howled, "You're toast!" and gone to war—lien on the property, declaration and seizure of assets, whatever—except they would have said, "See? They're all like that!" and completely lost sight of my daughter's damage and emotional distress. I am not a dentist.'

When Hoyt described what happened at his renunciation appointment at the embassy, I could see it all clearly because we had been there together such a short time before.

Those Vietnamese and Indians and Malays and other hopeful people were still waiting in the vestibule of the consular section when Hoyt arrived. He did not pay much attention to them. The irony that they were eagerly awaiting the very same passport that Hoyt was on the verge of renouncing did not impress him. When I mentioned it, he said, 'Which of those fruit pickers was taking a tax hit on a million-eight?'

'So you didn't think anything when you saw them?'

'For the first time in my working life I didn't resent them,' he said. 'I knew I didn't have to pay their medical bills any more, or educate their kids, or listen to them bitch about affirmative action.'

I saw him fidgeting, knocking over a stack of leaflets as he snatched a magazine from a table. I saw him scowling at the seated people—no chair for him. I saw him winking at the president's picture.

Scavola appeared with witnesses. The witnesses goggled and seemed nervous, as though they were unwilling accomplices to an illegal act. It was an undramatic ceremony—paper shuffling, oaths, signatures, rubber stamps. The only detail that made it memorable, Hoyt said, was that a plump, dark secretary in a sari was eating some food she had hidden in her handbag. While Hoyt was signing the renunciation papers and swearing his oath, and witnesses were conferring, this Indian woman was reaching into her propped-open handbag and eating—prawn crackers, he thought, from the sound of them.

'Don't we have some rule about that?' Hoyt asked.

Scavola smiled, welcoming the comment and wanting more.

'Rule about what?'

'Eating on duty. She's a federal employee. She works for Uncle Sam.'

'You're not an American, Mr Maybry. It's no concern of yours.'

As he spoke he brought his hand down—a bit harder than was necessary, Hoyt thought—and stamped VOID on Hoyt's passport.

'One last document,' Scavola said. 'Raise your right hand.

Repeat after me. "I hereby renounce my citizenship of the United States of America, and all rights, obligations and privileges."'

Hoyt repeated the formula, sealing his renunciation.

Far from being the solemn ceremony he had expected, it was the sort of business that Hoyt always referred to as 'bureaucrap'. The fans were croaking, the paper fluttering, the stacks of files were sweat-stained, the Indian woman was still covertly munching prawn crackers out of the crackling cellophane wrapper in her bag, as Scavola said, 'I trust you are aware of the implications of this.' Hoyt hated him all the more for that 'I trust', a kind of wordy and meaningless pomposity that made Scavola seem even more stupid.

The paperwork was mostly signatures and initials. It was a legal act in which blanks had to be filled in on the standard forms. Horrible music was playing—someone's radio. They allowed this? It reminded Hoyt of his first divorce. His only annoyance was that he had found himself tapping his toe to the music.

'Afterwards I was the same person,' he said. 'Except happier. I knew I was free.'

Lighter, freer, stronger—but these were hard-to-define feelings. He felt in control. He felt liberated. He felt wealthier. In the days before income tax and welfare and parasitic fruit pickers and criminal rappers, he said, men must have felt just this way when they closed a deal and made a profit. The whole amount was theirs—a big chunk of cash. They had then been able to act more boldly—start a railroad or a steel mill, dig a canal, found a city.

'Grillo, that is a very American feeling.'

'But you're not an American, Hoyt.'

'I'm American,' he said, and then as though to a child he said slowly. 'But I'm not *an* American.'

I must have looked sceptical, because he then repeated it and said, 'You understand the difference between essence and status?'

'What did you do after you renounced it?' I asked.

But he had already streaked past my question.

'It's like the difference between the flag and a flag. You can't burn the flag. It is a large and noble symbol. But you can burn a flag. That's just a piece of cloth.'

'What flag are you talking about?'

'Ours. Stars and stripes. The American flag.'

'But it's not your flag. You're not an American.'

'Not an American.' He raised his shoulders and smiled. 'I'm American.' He dropped his shoulders. 'You call yourself a lawyer?'

He peered at me, pitying me for my stupidity, and then he answered the question I had asked a few minutes ago.

'I went back to work,' he said sharply.

He was impatient. I had missed the subtlety of his philosophical distinction.

'You have some idea that by giving up my US citizenship I dropped out of the world—just tuned out. Bye, everybody! No, I'm working harder than ever. I have never worked like this in my life. I feel pure, I feel strong. I am free.'

He said he had stayed late, and his saying it made me recall passing his office when I left and seeing him inside, tapping away at his computer, smiling at the screen.

'When I was done, about two a.m., I clicked on my calculator,' he said. 'I figured out my savings in tax for that day alone. I did the billable hours, the expenses, the profit projections. And I realized that every penny was mine.'

The following evening, he and Vickie and their twins, Mallory and Dana, went out for a meal. They chose the Singapore Hilton, because of the restaurant there, called Main Street, which served all-American food. The twins were not told what their father had done—it was a business matter—but they were well aware that the meal was a celebration. They called Alison at Willard and told her they loved her and that they were eating her favourite food.

'The fish is good there.'

'The only fish I'd eat is a cow that had drowned,' Hoyt said. 'I had prime rib. The kids had burgers and fries. I had two Buds. They had shakes. We had hot fudge sundaes for dessert. I haven't had a sundae for years.' He shook his head. 'OK?'

'It sounds like fun.' Odd though: one of the few virtues of Singapore was its peculiar cuisine and its noodle stalls.

'What did Vickie think about you renouncing your citizenship?'

'She has this superstitious idea—a lot of people do—that renouncing American citizenship is the equivalent of damnation,' Hoyt said.

Deep down it was the way I felt. When Elfman brought the subject up he had sounded like the devil. I did not say so, because the deed was done, and nothing could undo it. And Hoyt was saying this, I was sure, as a prelude to telling me that it was not so.

'Give it up, and you'll go to hell—that's what she thinks. That you're a kind of outcast, the man without a country, wandering the earth,' he said. 'She's a Catholic. She believes in Original Sin.'

It sounded convincing, but I did not contradict him; he was still talking.

'She does not yet understand that it's the opposite—an elemental and purifying act,' Hoyt said. 'I'm like the guy in the soap commercial. For the first time in my life I feel really clean.'

'I guess she'll understand it eventually.'

'She surely will,' Hoyt said. 'All my American assets are in her name now. Vickie's going to realize that I've made her a very rich woman. Hey, she's high maintenance.'

Victoria Maybry was the sort of woman I wanted to marry. She was attractive, she was bright, she was a great cook and had a cheerful disposition. She had a warm way of saying, 'Hi, gorgeous'—even to me, and later, smilingly, 'M'bye-bye.' Yes, it must have been an act, but it was a good act. She was secure and tolerant. And so her pretence of being submissive and of letting Hoyt hold forth was a sign of her strength. She was in all ways the perfect wife and mother, for that was what Hoyt needed most. She did not complain about Hoyt's long hours or his travel, nor the many clients he brought home to entertain.

She did not have an easy life, and sometimes it showed—she had begun to go a bit grey—and more than ever she had begun to look and act as though she was his mother. Hoyt's talking had turned Vickie into a listener, and she was so silent at times it was as though he had talked her personality away and simplified the poor woman, the way rushing water smoothes a boulder.

She was a trained nurse who had never worked as a nurse— Hoyt had married her just after her graduation from nursing school. But given Hoyt's proneness to accidents, her medical knowledge was helpful, and she was often called upon to give him first aid. More than that, she understood his ailments and ministered to him. Like Hoyt she was from California, was a competent scuba diver, spoke Spanish, read the new novels and, even if she did not agree with all of Hoyt's political opinions, at least she did not contradict him in public. She became prim, pressing her lips together, when Hoyt said 'fruit pickers'.

'Caning is good—it teaches a lesson,' she said once. It was the eternal Singapore topic.

'Hanging's even better,' Hoyt said. 'There's plenty of that here, too.'

'I'm for gas,' Vickie said. 'Or lethal injection.'

'Too humane,' Hoyt said. 'My father had a collie dog. Lovely creature. The dog began killing our chickens. My father hung the dead birds around the dog's neck. Broke my mother's heart, but it taught the dog a lesson. "Whip 'em with barbed wire," my dad used to say.'

Hearing these stories I often tried to imagine old Mr Maybry, Hoyt's father.

Hoyt said, 'I frankly don't understand why they don't have public executions. There's your deterrent.'

When Vickie was asked to think for herself she deferred to Hoyt or else went silent, her gaze faltering, and clasped her nervous fingers. In this fear she became stubborn and sure once again and, with an irrational certainty, spoke in her husband's voice. Lorelei—Lori—Elfman was a spender with a coarse sense of humour. She called oral sex 'making jewellery'. Warfield's wife was a golfer. Loong's was a partner in another Singapore law firm.

Although Vickie called herself a homemaker, her servants had usurped her role in Singapore. Each summer she arranged a rental in Martha's Vineyard, yet instead of spending those three school-vacation months there she dutifully followed Hoyt back to Singapore with Alison and the twins after two weeks. Each winter she supervised the condo rental in Telluride, for skiing. She flew ahead of Hoyt and put the place in order in anticipation of his brief and frantic visits.

Hoyt loved her, but that was beside the point. It was an unequal marriage of an old-fashioned and unfair sort, full of understandings and trade-offs. It seemed indestructible because she accepted her submissive role as handmaiden, and because her submissiveness was an illusion. Once, returning from a snorkelling trip to one of the outer islands of Singapore harbour, I saw Hoyt sit next to Vickie; then he slipped down and hugged her like a little boy. He was tired from the sun and the swimming, and blotchy with sunburn. When Vickie held his head against her breasts and looked down at him with a slit-eyed Madonna smile, I understood her power.

Vickie kept her American passport. Hoyt was alone in his renunciation, he said. Only then did the obvious question occur to me.

'If you're not an American, what are you?'

'Ever heard of Guinea-Bissau?'

3

Squinting at the small print in my *World Almanac*, I read that Guinea-Bissau (capital Bissau) was a tiny West African country, formerly a semi-destitute Portuguese colony, now a destitute independent republic, containing almost a million people, four per cent of whom were classified as 'white'. One of those white Guinea-Bissauans was now Hoyt Maybry, who used to describe the inhabitants of such places as 'cannibals and communists'. More than half the native Guinea-Bissauans were illiterate, most of the roads were unpaved, the life expectancy for men was thirty-eight years. There were no daily newspapers. The average per capita income was two hundred bucks a year in pesos, the local currency. I imagined many people being shocked, but the more I read, the greater my belief that Guinea-Bissau was Hoyt's kind of place. They exported cashew nuts. Hoyt liked munching cashews!

Hoyt's passport was dark green, its text was Portuguese, he had bought it for forty thousand dollars from the Guinea-Bissau Consul-General on Orchard Road, behind Tang's. Hoyt secured investor status in Guinea-Bissau, a country whose resources (apart from cashew nuts) were salt, sugar cane, bananas, coconuts, pozzolana ('a siliceous volcanic ash used to produce hydraulic cement') and peanuts. But the briskest business these days was the trade in passports. Kinglet Chee's Tongan passport was a hedge against Hong Kong's handover to the Chinese, and it had clearly influenced Hoyt's decision.

Hoyt said that he had been bold and that he felt free. But almost from the first this Guinea-Bissau passport seemed a nuisance.

Most Saturdays we went to Johor Bahru, just across the causeway in Malaysia, to play golf at the Royal Johor. Returning, we normally flashed our US passports and sailed through the immigration check. Not today. Hoyt's green one interested the immigration officers. They stopped us. They asked to see this odd-coloured document. They passed it around and muttered over it. It was no reassurance to hear one of the men laugh out loud. They ordered Hoyt out of the car and asked him where Guinea-Bissau was and why he had no Singapore entry stamp in his passport.

'Fill up this form, Mister,' one officer said.

Hoyt did so, standing in the heat, scribbling on the clipboard, looking absurd on the causeway in his golfing gear: yellow pants, two-tone shoes, pink shirt, cowboy hat.

'Your address is—what is this place called?'

'Bissau.'

'You live in this place?'

It was a cruel question.

'Obviously.'

'Not obvious to me, lah,' the officer said, his goofy grin masking his shrewdness. 'Why you put down your residence care of this business?'

'It's a bank.'

'You live in a bank?'

'That's my mailing address.'

'Not postal address, we want your home address.'

'I don't have a home address.'

'So where you live, lah?'

'I don't live there.'

'You say you live in Bissau'—the man pronounced it 'Bissoo'.

'That's a figure of speech. I am a citizen of Guinea-Bissau.'

All this time, Indians and Malays and Singapore Chinese were driving past the checkpoint in cars, staring out the window

at the large hot man in the golfing duds being interrogated by—
so his badge said—Officer Tan.

'You're a Guinea-Bissau person?'

'No. I am a citizen.'

'That means you are a Guinea-Bissau person.'

Hoyt's pink face seemed to swell as he compressed his lips. A
grunt came out of his face.

'Right.'

But this dispute had only made Officer Tan more suspicious.

'I never see one before.'

Hoyt was told to wait. I parked the car and joined him. He
apologized for the delay, and we watched what appeared to be a
little family being shouted at by another Singapore policeman.
They were Indians, probably Tamils, the sort of people we saw
all the time doing menial work. This being Singapore, the quarrel
was in English.

'I am not in possession of documents because I am leaving
pouch of documents at my residence.' The dark man had close-
set bloodshot eyes and he gestured with bony fingers that had
claw-like nails. 'For sake of safety.'

'How do I know that? Just because you say it doesn't mean
it's true. You can say anything. People say anything.'

'I am speaking the truth!'

The Indian woman, his wife, shrieked; the children cried and
clung to her sari.

'You are making my lady wife upset!'

'Go back to your country.'

'My home is there,' the man said, pointing past the far end
of the causeway, his voice rising and becoming hysterical as he
stepped forward to plead.

The Chinese policeman pushed the man's chest, making him
stumble. The wife wailed again, the children joining in a
miserable chorus.

Hoyt said, 'What in the hell is going on here?' and looked
combative.

But I tugged his arm. I said, 'Stay out of it.'

'This is ridiculous. It's simple for them to run a check on his
Singapore ID.'

I said, 'Do you really want to call attention to yourself? You could be next.'

Hoyt took a breath, as though to speak, but he said nothing. I had never seen him identify with a victim like this before. Such people were usually the targets of his bitter sarcasm. Only if you were billable were you a true victim. Yet this encounter interested me, as a display of Hoyt's sudden outrage, and for the way it vanished, as though this tough man had just discovered a survival instinct.

Singapore looked more severe if you were not American, and it looked very bad indeed if you were, as Hoyt was now, a citizen of the Third World. Really the planet was so simple. There was America, and there was everywhere else. Singapore, for all its modernity, was not America, and not very snug. Hoyt seemed to understand—perhaps too late—that he had chosen this world, and he did not like it much.

For one thing, it was small. We had business all over Southeast Asia, but it involved only short trips to big cities, usually the same ones. There was something so swift and hectic about these trips that we had no idea of the weather or seasons— the winter in Hong Kong, the monsoon in Jakarta, the stifling heat in Bangkok. We had client business in Russia and China. On the map Russia was vast; in business terms it was tiny, just one city and a few streets. We did business in China all the time. 'China's a closet,' Hoyt said. 'Russia's a toilet.'

'Don't bring a coat to China,' I heard Hoyt telling someone on the phone one day. It was the dead of winter in Shanghai, there was snow in Beijing, Harbin was frozen as hard as a cryogenic corpse. 'You never need a coat in China. You're always in taxis or meetings.'

The time we spent in America was not billable, and so our vacations seemed unreal and a bit frivolous. But real travel, real space and freedom was available in the United States, which seemed, with all its possibilities, the biggest country in the world.

'That's why aliens want to come to the States,' I said to Hoyt once, 'because there's room for them and opportunity and money. And you can drink the water.'

Hoyt had set his jaw and looked away and said, 'Serve them right if I took up residence where these fruit pickers came from. One of them tropical toilets full of soldiers and shoeshine boys and tax breaks. I'll live on orange juice. I'll get a tan. My kids can go swimming.'

He must have been thinking about renunciation for years and now he had done it. He kept saying he felt free, but I suspected that he was confused and now understood the true size of his world. There was no Second World any more—Russia was a welfare scrounger, Eastern Europe was just another basket case like Kenya or the Philippines. Beyond America was the Third World, of which Guinea-Bissau and Singapore were members. Never mind the way they looked: their thinking was the same.

The Singapore justice system was as primitive, as unfair and arbitrary as that in any banana republic. Guinea-Bissau had no newspapers; the Singapore press was gutless and unreadable, no more than convenient bum fodder for a repressive nanny government that rigged the courts and advocated caning and hanging. I hated caning most of all because it was the only topic at Singapore dinner parties; Hoyt seemed to like it for that reason, until he became a Guinea-Bissau citizen, for then it was his caning, not theirs. He had opted to belong in this world, and that's what they did in countries like his.

He said, 'It makes me want to litter.'

The incident at the Johor Causeway showed him that he had no authority any more. He had caved in to the unimpressed cops—very uncharacteristic for Hoyt. He had lost a tangible thing, his American confidence in the shape of a US passport. He watched his mouth these days. He had no one to back him up.

The other partners noticed this change in him, how subdued he was, as though he was nursing a cold: not talking so much, a bit fragile. Hoyt! There was not much sympathy. They knew about his million-eight; they knew about his passport.

Elfman said, 'You gotta feel sorry for the guy. It was this impulsive thing, like the fairy tale where the guy gets three wishes and totally fucks them up.'

The words were compassionate, but this tone from one of the men who had first suggested Hoyt's renunciation was a bit too strident for sympathy. It was the sort of calculated sarcasm Hoyt himself often used when he was talking about the United States, and you did not know until a moment later that he was mocking. By then Elfman was back in his office.

That was in February, the week of the party at the US Embassy to celebrate Presidents' Day. A typed sheet enclosed with the invitation stated that the party was also intended To Welcome the Secretary of Commerce, the Honourable Mr Ron Brown, and his Delegation.

We soon discovered that Hoyt had not been invited.

'You don't mean to tell me you're actually going,' he said.

'Brown's travelling with about twenty CEOs,' I said. 'There's definitely action there.'

'Who needs it?' Hoyt said.

'Some of us do,' Warfield said.

'Not me,' Elfman said. He was smiling. His sparse moustache made the smile worse. 'I'm going because it's Presidents' Day. To honour my country.'

In that moment I felt sorry for Hoyt, but as he went back to his office I saw the others exchanging glances and thinking the thought that had just occurred to me: Hoyt had recently become a multimillionaire.

'These wealthy foreigners,' Elfman said.

That evening Hoyt was working late again, and I saw that he was furious. 'I can't believe it. Those embassy bastards are actually discriminating against Vickie. My wife's an American!'

The fact that Hoyt had not been invited to the ambassador's residence made me view the whole evening with his eyes, and I saw the cruelty of it; it was an opportunity he would have relished. Ron Brown was in the receiving line, the ambassador next to him and, further down the line, a car-maker, a drink-bottler, the president of a network, a computer tycoon and a dozen more—fresh from China, with deals on their mind.

Watching from the side, his smooth face lit with concentration, was Kinglet Chee. He stood compactly, as though steadying himself by clasping an untouched glass of mango juice. He smiled uncomfortably when he saw me, or perhaps it was my name—saying the word Grillo makes people smile, or at least show their teeth.

'What do you think of our secretary of commerce?' I said.

Kinglet said, 'He works hard. He has a good face. I think he is a good man.'

It was not sarcasm, though my first reaction was that Kinglet was mocking—after all, I was listening to this unexpected praise with Hoyt's ears. I looked at Ron Brown before I said, 'I'm sure you're right.'

'I am so fortunate to be invited,' Kinglet said.

He meant it, the light in his face said that. There was also something so careful in the way he was dressed, as though the grand occasion merited his best silk suit, his most expensive tie, his handmade shoes.

'This is American soil,' Kinglet said. He spoke with the utmost seriousness. 'I am happy to be standing on it.'

Just then, Vic Scavola passed us, deep in conversation with one of the members of the Singapore Parliament. The last time I had seen Scavola I had been with Kinglet and Hoyt and I understood why, seeing Scavola, Kinglet then said, 'I don't see Hoyt Maybry here.'

'Hoyt's on the other list now,' I said. 'Of people they don't invite.'

'I heard that he renounced his American citizenship,' Kinglet said in a level tone, giving nothing away. And when I nodded he said, 'Very interesting.'

'But what do you really think?' I said.

'Strange that he did it for money,' Kinglet said, and faced me.

'Why is that so strange?'

'Because money is so easy,' Kinglet said. 'To gain it or lose it. But you Americans are the luckiest people in the world. China was once the Middle Kingdom—centre of the world. Now it is America.'

I said with enthusiasm, 'I agree.'

'To lose your country can be a curse,' Kinglet said.

But then, wincing in a kind of reflex, as though he had just realized he had said too much, he fell silent and became watchful. When he spoke again it was in a chastened tone.

'My opinion is of no value. I am a refugee. I have a Tongan

passport,' Kinglet said. 'I have never had to face such a choice, because my citizenship was of no value. The British have betrayed Hong Kong.'

At this noisy gathering of bureaucrats and businessmen, the unlikeliest occasion for candour, the visceral passion of this man was touching. Through two previous deals I had done with Hoyt I thought I had known Kinglet. But until now I had not had any idea of his strength of feeling.

I said, 'I was kind of surprised that Hoyt went through with it.'

Kinglet smiled, perhaps doubting me: his eyes were flinty. He said, 'I was not surprised. When we rode together to the embassy that day I heard his real voice.'

'When he was talking about the States?'

The memory of Hoyt's ranting made me cringe.

'That was sarcasm,' Kinglet said.

He surprised me, using that accurate word to nail Hoyt's monologue. It was clear that he remembered everything Hoyt had said and he easily characterized it.

I said, 'Hoyt lays it on a little thick.'

Kinglet's face was impassive and rather frightening for the sudden blankness that revealed nothing of his feelings. He said, 'He thought I did not understand.'

Kinglet did not say any more than that, nor did he suggest that Hoyt had mocked him. Yet it was apparent in his voice and manner that he understood everything. On the short ride to the embassy, Hoyt had lost him.

I said, 'I'll tell you frankly that I would never give my American citizenship away. Never, ever.'

Kinglet stepped back, because of the force of my words, but he said nothing, and that made me feel worse. Afterwards I wondered why I had blurted that out and I regretted that I had shown my feelings. Oddest of all was that I had not known how I had felt until I had heard myself saying it. It disturbed me to realize that, without planning to, I had probably told him the truth.

Nor was Hoyt invited a few weeks later to a poetry reading given by the visiting Maya Angelou at the American Cultural Center. He said he was glad to be excluded. 'When I heard her recite her horrible poem at Clinton's inauguration I knew we were in for a bad four years. God, that was embarrassing.'

Someone—it had to be a partner, though it could have been a secretary—taped an item from the *Straits Times* on to Hoyt's door: CHOLERA EPIDEMIC SWEEPS GUINEA-BISSAU. It was a lame joke but it made Hoyt defiant. He began talking about the infant-mortality rate in Mississippi. On the bulletin board in the room where we kept the coffee machine and the photocopier, strange little newspaper stories began to appear, on one occasion a list of sugar-producing countries with Guinea-Bissau near the bottom, highlighted in yellow; another day, a list of hopeless debtor nations, Guinea-Bissau near the top. An item from a Rhode Island paper, the *Providence Journal*, concerned a serial rapist and murderer who had been convicted and given a sentence of four hundred and twenty years: ' . . . is of Guinea-Bissauan nationality' was underlined, and in the same ink was written, Send them all back!

'Just a joke,' I said.

'Sure, I miss the United States a lot,' Hoyt said, 'but my aim is getting better.'

It was another of Hoyt's sayings, but did he mean it? I saw more of Hoyt than the others did, so I knew that these days, perhaps as a result of his renunciation—and his new wealth—he took a much greater interest in American politics, in the progress of the stock market, even the weather. He had sworn off skiing this year—our rowdy haunts at Telluride seemed quieter without him—but he said that he was intending to go to the States fairly soon. He did not mention this again. And before I left for this ski trip he asked me to bring back his favourite peanut butter, some new movies on video and a case of a particular type of Mexican salsa that was unobtainable in Singapore.

Hoyt bought a Jaguar Vanden Plas, white with gilded trim and spoke-wheels and blacked-out windows. When I complimented him on it, he said, 'I was going to get a Roller, but they're too conspicuous.'

After work one day all the partners met at the Mandarin to discuss an outing to a resort in Malaysia. The idea was that we would bring our families so that they would not feel so alienated by our long hours.

While we were drinking and talking in the bar, a group of men, Africans perhaps, were talking loudly at the next table. Hoyt called the waiter over and told him to quiet the table.

'It is the United Nations delegation,' the waiter said.

Elfman said to the waiter, 'Ask that guy in the blue suit, the guy who looks like Louis Armstrong, if he's from Guinea-Bissau.'

In the end Hoyt did not take Vickie and the twins to Malaysia. He said they had other plans, but I felt sure he feared being held up by Singapore immigration on the return journey. Hoyt lived the way many other non-American aliens in Singapore lived, especially the Third Worlders like the Filipinos and Indians and Bangladeshis. He stayed put. He tried to be inconspicuous. He joined the Singapore Swimming Club. He did not travel.

'I can cut down these days,' he said to me, though I had not asked him for an explanation. 'I don't have to stay up all night servicing clients like I used to. I don't have to chase business. Hey, I was asked to give a talk at a business lunch in Tokyo. I turned it down.'

Elfman put a different spin on this. He said, 'How many visas do you suppose the Japanese hand out to Africans?'

This sort of remark reached Hoyt. He responded by spending money, buying clothes, buying jewellery for Vickie and talking about his new investments. The others said: Exactly what a real Guinea-Bissauan would do—when these simple people get rich they just blow it. Elfman said, 'Know the expression "nigger rich"?'

'Back off,' I said. 'You're disgusting.'

Hoyt was not bothered. He said, 'It's ironic. Now that I've given up my US passport I can at last afford a really good house in the States.'

It was about that time that he said casually—but knowing that it would be repeated—that Vickie had gone to the States, to Florida, the little town of Boca Grande on Gasparilla Island, just off the south-west coast, and not far from the Dupont Mansion, and had bought an ocean-front house for just under three million dollars. It was a select and sunlit island of second homes, connected to the mainland by a narrow bridge.

'Little island, a causeway, great fishing, no crime, no litter.'
'Sounds like Singapore.'
'No Chinese,' he said. 'It's a white-bread community.' He raised his eyebrows and looked down the corridor. 'Elfman could have a problem there.'

He showed me pictures of the house, a pretty white-frame mansion on seaside stilts, with porches and a cupola. He told me about the hotel in the town, the tennis courts, the restaurants, the marina, the Intra-Coastal Waterway, the ospreys that nested near it, the pelicans that roosted on the mangroves, the dolphins—even manatees.

'George Bush went marlin fishing there after he lost the election,' Hoyt said. He must have seen me smiling, because he added quickly, 'But I'm going there because I have a lovely home on the Gulf. And I didn't lose anything.'

The 'Elfman could have a problem there' remark must have got back to Elfman. Soon after, at a partners' meeting, Elfman looked up from *US News and World Report* and said, 'It says here that there are a large number of Guinea-Bissauans in the United States employed in the offshore commercial fishing industry in the north-east.'

'Grillo will back me on this, Burton,' Hoyt said to Elfman, and he stared at him and silenced the table. 'You bring this subject up a lot. I am not particularly interested in these references. It can't be a joke—no one's laughing. Are you laughing, Warfield?'

Warfield was stony-faced; Loong looked disgusted.

Hoyt said, 'When you look at me, I don't want you to see a Guinea-Bissauan. My passport is a detail. It helped me through a personal crisis. Do me the courtesy of seeing me as I really am, a colleague and a fellow human being.'

Lectured to in this way, in front of the partners, Elfman was furious, his eyes were dancing in anger. He smiled a wild carnivorous smile. He said, 'And reciprocation will be highly appreciated.'

Hoyt laughed and looked away. 'When someone gets as pompous as that, you know they're in the wrong.'

But Hoyt knew that he was a subject of gossip. He had more money than any of us now, but he was also aware that we were curious to know how strong that money had made him. He was restless too. In this way he was like the local Filipinos and the Thais and the Malays and the Indians who longed to go to the States but never brought the subject up. Because it was their most profound desire, it was the thing they never mentioned. Elfman explained all this to me, hoping that I would goad Hoyt by telling him.

At last Hoyt did what many Guinea-Bissauans did—though no one risked his anger by reminding him. He applied for a United States visa. And like many other Guinea-Bissauans, he was turned down.

4

Hoyt had said, 'Don't bother, Jim,' when I said that I would go along with him the day he applied for his US visa. I wanted to reassure him of my loyalty to him—too many bad jokes had made the office seem negative and contentious.

I tried to hug him and insist on going to the embassy with him, and he quivered and then exploded. It took three distinct forms, like a beach toy blowing up. There was first my insistence, my pushing just too hard at the wrong time, murmuring 'Hoyt'. Then his howl, like the thing breaking with a bang, my name spoken in rage, 'Grillo!' Finally, a funny whimper of self-pity, not words, but a rubbery hiss of deflation.

'I have to do this alone,' he said after a while.

It seemed dangerous for me to say anything more.

'I am too ashamed to do it any other way,' he explained.

He was still breathing hard from his first outburst. I knew there was more to come.

'This isn't my first time,' he said.

I gave him a little space and then asked, 'Want to tell me what happened the first time?'

He smiled at me, his old Hoyt smile of utter contempt. He smiled like this whenever he said I was a lucky sperm. This time he said, 'They turned me down. Scavola, that scumbag.'

'On what grounds?'

'See, you're asking all the wrong questions, Grillo. They turned me down twice.'

He looked sad when he saw the disbelieving expression on my face. He had no answers. He was angry and incoherent. Twice?

'Scavola's got his own agenda,' Hoyt said. 'I'm in a lot of pain.'

He walked past me kicked his office door shut and then stood in a tragic posture, talking to a picture of his late father.

'I never had enemies before. Strong men don't have enemies,' he said. 'Now I have enemies. Does it mean I am getting weak?'

He needed to tell me the story, but I let him take his time, and he did so, as though grieving.

It had started badly. Elfman had offered to help deal with it, since the impending trip to the States concerned a client they shared. He had sent Elfman's messenger to the consulate with the forms and the photographs and his distinctive passport. Elfman had assured him that it would be no more than a formality since he had already secured a visa for his client, a Taiwanese named Lee. The messenger returned empty-handed, and it was for Elfman to tell Hoyt that he would have to appear in person.

'The line was down the driveway,' Hoyt said. 'I told them I had meetings.' That smile again. 'You'd think the American Embassy might consider hiring English-speaking security officers.'

He went to the end of the long line and stood there an hour in the heat with all the other hopeful nationalities. As he stood, shading his head with his application form, the ambassador entered in his official car, his Malay chauffeur tooting the ambassadorial horn, the Marine guards at attention.

'You know how big the commercial section of the embassy is, Grillo. You know how much business we've generated here,' Hoyt said. 'I was going to say something, just "Hello!" Then I'm like, "Why give him the satisfaction of seeing me?"'

At last, inside, he got to the visa window and handed his application to the clerk and was given a number. He was told to wait.

'Why is it that people always sound so rude when English is their second language?'

Witnessing other applications being processed ahead of his, he complained. Still his passport was not returned. Chinese? Thais? Filipinos? Indians? He stuck his head in the window again. The clerk said, 'They are Canadians.'

'What's the problem with my application?'

'Just wait.'

They weren't taught to say please?

'I want to see Mr Scavola.'

'He is in a meeting.'

'Who is the supervisor?'

'I am the supervisor.'

'I demand to know what the problem is,' Hoyt said.

'Maybe insufficient supporting documents. Did you submit a return air-ticket, and the names of three referees in the United States? In addition, a letter from your American company? And your birth certificate?'

As he experienced the shortness of breath and the tightness of his scalp that was like flammable vapour building in his brain, all of it indicating that he was about to scream at the woman, he saw Scavola walking past. He called out, and hearing his own voice was disturbed by its similarity to a cry of pain.

'You're an African,' Scavola said.

'Listen—'

'Those are the requirements for Africans.'

Scavola had not even slowed down and now he was out the door.

'Sit down, sir,' the clerk said. 'Your paperwork is—'

'No,' Hoyt said, and he left so suddenly he forgot to collect his passport and visa application and did not remember them until he was in the taxi, on his way to the office. Back at his desk, he realized he would have to go again and reapply. He had accomplished nothing. Much worse, this delay meant that he would not be able to do the joint negotiation with Elfman.

That was the first failure.

'So Elfman got the contract.'

'You don't need it.' I felt it was what he wanted me to say, and yet he looked morose.

'I was going to stay on so that I could speak at Alison's

graduation. They asked me to be the commencement speaker.'

On his second try his papers were in order—the pictures, the application, the letters, the names, the birth certificate, the air ticket: a thick file. He stood near the counter, his flimsy numbered ticket wilting in his palm.

Scavola leaned on the counter, notarizing documents for a Chinese man.

Hoyt said, 'I see. If you're Chinese you get service.'

'This American citizen is ahead of you,' Scavola said.

Hoyt said, 'I know my rights.'

'You have no rights here.' Scavola stamped the document. He did not even look up. He signed and dated each document, taking his time.

'This is not a commercial matter,' Hoyt said. 'I am speaking at a college graduation. I was asked to do this. I am the commencement speaker at Willard College.' He was about to add that his daughter was in the graduating class, but then thought better of it. 'I must have this visa.'

Still notarizing the documents, still looking down, Scavola said, 'No one can be guaranteed a visa. They are dealt with on merit.'

'If I don't show up,' Hoyt began.

'They'll find an American speaker,' Scavola said.

It was clear to Hoyt that he had been singled out for persecution. It made him angry, but what could he do? He regretted renouncing his citizenship in that hot, over-familiar little island. That had made him a marked man. He was thinking: I have always felt these people were mindless and robotic bureaucrats, but really they are vindictive, shallow, envious and disgusting human beings.

That was the second failure. Was it any wonder that he had not wanted me to go along with him the third time?

I left him to his bitterness and avoided him for the rest of the day. Going home that evening, passing his office, I was surprised when he called me in and told me that he had been granted an American visa. Yet he was sour.

'They gave me ten days,' he said. 'I own a three-million-dollar home in the United States—and I get ten days. "British businessmen get three months," I told them.'

Even with all his papers in order, Scavola had said, 'I'll need to see three forms of identification.'

'Look at me, Vic,' Hoyt had said.

'And when you produce them I will record the relevant numbers in your file.'

'It's me, Vic. Remember me?'

Under Scavola's fishy and disbelieving gaze, Hoyt took out a California driver's licence, a pistol permit and his American Express Card.

'Credit cards are not a valid form of ID, I'm afraid,' Scavola said. And it annoyed Hoyt that the consular officer did not look squarely at him. 'Perhaps a bill or receipt with your name on it?'

Hoyt snatched in his briefcase and brought out a tax file. He showed Scavola his most recent tax return. It delighted him to be shoving this into Scavola's face. 'And you'll see what I've paid to the US government.'

Scavola blew his nose. He was looking at his soiled handkerchief as he said, 'Is that your signature, Mr Maybry?'

Scavola photocopied the documents and stapled them. He told Hoyt that he would be granted a ten-day visa and that he could pick it up at the visa window at a specified time the next day.

'Ten days is not enough.'

Scavola smiled at Hoyt's futile protest. He said, 'The consulate determines the time period.'

'I have a home in Florida. I am giving a speech in Oregon.'

Scavola said, 'Over the years we have found that certain nationalities overstay. Guinea-Bissauans are serious offenders.'

Hoyt flew to the United States, his first trip as a Guinea-Bissau citizen. Vickie had gone the week before with the twins and was waiting in the small Oregon town that was home to Willard College. On his arrival at what he always called Tom Bradley Airport in Los Angeles, Hoyt found himself directed to the non-US citizens line, 'And there I waited for two hours with half the population of Asia.' The immigration officer, a Hispanic woman, reminded him in barely comprehensible English (he said) that his visa was non-renewable, and then it was another three-hour flight to Portland.

An honorary Doctor of Law degree was conferred upon Hoyt the next day on the green lawn of Willard College while his family cheered; he delivered his commencement address; and afterwards, at a lunch at the president's house, he was asked in a fairly direct way, by the president himself, for a substantial amount of money to endow a scholarship in his name. So that was what it was all about: they gave you an honorary doctorate, and you gave them money. It was like the old wicked Vatican that had outraged Luther by its sale of indulgences.

Hoyt said, 'You can't have paid much attention to my speech.'

He had called it 'Unsung Heroes', and the example set by each of these heroes—a particular policeman, teacher, scoutmaster, as well as his own father—was one of self-reliance. His father was a proud, stubborn man who was entirely unsentimental, and his stories gave colour to the speech. The concluding story concerned a dog his father had owned.

'It was called a basenji, a strange little sharp-faced and short-haired dog that had been bred by the ancient Egyptians,' Hoyt told the audience. 'It had two unusual characteristics. The first was that it didn't bark—couldn't bark. It is the most silent dog in the world—the most it does is grunt. And its second odd feature was that whenever it saw a cut or a sore on a person's leg or ankle, it crouched and began licking. It licked any wound it saw—kept at it with its rough tongue. It was happiest when it was around injured people—it needed their wounds, even though for all its attention the dog made no difference to them.'

Hoyt described the barkless behaviour and the wound-licking, and he quoted his father as saying, 'Don't be a dog like that.'

'That lesson made me a lawyer,' Hoyt told the audience at Willard College. 'And when I see a basenji I often think, "I'd like to own half that dog." Because if I did I'd shoot my half. Thank you very much ladies and gentlemen.'

'Given the message of my speech,' Hoyt told the president of Willard, 'you sure asked me a funny question.'

The president, not certain he had been rebuffed, went on to ask Hoyt whether he was able to attend a seminar on US trade that the college was sponsoring for the summer session.

'I'll have to get back to you on that,' Hoyt said.

Hoyt wondered if the man was mocking him, for the fact was that although he wanted to be part of the seminar—there were always potential clients at such gatherings—Hoyt had no idea whether he would be granted a visa for another visit. A request for money, a request to return. All this awkwardness. Did the president know something?

At the lunch itself Hoyt was seated between a student from South Africa—a young black woman who had just-visible freckles—and an elderly trustee, still wearing her robes and her purple Willard hood.

'I read that story in Mark Twain,' the young woman said. '*Pudd'nhead Wilson*. It's a good novel about racial paradoxes. "I'd shoot my half." Pudd'nhead says that.'

'My father taught me that,' Hoyt said.

'He must have read the novel,' the young woman said.

'Or perhaps Mark Twain got the story from my father.'

The young woman stared at him. Yes, they were freckles, mostly on the bridge of her nose, but also on her cheeks.

'We did a lot of work in South Africa in the seventies,' Hoyt said, but thinking: I need a lesson in American literature from a Hottentot?

'My country was not free then,' the student said. 'We were suffering the twin evils of apartheid and political oppression.'

'What exactly does that mean?' Hoyt asked, smiling at her, though she could not have known the meaning of his smile.

The elderly trustee leaned over and said, 'Nelson Mandela was in jail then, is what she means.'

'My background is mainly Asia,' Hoyt said, hating both women. 'I wonder whether you realize that China is an economic giant.'

The student said, 'Africa's colonial past kept her from realizing her potential. Not just South Africa, but all over.'

'So Africa is a sort of unwed single mother on welfare with too many children, is that it?' Hoyt said. 'And we're paying the bills.'

As he spoke, he remembered his tax position and his Guinea-Bissau passport and felt light-headed, not angry any more. He was in the mood to tease and laugh, like an escape artist who has just freed himself of the handcuffs and the chains and the coffin.

The South African student was trying to reply, as Hoyt interrupted and said, chewing his food, 'What will you do when you go back to South Africa?'

'I am going to grad school here. After that, I might stay.'

'Just like that. "America's kind of a neat place. Think I'll just stay."'

Sensing the dark heat of Hoyt's hostility, the student frowned and became silent.

He left the next day with Vickie and the children to go to Florida, to the house in Boca Grande. It took a whole day to fly to Tampa, and by the time they had rented a car and driven it the hundred miles to Boca it was dark. Four days in this splendid house, then a meeting in Seattle, and his visa days were used up. He flew to Vancouver.

'I've never seen one of those before,' the Canadian immigration officer said. The green passport again. Why did they all say that? 'But your English is excellent.'

Hoyt tried to drive back to Seattle to see whether he would be allowed over the border. On the American side he showed his driver's licence. The officer ran a computer check. Hoyt was escorted to a secure room, where he waited, with a woman from Pakistan. Hoyt knew from the way she was dressed that she was Pakistani: white veil, purple gown, yellow pantaloons; no dot on her forehead. She held a US passport in her skinny fingers.

'But why won't they let you through?'

'Sorry.'

She fanned him away with her passport to indicate that she did not speak English. She looked anxious. Then she smiled, seeing her husband appear in the room. The bearded and sandal-wearing man in a grubby gown gave Hoyt a malevolent look and helped his wife from the room and into the United States.

Soon after, Hoyt was turned away. 'I'm in the computer!' He called Vickie in Florida and flew to Singapore, where he told me this. He was limping. 'Somewhere along the way I pulled a hamstring.'

5

You know that an American is truly rich when he tells you how poor he is. Hoyt could not say that any longer, and I think it bothered him. When he said these days, 'I've got money,' it always sounded as though he had a problem, for the fact was that he had very little else. He had no hobbies, didn't collect things, didn't read. His golf game was too amateurish to be regarded as anything but a humiliation. In a working life of servicing clients and taking business trips he had developed no other skills and no pleasures. Hoyt's preoccupation with the Asian market had cast a spell on him, making him believe that he did not need a US passport. He soon realized that he could not be an effective lawyer without it. He said he didn't mind. He had money.

But without the passport it was almost impossible to use the money. He could of course buy anything he wanted. There was a brisk trade in Singapore and Hong Kong in Chinese porcelain and carved wood furniture and jade and Japanese prints and netsukes. Hoyt had worked so hard he had had no time to study the nuances of such collecting. He bought an expensive sound system and a video camera and had a wet bar installed in his Singapore house.

The Boca Grande house was shut much of the time, but still Vickie went there with the children and they played on the beach. She seemed to enjoy it and to manage without Hoyt. But he could not go to the States impulsively, as he once had, and he was an impulsive man—it was his most American quality.

Once, at a party for some Japanese automotive clients, an elderly Japanese with thick glasses and a hearing aid was introduced to Hoyt. They talked about cars. Hoyt mentioned his Jaguar.

'That's patriotism,' the Japanese man said. 'Because you are English man!'

A bad joke but a harmless one. Hoyt was livid. 'I'm not English—I'm American!'

Still feeling insulted the next day, he brought the subject up again, saying, 'Only a deaf and blind Jap would take Hoyt Maybry for an Englishman.'

It was true: no one was more American than Hoyt Maybry. It was not just the cowboy boots and the silver belt buckle and the aviator glasses and the turquoise stones in the silver bracelet that served as a watch band; it was his whole manner, his way of saying, 'I'm currently busy' and 'Thank you very kindly' and 'At this juncture'. It was the unhesitating way he shook hands—in his grip you felt your hand had disappeared. It was his generosity towards friends, his ruthlessness towards enemies, his blue shirts, his big feet, his obsessional cleanliness, his appetite for work. His very name was American, probably a corruption of a picturesque English name, for 'Maybry' grunted out of the side of an illiterate immigrant's toothless mouth was probably 'Mayberry'.

I have mentioned that Hoyt was accident-prone—probably as a result of his hurrying and divided mind, always seeming to hold two conversations, no matter what the topic, one for the defence and one for the prosecution. It was an occupational hazard but it was also related to his being an American. Was it also related to fatigue? That hamstring business after the Willard speech was typical. Hoyt often returned from a trip with a sore back or a sprained ankle. 'It's a strain,' 'It's some kind of rash that's going around,' 'Pulled a muscle in my groin.' As a lawyer who had worked on personal injury cases Hoyt knew the names of any muscle he injured. He was a scrupulous litigator, and yet settling into his desk he had a tendency to flip open the lid of his laptop at the same time he set down his coffee cup. As he fumbled the coffee cup and tried to right it he would knock his laptop to the floor.

'Stress weakens the immune system,' I said one day to my secretary, and I laughed when I realized I was quoting Hoyt again, who always said that when he caught a cold.

At one time he had been preoccupied with thinking of ways to save money on taxes. Having solved that with different citizenship he became preoccupied with ways to get into the United States. Being sent back to Vancouver had stung him.

'Imagine being sent back to Canada. Think what that does to a person.'

I said, 'There must be lots of countries that welcome Guinea-Bissauan citizens.'

'Probably,' he said. 'But I wouldn't go to any country that did.'

He did not say that he regretted giving up his US citizenship. He did not question the wisdom of having become a Guinea-Bissau citizen. He had not imagined how valueless that passport was as a travel document. It was questioned, or smiled at, or held up to ridicule at many airports in Southeast Asia.

Hoyt said, 'I was under a lot of stress over Kinglet's memory-chip deal. If I had to do it again I probably wouldn't choose Bissau.' And he made a point of saying that he knew nothing about Guinea-Bissau—had no idea where this place was.

He said to Elfman, 'Does every passenger on a Liberian-registered ship know where Liberia is?'

Elfman annoyed him by replying, 'Liberia is near Guinea-Bissau.'

So he schemed. He arranged for Vickie to be a director in a company that needed her to vote at semi-annual board meetings. Rather than find a willing company, he gave her the money to start one. I knew this because I was also a partner in New World Investments. We even held a meeting in Honolulu—Vickie and Elfman and me, though all we discussed was Hoyt's rage, because he could not be there. The meeting had an odd effect on Vickie, but in any case Hoyt was not granted a visa.

'My spouse has a business meeting in Hawaii!' he had told Scavola.

But all the consul said was, 'It doesn't follow that you need to go. She has the meeting, not you.'

'I am married to this woman!'

Scavola said, 'When you're doing business in Shanghai, do the Chinese recognize this as a valid reason to grant a visa to your wife?'

'I thought I was dealing with the United States government.'

'You are an African,' Scavola said, seeming to take pleasure in saying it, 'and therefore subject to all visa requirements governing Africans.'

'Guinea-Bissau is an independent republic.'

'And a member of the Organization of African Unity,' Scavola said. 'My last post was Senegal. It's next door.'

The directorship didn't work. A moment ago I used the expression 'had an odd effect on Vickie'. What happened was that Vickie invited me to her room at the Kahala Hilton and gave me a drink. We sat on the *lanai* looking at the moon on the water. I was talking—about Hoyt, of course—when I noticed she was crying. When I tried to console her and hugged her, she said in a throaty way, 'God, it's been so long since I've been held by a man.' And she was smiling.

Then she said, 'Jim, do you know how many women in Singapore wonder whether you're gay?'

There is a grinning Hindu goddess with about thirty arms. At that moment I felt I was being embraced by her. It took all the strength I could muster to disengage myself.

Hoyt had another scheme. He had noticed ('a bit late in the day,' Elfman said) that our British and European clients visited the United States with relative ease. Inspired by that freedom, Hoyt decided to apply for a second passport, one from a country in the European Union. Ireland granted passports to individuals who invested one hundred and sixty thousand dollars. The money was handed over in instalments, and after five years could be withdrawn. Hoyt put down forty thousand dollars and was put on a waiting list.

'If I get an Irish passport, I'm fine,' he told me. 'I'll have access to the whole of Europe, and it'll be easier to get into the States.'

He regretted that he had no Irish relatives, which would have made it easier. An Irish grandfather would have done the trick. Yet he knew that an Irish passport was available, at a price. In the meantime, because he could not see Vickie and the children in the States, they met in Mexico, stayed for a week at a time at hotels in Acapulco, got sick with stomach upsets, and he ranted over the hotel bills.

It was expensive to travel on the periphery of the United States, involving rental cars and two hotel suites and restaurants. Formerly he had broken his journeys in Honolulu. This was not possible any more. He got to know Vancouver well, which seemed to him a shabbier, less fireproof version of its sister city, Seattle.

There was an edgy and irritable atmosphere at partners' meetings these days. Warfield felt it too. 'It's our foreign colleague,' he said. Then, 'No, not Ernie Loong.' One typical meeting concerned our effort in organizing a Chinese–American joint venture by a large American pharmaceutical company (which had a division in Singapore) to market an asthma medicine. Hoyt had done his homework. He found a Rand report stating that because of the bad air produced by China's successful manufacturing industry, China was full of asthmatics, almost a tenth of the country gagging. It was the sort of image that Hoyt loved presenting to clients: a hundred million Chinese gasping for breath, and we own the inhaler!

'It's like owning air,' he said. 'So let's do the deal.'

'It means meeting the principals,' Elfman said.

'It could be a conference call.'

'You call that service? Hey, I've lined up three days of discussions in San Francisco.'

'Why not Seattle?' Hoyt said. And I guessed what he was hinting: 'Why not Vancouver?'

'The Chinese want to see the sort of plant our people have,' Elfman said.

'And they like going to the States,' Warfield said. 'We'll probably fly them down to Disneyland on their free day.'

'This has to be next week?'

'Snooze, you lose,' Elfman said.

'You have this gift for phrase-making,' Hoyt said. 'Listen, I can't go next week. I think you know that.'

'Grillo can take your place.'

Afterwards, when he did not ask me about the deal, nor inquire how much my cut was, nor mention Elfman's commission, I realized how much it mattered to him and how it had hurt.

'I have plenty of money,' he said one day at lunch. He was chewing, taking his time, knowing that a statement like that got my attention. 'So I don't have to chase every deal that comes up.'

'You can stop and smell the flowers,' I said.

'Ever notice, Grillo? Flowers in the tropics have no aroma,' Hoyt said. It was indignation rather than remorse. 'These Singapore orchids look gorgeous but they smell like potting soil.'

Hoyt was pleasantly surprised to find that he had no serious problem going to Europe. This discovery came about during a business trip to Hong Kong. He had taken the jetfoil across to Macau and had easily gotten a visa to Portugal. From there he could travel anywhere in Europe. He called Vickie from Paris to say that they might consider meeting there, but when he saw that his hotel bill for three days was more than four thousand dollars, he said it was out of the question.

Vickie said, 'I thought the whole point of your citizenship thing was to make us rich.'

'Cut me some slack!' he shouted and flew to Dublin. Once again an immigration officer smiled at his passport. He rented a car and drove to Cork in the rain and tried to imagine himself living in a house there, looking out of the window at the drizzle. He went to an agency in Cork, he looked at some houses and he marvelled at how clammy they were. This country existed in another century: a cold damp century of stinking woollens and rotting plaster and toothless old men.

Travelling back to Singapore by way of Lisbon he had a giddy thought of stopping in Guinea-Bissau. Why not? He had the passport. He knew the place was not expensive. What if it happened to be palm trees and white sand beaches and outdoor cafés? He saw himself with a drink in his hand, at a café table, writing something. He heard himself on the phone. *I'm doing a book.*

The woman at the Tap Airlines counter at Lisbon printed an itinerary for him. Hoyt examined it. He said, 'Why do I have to come all the way back here? Can't I just go from Guinea-Bissau to—anywhere else?'

'You can go to Africa,' the clerk said. 'But this is the most direct route.'

'It's about two thousand miles out of my way,' Hoyt said. 'Where else can I go from Guinea-Bissau?'

'Just Lisbon,' she said, 'or Africa.'

Nowhere, he mumbled to himself, and he thought of that arrogant student he had met at the lunch at Willard College. I might stay.

And yet Hoyt still had a desperate curiosity to see what Guinea-Bissau looked like. The fact might be crucial. He imagined it as looking like a West Indian island. He said so to the clerk, who smiled, just the way strangers smiled at his passport. She said it was a terrible place, of deforestation and drought and bad soil. Now he imagined cindery beaches and isolation and hunger. They all want to leave. They are a problem here. You see?

What was she talking about? She had lifted her eyes to the people behind him in the line, perhaps a family, and yet there was just the merest resemblance, not in their features but in their coarse skin, a kind of acne Hoyt had never seen before except on the skin of certain blighted fruit. The women's hair was in plastic curlers, the men wore stained baseball caps and rags, their luggage was sewn in bales and bundles. Entering the ticket area half an hour ago, Hoyt had seen these people stretched out on the floor. He stepped aside and listened, and he gathered that only one of them was travelling, a young man in a shiny nylon tracksuit and torn shoes.

The ticket agent was shaking her head and saying, No, no, and showing them a circled paragraph on a printed piece of paper. The young man had a problem. He waved his ticket irritably while the clerk indicated that his passport was blank— no visa. The word was the same in Portuguese and English.

He knew what the woman was saying. He heard certain familiar words—'JFK', 'New York', 'Lishboa', 'visa'. He understood the gestures.

The clerk, who would not accept his ticket, was probably saying, 'Yes, you have a ticket to New York, but when you get to JFK airport they will not admit you. You have no visa. You will be put on the next plane and sent back to Lisbon.'

The language of rejection and humiliation was easy for Hoyt to follow.

The ragged family complained. They took turns whining. They muttered. They crowded the counter. The young man was the shrillest, his eyes shining in a fever of misery. But this was just futile noise, a kind of squawking: they knew they were beaten.

The young man's green passport was familiar to Hoyt, and just seeing it in their skinny fingers demoralized him and ended his desire to go to the place of his citizenship.

His European trip was an expensive one, no billable hours,

no client meetings. It was a journey into frustration. 'There's so much emotion in airports,' he told me. 'People crying, people holding hands and hugging. People looking petrified, as though they're going to crash. That's taken its toll on me.'

Back in his office he calculated that eight months after his renunciation of citizenship his income dropped to a third of what it had been. He had been granted one US visa—the commencement speech. Alison now had an internship at the *Wall Street Journal*.

'I can't even see my own kid!' he said to me.

He said he could not trust anyone else in the office. They were stealing his clients, he said; they had muscled in on his accounts. Losing the pharmaceutical deal had been crucial; it was the first of many such losses for Hoyt. He was not imagining the attitude of the other partners. They had begun to treat him with the mixture of off-hand courtesy and evasiveness that they reserved for foreign partners who were not involved in our deals. Maybe it was better to tell them nothing, we thought, and because we were keeping them at a distance we were polite to them in a formal and unconvincing way.

'I've got a beautiful home in Boca! I never go there!'

These days Vickie was living in it with the twins and taking tennis lessons; but that was not the way Hoyt saw it.

This house, in his odd, resentful description, lay on the Gulf of Mexico, on a barrier island of multimillionaires. The rooms were in darkness, the shades drawn, the sun visible in knife-like slashes in the blinds. The tiles were white, the beams varnished, the furniture covered with sheets. 'Vickie chose all the accessories'—a giant paper parasol from Bangkok, some Mexican pots, a rocking chair. Empty rooms. The microwave clock blinked green, the burglar alarm blinked red. Dusty hibiscus bushes had been planted among woodchips. Many deserted houses were like that, but this was slightly different. This house had its own sound—the loud drone of air-conditioners, audible from their shelf just outside a rear window, cooling the house, month after month, cooling the Mexican pots, cooling the rocking chair, cooling the empty rooms.

The grinding sound was the same an office shredder made when it was chewing on something that offered no resistance, like hundred-dollar bills. That air-conditioner on that hot American island made the sound of money being shredded.

'So it's settled,' Elfman was saying. More and more he was taking charge of the partners' meetings. 'Lake Tahoe for the holidays. Something for the swimmers, something for the skiers.'

Woe had turned Hoyt's face a bloodless, corpse-like grey. We discussed the annual meeting in a circumspect way, knowing how keenly Hoyt was watching. He had become more intimidating as a listener than he had been as a talker.

'I know I can get ten days,' he said to me the next morning. 'I might get a month. But that's not the point. It's when my time's up—that hurts. When I have to go.'

'But you can always go back.'

'I like to do things in my own time, when I want.' That was another of his American qualities—impatience.

'Think of all the money you've saved.'

He did not reply to that. Wealthy people talked about being poor because they concentrated on what they spent rather than what they saved.

He said, 'When this Irish passport comes through I think I'll be in the clear.'

Alone of the partners, I knew that his reason for not going to Lake Tahoe was that Vickie had left him and decided to stay in Boca Grande. Their separation had proved to her that she did not need him, and she told me frankly that she resented his giving up his American passport. The lawyer I found for her was a shark. I hated his method, I admired the result.

Even the marital crisis was no help in his securing an American visa, and the Irish passport was so long in coming that Hoyt developed a set of Mexican clients. He seriously thought of becoming a Mexican citizen. 'After all, they seem to have free access to all parts of the United States.'

But no, he could not do it. 'I can't bring myself to become a fruit picker.'

Not long after the news of Hoyt's divorce, I received a call from Kinglet Chee, asking me to come to his office. He seemed relaxed; he showed me the panelling he had removed from our

Harborfront Tower offices. It was a superb example of colonial workmanship, he said, but all I could think of was Hoyt's crack, 'You might have to sue me,' and the rest of the rant. I squirmed at the memory of Kinglet's telling me, at the Ron Brown party, how Hoyt had mocked him. I could not recall the exact words, only my feeling of discomfort, his eyes on me, his face impassive. And I had blurted out how I had felt.

But today, Kinglet was talking about my negotiating the terms of this new generation of memory chips. The great thing about this world was the way technology became so quickly dated. The typewriter hardly changed for a hundred years, but computers and chips became obsolete and worthless every year or so. This was another very big deal.

I said, 'Hoyt should be in on this.'

'He is not an American,' Kinglet said.

'He'll never speak to me again.'

'If so, then he is not your friend and never was.'

He chose me over all the other partners because of what I had said to him at the ambassador's house, that I would never renounce my citizenship, never, ever. Odd that a businessman should be such a sentimentalist, but he explained that it was his dream to become an American, and Hoyt was a liability there. Perhaps I might help with that? The profit for me was a million-two.

Hoyt stopped speaking to me. It was the money—so far, that was all he knew about, and just as well. The talk in the office was that he had begun to refer to me as a 'cheese-ball', and to how Elfman had set him up.

All this I got second-hand. I was no longer in Singapore. At last I heard through Warfield that Hoyt, who was almost broken by the Irish passport he finally got, was applying for a Green Card.

I hope that he is turned down. Vickie and I are very happy in Boca Grande. 'I'm doing a book,' I say. 'Words for sale!' she calls out. Just a joke, but it disconcerts me that she uses so many of Hoyt's expressions. And I do too. I have begun to understand the meaning of the expression, 'not a lot of money in my tax bracket'. With all the assets in her name Vickie was now regarded as a very wealthy woman, but as a married couple living in America the fact is we don't have that much money.

NOTES ON CONTRIBUTORS

PAUL BEATTY is the author of two collections of poetry, *Joker, Joker Deuce* and *Big Bank Take Little Bank*. His first novel, *The White Boy Shuffle*, from which 'Taken out of Context' is taken, will be published in the United States in June by Houghton Mifflin and in the UK in November by Secker and Warburg.

GORDON BURN's books include *Somebody's Husband, Somebody's Son: the Story of the Yorkshire Ripper* and the novels *Alma Cogan* and *Fullalove*. He is working on a book about the Wests.

ZOË HELLER is a columnist on the London *Sunday Times*. She lives in New York.

ERIC JACOBS is a journalist, broadcaster and writer. His most recent book, *Kingsley Amis: a Biography*, was published last year.

DAN JACOBSON's most recent book is *The Electronic Elephant*, an account of a journey through southern Africa.

PHILLIP KNIGHTLEY's work for the *Sunday Times*, for which he was twice named Journalist of the Year in the British Press Awards, included investigations of Kim Philby, Robert Maxwell and the Thalidomide affair. His books include *The First Casualty*, on war correspondents, and *The Second Oldest Profession*, about intelligence agencies. He is working on his autobiography.

FINTAN O'TOOLE is on the staff of the *Irish Times*. His books include *Black Hole, Green Card: The Disappearance of Ireland* and *Meanwhile Back at the Ranch: the Politics of Irish Beef*. He lives in Dublin.

TOM PILSTON is a staff photographer on the *Independent on Sunday*.

LYNDA SCHUSTER has reported from Central and South America, the Middle East and Africa for the *Wall Street Journal*. She is working on a non-fiction book about a South African family. She lives in Mozambique.

PAUL THEROUX is the author of numerous books, among them *The Mosquito Coast*, *My Secret History*, *The Great Railway Bazaar* and *Riding the Iron Rooster*. His latest book, *The Pillars of Hercules*, is an account of a journey around the Mediterranean. He lives in Hawaii.

PATRICK WRIGHT's books include *On Living in an Old Country*, *A Journey Through Ruins* and *The Village that Died for England*.

DAVID XIAO was born in Hong Kong and now lives in Seattle. He is writing a novel set in Changsha, China, on the eve of the Cultural Revolution.